United States
Postal History Sampler

By Richard B. Graham

Published by *Linn's Stamp News*, the largest and most informative stamp newspaper in the world. *Linn's* is owned by Amos Press, 911 Vandemark Road, Sidney, Ohio 45365. Amos Press also publishes *Scott Stamp Monthly* and the Scott line of catalogs and albums. Copyright 1992 by Linn's Stamp News.

On the cover: An immaculate brown gloved arm extends through a tattered hole in the front of this "trompe-l'oeil" advertising cover, to present a card with Adlers Gloves' address and return legend. This cleverly designed cover and other turn-of-the-century advertising covers are described on page 156. Cover design by Veronica Schreiber.

Contents

Introduction

By Michael Laurence

Richard B. Graham is the dean of United States postal historians. Over the last four decades, his writing has appeared in a wide range of stamp journals and publications, and his behind-the-scenes editorial hand has shaped many excellent and important books. The quantity of Graham's output on postal history subjects is simply staggering.

A retired engineer, Graham established his reputation for dispassionate research and accessible prose in the pages of such scholarly publications as *The Confederate Philatelist* and the *Chronicle* of the U.S. Philatelic Classics Society. To the stamp collecting community, he is best known as the author of the weekly Postal History column in *Linn's Stamp News*. Begun in 1982, this column has appeared in every issue of *Linn's* since then, a total (as of this writing) of almost 500 columns. A complete listing of Graham's *Linn's* columns through the end of 1991, compiled by Douglas A. Kelsey, appears on page 171.

As early as 1983, when Graham and I first discussed the possibility of reshaping some of his *Linn's* columns into a book, we realized from the outset that the project would have to overcome some substantial obstacles.

We both shared the same goal. We wanted to accomplish, in book form, what Graham's very popular column does weekly in the pages of *Linn's*: combining text and illustrations to bring postal history to life, reaching out to make collectors aware that covers and their markings can be just as fascinating — perhaps even more fascinating — than stamps themselves.

But sharing a goal doesn't necessarily achieve it. Postal history, Graham is fond of pointing out, is a never-ending cycle of updates and new discoveries. In a field in which the last word can never be written, the permanence of a book may not be the best way to convey information. Moreover, given the limited space available in *Linn's* weekly newspaper format, many of Graham's columns are hardly more than encapsulations of subjects that individually can justify entire books. So here too, the transition from ephemeral newsprint into permanent binding faced obstacles.

And as the years passed, selection and organization became a growing challenge. Graham has contributed a Postal History column to every issue of *Linn's* since November 15, 1982. Obviously, only a fraction of these could be included in a book.

Most of the obstacles were overcome when Graham conceived the idea of creating an introductory work that could be called a *Postal History Sampler*. This allowed the freedom to choose certain subjects and exclude others without appearing to be arbitrary. Subjects were selected on the basis of their inherent interest, and to hint at the vast range of U.S. postal history topics around which collections can be formed. The word "sampler" implies an introduction to many different subjects, and suggests that the material presented is at best a partial and fairly limited selection. If this book is well received, we hope to follow it with additional works from the Graham output, devoted to more specialized subjects. The postal history of World War II is just one such subject.

A few technical notes: This book consists of 15 chapters, based on approximately 60 *Linn's* columns created by Graham between 1982 and 1991. The specific columns and dates are noted marginally at the conclusion of each chapter. Corrections and updates published in subsequent *Linn's* columns have been incorporated into the text where appropriate. The whole has been edited to stand alone as a book and the illustrations have been numbered consecutively. But beyond this, little attempt has been made to mask the fact that the material herein was originally created for weekly publication.

This is the second book in the Linn's Handbook series. The first is *Classic United States Imperforate Stamps*, by Jon Rose, published by *Linn's* in 1990. The Linn's Handbooks are a continuing series of original works, in a common format, on a broad range of stamp collecting subjects, conceived, created and priced to be within the grasp of ordinary stamp collectors. The overriding objective of the series is to bring useful information to the widest possible audience.

Chapter 1

Domestic Letter Rates

High rates on early stampless covers

Prior to 1847, letters in the United States were rated on a combined basis of distance and number of sheets of paper. Only when a letter weighed more than an ounce was weight considered. Letters having four or more pieces of paper or weighing over one ounce were charged four times the single rate and "in that proportion for all greater weight." Which is to say, above one ounce an additional rate was charged for each quarter ounce. Postmasters were instructed ("Instructions" of 1832) that "less than one fourth of an ounce need not be noticed when the letter or package weighs more than an ounce. Thus, a packet weighing 1 1/8 ounces should be rated with quadruple postage, only."

The early years of our country saw several postal rate structures, all with complex mileage zones (from the point of origin) having successively higher rates. For example, the postage table of 1792 had

Figure 1. A seven-times-single-rate cover from New York City to Albany in December 1815, sent during the brief period of 50 percent higher postal rates to help finance the War of 1812.

Table A: Postal Rates 1799-1816 (for single letters)		
Distance	**Rate, 1799-1815**	**War Rate, 1815-16***
Not over 40 miles	8¢	12¢
41 to 90 miles	10¢	15¢
91 to 150 miles	12 1/2¢	18 3/4¢
151 to 300 miles	17¢	25 1/2¢
301 to 500 miles	20¢	30¢
Over 500 miles	25¢	37 1/2¢
*Effective February 1, 1815; repealed, effective March 31, 1816		

nine distance zones with 2¢, 2 1/2¢ or 3¢ increases in the single-letter rate for each additional distance increment of from 30 to 100 miles, up to 450 miles. The rates ranged from 6¢ to 25¢ per single sheet. It isn't difficult to find covers from those years showing postage equivalent to a day's wages for a clerk in a counting house.

In 1799, the postage table was simplified somewhat, being reduced to only six zones. Single-letter postage then ranged from 8¢ for under 40 miles to 25¢ for letters sent over 500 miles. This rate structure is shown in Table A.

During the War of 1812, the major government revenue source — customs fees — sank to practically nothing. One of the many attempts to raise money for the war was a 50-percent increase in postal rates, also shown in Table A. These war rates applied during the period of 1815-16. Figure 1 shows a cover sent at this time from New York City to Albany, on December 11, 1815, by Dirck Ten Broeck, a lawyer from one of the old Dutch patroon families.

The enclosed letter on legal matters is written in huge script, capped by a gigantic signature stretching across the page. The letter also enclosed a court document, and the scribble (in red ink) in the upper left corner of the cover deciphers as "1 3/4 oz." The letter is addressed to a court official at Albany, and Ten Broeck prepaid the postage, whether because the court wouldn't pay postage on due letters or for other reasons not evident.

Postage of $1.78 1/2 computes for a letter over one ounce, weighing seven quarter ounces and requiring seven times the single-letter rate. The single-letter rate was for over 150 but under 300 miles. The distance from New York to Albany is given on today's road maps as 154 miles. This distance, relative to mail routes, was an occasional source of controversy in the early 19th century. The Post Office was pressured to consider the distance less than 150 miles. This would reduce rates on mail between the two cities. However, the distance calculation was based on the route by which mail was actually carried, not as the crow flies. The single-letter rate for 151 to 300

Table B: Postal Rates, 1816-1845 (for single letters)	
Distance	**Rates**
Not over 30 miles	6¢
31 to 80 miles	10¢
81 to 150 miles	12 1/2¢
151 to 400 miles	18 1/2¢*
Over 400 miles	25¢
*Increased to 18 3/4¢ in 1825	

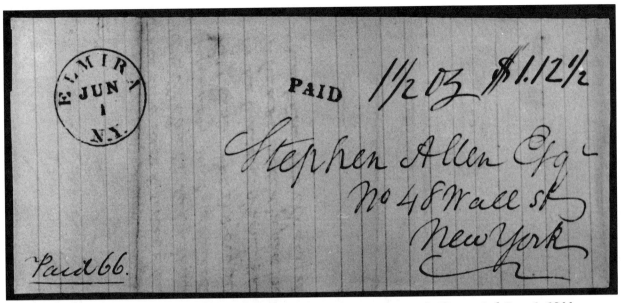

Figure 2. A six-times-single-rate cover sent from Elmira, New York, to New York City, posted June 1, 1844.

miles, prior to the War of 1812, was 17¢. The war rate increase of 50 percent brought it to 25 1/2¢. Thus, postage on the Figure 1 cover, seven times the single rate, was correctly figured at $1.78 1/2.

After the war rate was repealed, on March 31, 1816, the rates reverted to the old prewar rates for just a month. Then, effective May 1, 1816, a new rate structure was introduced. This is shown in Table B. Figure 2 is a folded letter sent from Elmira, New York, to New York City, posted June 1, 1844. According to its rather brief contents, it contained legal documents sent from one lawyer to another. The outside of the cover is endorsed "1 1/2 oz.," and "$1.12 1/2" postage was prepaid by the sender. A weight of 1 1/2 ounces or six quarter ounces would require postage six times the single rate. The distance between Elmira and New York City was between 151 and 400 miles, measured as the mails were carried over the post routes. Thus, as shown in Table B, the rate was six times 18 3/4¢ or $1.12 1/2, which is the rate shown on the cover.

The fractional 12 1/2¢ and 18 3/4¢ rates seem a bit strange as viewed today, even though today's postage-rate structure has its share of fractional rates. In the 19th century, U.S postal rates were based upon the coins then circulating. These were a rather random mixture. The Spanish milled dollar, which could be broken into eight pieces or "bits" and was the basis of the "pieces-of-eight" in *Treasure Island*, was a very common coin in the United States. Thus, 12 1/2¢ was an eighth of a dollar. A "bit" mark, much the same as the English shilling mark, was commonly used by the express companies to show their charges. The term "two bits," meaning 25¢, stems from this source. The postal rates of 1816 didn't quite jibe with the "bit" divisions. The 6¢ rate should have been 6 1/4¢ and 18 1/2¢ should have been 18 3/4¢. The 18 1/2¢ of 1816 was changed to 18 3/4¢ in the new postal act of 1825. The rates shown in Table B remained in effect until they were lowered and simplified in 1845.

1851-55 rates: 3¢ if prepaid, 5¢ if collect

The cover shown in Figure 3 has a Columbus, Ohio, 5¢ marking

Figure 3. Cover from Columbus, Ohio, sent in 1853, bearing a "3 PAID" marking, struck in error and overstruck with the correct 5¢ due datestamp, repeated at the left of the cover for clarity.

struck over a 3¢ "PAID" handstamp with a second example of the 5¢ marking applied elsewhere on the cover. A tracing of the 5¢ marking is shown in Figure 4. Also shown in Figure 4 is the similar marking reading "Columbus, O./3 PAID." These markings were issued in late 1851 and after for postmasters to use in connection with the new postal law that went into effect July 1, 1851. The new law provided that prepaid letters not weighing more than a half ounce and sent in the United States a distance of less than 3,000 miles would require just 3¢ in postage. Similar letters, sent collect, would be charged 5¢ postage due. The previous rate, from July 1, 1845, had been 5¢ per half ounce for letters sent less than 300 miles and 10¢ for those letters sent further.

The 1851 law also established a rate for letters sent more than 3,000 miles, which applied to letters between the West Coast and the eastern parts of the country. This rate was 6¢ per half ounce for prepaid letters and 10¢ for unpaid. Thus, while new postmarking devices were needed to show the 3¢ or 6¢ prepaid rates, the 5¢ and 10¢ rates of the previous era continued in use as postage due rates.

Prepayment of postage on all domestic letters was made compulsory effective April 1, 1855. Prepayment by stamps became compulsory as of January 1, 1856. These requirements brought to an end the long-established custom of sending letters unpaid. Until the 1850s, all letters were automatically considered unpaid except those with a "paid" marking and the correct rate, or (beginning in 1847) those prepaid by postage stamps. Thus, the stampless period actually lasted in the United States until January 1, 1856, even though it was forbidden to send domestic letters collect after April 1, 1855.

Another distinction to remember is that prior to July 1, 1851, postage was the same whether prepaid or not — and a very high percentage of letters were sent collect. Of the smaller portion sent prepaid, relatively few covers were prepaid with the postage stamps of 1847. There was little incentive to use stamps. Use of a stamp would permit a sender to mail a letter through a slot in the post office — the same way collect letters were mailed. To mail a prepaid letter otherwise, one had to wait in line to pay cash at the post office counter or maintain a charge account with the postmaster — a common business practice at that time. Thus, prior to July 1, 1851, it was more convenient to send letters collect, and there was no incentive to do

Figure 4. Tracings of the markings on the cover in Figure 3.

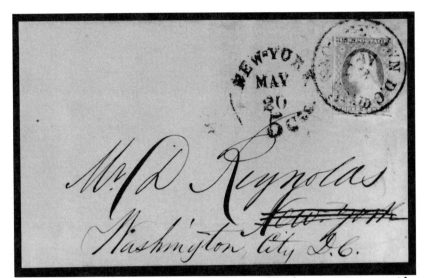

Figure 5. A cover sent on May 12, 1853, from Georgetown, D.C., with 3¢ prepaid by stamps, forwarded back from New York with 5¢ collect. Thus, this one cover shows both the prepaid and due rates of the period.

otherwise. Furthermore, some people considered receiving a prepaid letter an insult to their financial standing, implying they couldn't afford to pay collect postage.

The postal act effective July 1, 1851, changed all that. Since it provided a lower postage for prepaid letters, most businessmen were soon prepaying all their mails — and expecting correspondents to do likewise. Thus, the mails of 1851-55 presented a mixed bag of prepaid and unpaid covers at various rates. It became obvious to the post office that in the interest of efficiency, town datestamps incorporating the 3¢ prepaid and 5¢ due rates were desirable.

The Postal Laws & Regulations of 1852 provided that "marking and rating stamps of metal are furnished only to offices that collect in postages $300 a year, but stamps of wood are furnished to offices collecting postages of $200 a year." Applications had to be made to the U.S. Post Office Department to receive these government-issue postmarking devices. If procured elsewhere, they were at the postmaster's own expense.

Returning to the cover in Figure 3, it has an enclosed letter datelined Ohio Lunatic Asylum, Columbus, July 14, 1853. It was mailed at Columbus on July 15, 1853, as an unpaid, collect letter. The postal clerk at Columbus, who rated the letter, accidently struck the "3 PAID" handstamp on the cover, realized his error and overstruck the "paid" version with his 5¢ due marking. He then added an additional strike of the due marking to clarify that the cover was actually sent collect. Thus, the cover shows both styles of the similar set of stock townmarkings issued to Columbus for use during this time of mixed rates and handling.

Collectors cherish covers from the 1851-55 era showing both rates. Figure 5 shows an example. Addressed to New York, this cover was mailed at Georgetown, D.C., on May 12, 1853 (per the enclosed letter), with a Georgetown "3 PAID" postmark (see Figure 6) canceling the 3¢ dull red stamp. At New York, the cover was forwarded back to Washington with postage collect, indicated by the New York 5¢ due marking (again see Figure 6). Forwarding is the most common way in which both the prepaid and collect rates appear on one cover.

Figure 7 shows two more Columbus covers with stock townmarks. These are on circulars, so no date was provided. The item at the top,

Figure 6. Tracings of the markings on the cover in Figure 5.

Figure 7. A pair of circular-rate covers sent from Columbus, Ohio, in the 1850s. Both postmarks were probably made by the same townmark, with different indicia inserted.

Figure 8. Tracings of the markings on the cover in Figure 7.

addressed to Adrian, Michigan, in 1853, shows no rate at all. The circular rate was 1¢ on unsealed circulars sent anywhere in the country (for weights up to 3 ounces). This 1¢ rate, effective in September 1852, was probably the beginning of junk mail. It superseded a complex rate structure, involving both weight and distance, under which I believe the lower Figure 7 cover was sent: 2¢ per ounce for circulars traveling more than 500 but under 1,500 miles.

Although my tracings in Figure 8 don't indicate it, I believe the markings on the covers in Figure 7 were made by the same instrument. This instrument probably had a slot in its lower section, in addition to the slots for the date in the center, so that different rates could be handstamped with the same instrument. In fact, I've long had the idea that these government-issue instruments of 1851-55 were all made that way. A post office the size of Columbus, with nearly $3,000 in revenue in 1855 and having perhaps a half dozen clerks, would have been given at least four such flexible instruments. (Or, if they didn't have the slots, they at least had two and probably more of the paid and due types.)

With the abolition, legally at least (it died hard), of the unpaid letter as of April 1, 1855, the ground rules changed. Letters were considered prepaid (after January 1, 1856, by the stamps) unless marked due, which could only happen in special cases.

U.S. domestic airmail rates, 1918-1926

"Fractured" first-day covers refers to covers to which something has happened to lessen their appeal as immaculate first-day covers, but which in the process converted them into postal history artifacts. One such cover is shown here as Figure 9. This was mailed from New York on May 29, 1926, the first day of use of the 5¢ Ericsson commemorative stamps it bears.

The cover was intended to be sent on the first flight of a new U.S. airmail contract route from Cleveland to Pittsburgh, via Youngstown,

Ohio, to which the cover was addressed. However, that flight wasn't made until April 21, 1927, almost a year later!

When the cover was mailed with 12¢ postage prepaid by the pair of 5¢ Ericsson stamps plus a 2¢ Liberty Bell commemorative of 1926, the rate was 10¢ for a 1-ounce letter sent by night airmail over the government-operated route from New York to Chicago, with intermediate stops in Pennsylvania and Ohio, including Cleveland. Mail could be taken off at least at some of these stops, including Cleveland, as may be noted from the endorsement on the Figure 9 cover, "Via Cleveland, Ohio," where the cover was to be held for the first-flight trip on Contract Air Mail (CAM) Route 11 from Cleveland to Pittsburgh.

At first, I speculated that the sender, J.M. Bartels Company (per a backstamp), had added the 2¢ stamp, over and above the 10¢ airmail postage, to cover the surface part of the route. But Philip Silver, who has made a thorough study and written extensively regarding U.S. airmail rates, corrected this assumption. Silver has called the era during which this cover was sent the "Period of Confusion." Surface-mail postage was always included as part of the airmail postage.

As a result of Silver's input, I started looking for explanations of early U.S. airmail rates. I found them, as written up by Silver, in an interesting article in the 1976 *American Philatelic Congress Book*.

Airmail service in the United States, barring one-time events and occasional experimental flights or spectacles, started during World War I, with the scheduled service between New York and Washington. This service commenced May 15, 1918, using Army pilots and wartime military planes. Figure 10 shows a cover carried on this route, bearing a copy of the 24¢ bicolored Jenny stamp, most famous in its invert version.

The service between New York and Washington was discontinued May 31, 1921. There were two rate changes during that period. A few other routes operating during those years also were discontinued by the end of May 1921. One example is a St. Louis-Chicago service that operated on an experimental basis between August 16, 1920, and June 30, 1921. Covers from these flights are listed in the *American Airmail Catalog*, fifth edition, Volume 1, published by the American Air Mail Society on a continuing basis.

The New York-Washington route opened with a 24¢ rate in

Figure 9. A first-day cover of the U.S. 5¢ Ericsson commemorative, issued May 29, 1926, on a cover intended for a first flight of one of the early contract airmail routes. The additional 2¢ stamp is superfluous for the night airmail flight from New York to Cleveland, for which the 10¢ rate also included surface-mail carriage. The cover has a Youngstown, Ohio, backstamp dated April 21, 1927, showing a long delay between the sending of the cover, apparently because of an announcement, and the actual flight.

Figure 10. The first scheduled air route in the United States was the New York-Washington route opened May 15, 1918, which was also the first day of the 24¢ Jenny airmail stamp. Sent from the airmail field at the intermediate stop of Philadelphia on June 27, 1918, this cover received special delivery at New York as part of the service.

effect, prepaid by the 24¢ Jenny stamp. May 15, 1918, the day of the route's first flight, was also the first day of issue of the new stamp. The 24¢ rate actually included 10¢ for special delivery service in the city to which the letters were addressed.

On July 15, 1918, the rate was reduced to 16¢, still including a 10¢ special delivery fee. A 16¢ Jenny stamp, printed in green, was issued July 1 for the new rate. On December 15, 1918, the rate was again reduced, by eliminating the special delivery service, leaving a bare rate of 6¢. This 6¢ rate for letters up to 1 ounce, prepaid by 6¢ orange Jenny stamps, remained in effect until special rates for airmail were discontinued July 18, 1919.

It has been remarked that the Scott catalog listings of the first-issue airmails are inconsistent, not only in terms of their sequence, which should have been as they appeared, in descending order of value, but also because the first two stamps issued (the 24¢ and 16¢ values) were actually airmail special delivery stamps — just like the 16¢ emissions of the 1930s, which have always been listed in a separate category.

Airmail service wasn't renewed on a regular, extra-rate basis until 1924. In the interim, various official experimental flights were made, carrying mail at the regular rate of 2¢ per ounce. Many covers prepared especially for those flights employ the earlier airmail stamps, with the rates considerably overpaid.

On July 1, 1924, a new scheduled transcontinental airmail route from New York to San Francisco was inaugurated. Figure 11 shows a cover carried at the single-zone rate of 8¢ per 1/2 ounce, from the airmail field at Bellefonte, Pennsylvania, to New York City. Bellefonte was one of the intermediate stops on the route between New York and Chicago, over which mail was flown only in daylight hours, with no passengers carried, in a government operation using military planes adapted for the service. A new set of three airmail stamps was issued to cover the rates for this service. Views of the DH-4 mail planes are shown on the 8¢ stamp (on the Figure 11 cover) and on the 24¢ stamp (Figure 12).

Rates were based on fixed zones into which the route was divided. The zones were New York-Chicago, Chicago-Cheyenne, and Cheyenne-San Francisco. The rates were 8¢ per zone or part of any

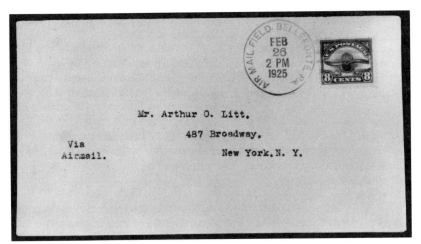

zone through which a letter was carried by air along the route. Surface-mail postage to or from points on the route was included in the airmail rate. Thus, the three values of the new set of airmail stamps, all issued in August 1924, were 8¢, 16¢ and 24¢ to cover rates for a 1-ounce letter carried over the one to three zones of the route. Regular postage stamps also could be used to prepay the airmail postage, but the airmail stamps weren't supposed to be used for regular service.

It should be noted that the postage wasn't based upon the miles involved, as is the case for parcel post zones. Instead, the zone boundaries governed, so that even if a letter was carried only just across a zone boundary, from the last stop in one zone, such as Cleveland, to the first stop in the next zone westward beyond Chicago, it still would have been charged two rates.

On July 1, 1925, overnight service was inaugurated between New York and Chicago. The rate for night service in that zone was raised to 10¢ per ounce, while the 8¢-per-ounce rate was retained for daylight service.

The 10¢ night airmail rate was the rate intended to be prepaid on the cover shown on page 7 in Figure 9 (per the printed/typed instructions on the cover), but it was also intended to serve as a first-flight cover on one of the new contract airmail routes being inaugurated in 1926-27. I suppose it was one of a supply of such covers prepared by Bartels in New York to be sent to their addresses as the new routes were put into operation.

Postal history in daily mails

When I ask about U.S. postal rates at a U.S. post office counter, clerks often hand me, or refer to, a pocket-size folder titled "Postage Rates, Fees, and Information." The folder often is available in post office lobbies, along with other material available to all at no charge. The folder from the 1988 rate change had, in fine print, "Notice 59/April 1988." A larger wall chart showing the same information, all on one side and inscribed "Poster 103, April 1988," also was available to postal patrons who could show need for the large version.

The rate charts display information needed to mail most items, except for bulk-rate or special fourth-class book-rate items. A collection of the charts from other previous rate periods would be quite useful. I suggest that those who don't have the current chart remedy this before the next rate change makes them unavailable.

Figure 12. The 24¢ stamp of 1924, showing one of the DeHavilland DH-4 planes that carried the mails.

Paul T. Schroeder called to my attention the pocket-size version of the 1988 rates. For months, I had been walking by the supply of them at my local post office. Schroeder sent a copy in response to my *Linn's* column of December 24, 1990, discussing rates used for Christmas cards, 1933-71. He commented, "Christmas card rate is still on the books." The chart Schroeder sent was marked to point out the "single-piece rates" under third-class mails, one of the sections covered on the charts.

He is correct in that this is the same Christmas-card rate, but as he also pointed out, using the rate creates no advantage unless a card weighs more than 4 ounces. Rates less than that weight per piece are exactly the same as first-class letter rates. I doubt the single-piece, third-class rate is ever used for mailings less than 4 ounces.

Another aspect also covered on the rate chart is pertinent to both first- and third-class rates. This aspect is the size of an envelope, as demonstrated by the cover shown in Figure 13. It is one of several similar covers sent to me by *Linn's* editor-publisher Michael Laurence showing the same usage.

The Figure 13 envelope measures 7 1/2 by 10 1/2 inches, but it didn't weigh more than an ounce. It was prepaid with a 25¢ Steamboat stamp. The large cover was assessed 10¢ postage due, because it was oversize rather than overweight. Had it been over-weight, postage due would have been 20¢ or more.

The portion in the rate chart titled "Size standards for domestic mail" is divided into two sections. One section gives size limits for matter to be acceptable in the mails. The other explains which large items are acceptable only with payment of an extra fee. The section "Minimum size" prohibits from the mails pieces that do not meet the following requirements: a minimum thickness of seven-thousandths of an inch, at least 3 1/2 inches in height and 5 inches in length, and a rectangular shape. An exception is any piece more than 1/4 inch thick.

The part "Non-standard Mail" refers to either first-class or single-piece, third-class mail weighing 1 ounce or less with any of the following dimensions exceeded: length, 11 1/2 inches; height, 6 1/8

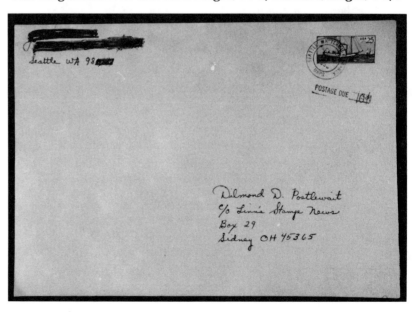

Figure 13. Large cover addressed to *Linn's* **precancel columnist Dilmond Postlewait in care of** *Linn's.* **It was oversize but weighed less than 1 ounce. The 25¢ postage was insuffi-cient for an oversize item, and the Seattle post office applied a "Post-age Due" handstamp and manuscript "10¢." The 10¢ was collected from** *Linn's* **at Sidney, Ohio.**

Figure 14. An oversize postcard mailed at the 25¢ first-class rate for letters because of its size.

inches; and thickness, 1/4 inch. Also, a piece's length divided by its height must be a ratio between 1.3 to 1 and 2.5 to 1, inclusive.

All non-standard mail is subject to a 10¢ surcharge per piece, except for first-class mail presorted by ZIP code or by carrier route, where the surcharge is 5¢. The Figure 13 cover was too tall and was charged 10¢ postage due. I have several other pieces with similar postage due charges. Excess height is the most common reason. I also have seen oversize pieces that should have been charged postage due but were not.

Figures 14 and 15 show two large postcards. Both are larger than the standard postcard. As stated in the "First-Class" section of the 1988 rate chart: "To qualify for card rates, a card may not be larger than 4 1/4 inches by 6 inches, nor smaller than 3 1/2 inches by 5 inches. The thickness must be uniform and not less than 0.007 of an inch." Thus, oversize postcards pay first-class letter rates.

The card shown in Figure 14 is 8 1/4 inches by 5 1/2 inches, and the card in Figure 15 is 8 1/2 inches by 5 1/2 inches. Both exceed the dimensions allowable to be treated as postcards and were prepaid as letter mail. On its back side, the Figure 14 card has a check-off list of maintenance items due on my car. The Figure 15 card has a photo of the Ohio State University marching band spelling out their Script *Ohio* in Ohio Stadium.

The Figure 14 postcard was sent in 1990 at the 25¢ first-class rate for letters and is franked with a 25¢ Creatures of the Sea stamp. The Figure 15 card was sent at the 21¢ basic presort letter rate. A 21¢ Railroad Mail Car coil stamp paid the rate. Had the card been of standard dimensions, it could have been sent at the basic presort rate for postcards: 13¢.

Among the material Laurence sent to me was a very large postcard measuring 10 1/4 inches by 6 5/8 inches and bearing an ad for a price guide to costume jewelry. This card has a Westminster, Maryland, meter imprint for 35¢ postage applied over a printed bulk-mail permit statement. The 35¢ postage is the same as for an oversize first-class letter, 25¢ plus a 10¢ surcharge for the excessive size.

The *Domestic Mail Manual*, Section 353.1, which defines non-

Figure 15. An oversize postcard sent at the 21¢ presort rate for letters. Had the card been standard size, it could have been sent at the 13¢ basic presort rate for postcards.

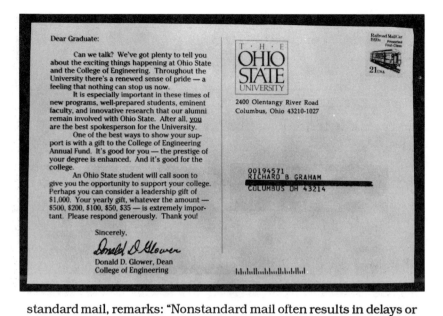

This chapter is based on the following *Linn's* columns: high rates on stampless covers, December 9, 1985; 1851-55 rates, December 5, 1988; domestic airmail rates, October 31, 1988; postal history in daily mails, January 28, 1991.

standard mail, remarks: "Nonstandard mail often results in delays or damage to mail because it does not lend itself to machine processing." The large number of damaged-in-handling oversize mail pieces delivered in clear enclosures confirms this. Postal clerks normally sort and handcancel oversize pieces. Large pieces fed into machines undetected often become damaged. The oversize fee is for the hand-sorting and handcanceling, although today's methods of collecting mail and sending it to processing centers makes detection of large flat items difficult.

The damaged, oversize pieces I've seen mostly are only slightly oversize and hence didn't get sorted out to be processed as flats.

The covers illustrated here all were received in either *Linn's* or my own daily mail. Most collectors would call them junk mail, but I don't think they'll be junk to collectors of future years.

Chapter 2

Town Datestamps

First government-issue (G.I.) town datestamps

As collectors, we usually think of fancy postmarks in terms of the fancy cancels to be found on U.S. adhesive stamps of the 1860s and 1870s — when certain postmasters gave their creative imaginations full sway. However, it should be recognized that fancy postmarks existed long before 1847, when the Post Office Department issued its first adhesive stamps that required cancellation.

We also seem to have cycles of misuse of the terms "postmark" and "cancel." Some people tend to call all postmarks "cancels." Obviously, while all cancels are postal markings, only markings that cancel something are "cancellations."

The U.S. Post Office Department came into being when the federal government was being organized under the Constitution. Like its predecessor organization, under the Articles of Confederation, it was called "the General Post Office." It was patterned after and in many ways a continuation of the British and Colonial postal systems.

The first postal markings were handwritten. Manuscript markings were used until mail volume forced some local postmasters to obtain handstampers, usually made from type fonts available locally. The postmasters probably had the type clamped into a wooden holder. In larger cities, perhaps a local craftsman would offer such on a commercial basis. Probably the first circular-style handstamps used in the United States were obtained from abroad, where they had been in general use for some time.

The first standardized or what might be called "G.I." (Government Issue) postmarking handstamps were distributed by the Post Office Department in 1799, according to research done by Arthur H. Bond. In a letter sent April 18, 1799, Postmaster General Joseph Habersham transmitted new brass hand datestampers to the postmasters of some towns, including Washington City (the early name of Washington, D.C.). The other towns supplied at that time were Newburyport, Massachusetts; Fredericksburg and Petersburg, Virginia, and Augusta, Georgia. A tracing of the Washington City postmark made by the new device is shown in Figure 16.

Habersham's letter of transmittal included detailed instructions as to how he expected the new instruments to be used and cared for: "The table on which the letters are stamped should be covered with cloth. Common writing ink is best. Printers' ink will clog the stamp too

Figure 16. This Washington City postmark is an example of one of the earliest standardized U.S. postmarks.

Figure 17. These Trenton and Pittsburg cancels are further examples of the earliest standardized U.S. postmarks, struck from the first postmarking devices furnished by the U.S. Post Office Department.

soon. It should be contained in a square piece of lead, hollowed and covered with sponge."

On June 8, 1799, Habersham sent out another shipment of the new brass postmarkers to postmasters at Newark, New Jersey; Alexandria, Virginia; Georgetown, "PTK" ("Potomack" — now, of course, District of Columbia); Newport, Rhode Island; Pittsburg (without the final "h"), Pennsylvania; Providence, Rhode Island; and Trenton, New Jersey. Tracings of the Trenton and Pittsburg markings are shown in Figure 17.

With his letter, Habersham went to considerably greater detail in the use of the stamps: ". . . (the handstamps) can be used with printers ink or common writing ink. The latter is preferable where much business is done, as printer's ink clogs the stamp sooner. For common ink a square piece of lead, hollowed in the middle and filled with sponge to contain the ink, is used. The stamp is dipped on the sponge, which prevents it taking up too much at once. The loose letters and figures should be kept in a box and proper care taken to prevent their being lost, as they are a dear article and it is troublesome to obtain new ones to fit the stamps."

The tracings in Figures 16 and 17 show postmarks made by three of these instruments. The Washington City and Trenton, New Jersey, tracings were made from covers franked by Benjamin Stoddert, the first secretary of the Navy, on November 26, 1800 (soon after the government moved to Washington), and Oliver Wolcott II, secretary of the treasury, on October 5, 1799. Wolcott had succeeded Alexander Hamilton as Washington's secretary of the treasury in 1795. He served until 1801, after the government had moved to Washington. Thus, Wolcott's franked covers can be found with postmarks of Trenton, when the government had moved from Philadelphia during the summer months to avoid the fever. They also can be found with postmarks of Philadelphia and Washington.

The Pittsburg marking, shown in Figure 17, abbreviated "PITTS^G," with the "G" higher than the other letters, is an early example of a practice the Post Office Department started with these standardized handstamps. They added the last letter of the town name, in smaller type, and raised it above the level of the other letters of the abbreviated town name.

In an article in the June 1962 *Postal History Journal*, Arthur H. Bond listed some 26 standard postmarks of different towns. Of these, the only major city using such was Baltimore. New York, Philadelphia or Boston are not mentioned as having been issued a standard device at that time. The basis of issuance isn't known, but neglecting the non-use by the largest cities, volume of mail was undoubtedly a factor, as it was in later years.

Probably the other key factor was a request for standardized instruments. At the time the standard instruments were issued, the three major cities had distinctive postmarks or were about to have such. Boston had a straightline marking in 1799. A few years later, a circular marking was put into use, but there wasn't anything standard about it, as it has a semicircle of stars at the bottom. Philadelphia used a small single circle with an abbreviated "PHI" and date, called by some a "thimble" marking. Its use continued for another 15 years. Not fancy, but still distinctive, somehow it seems to reflect Philadelphia's Quaker heritage.

The cover in Figure 18 shows the New York City marking in use

Figure 18. The New York "clamshell" marking of 1798-1802, which was quite distinctive and anything but standardized.

in 1799. This is the first of the two New York fancy "clamshell" designs. These are quite distinctive. The particular marking shown, dated March 5 (1801) seems to best fit the first of the two recorded types, but small differences indicate a new version was needed from time to time.

Obviously, long before stamps, the postmasters of many cities liked distinctive postmarks to appear on mail sent out from their offices. They were sometimes willing to go to considerable trouble to have this desire fulfilled. Figure 19 shows what is probably about the zenith of this approach. These are the Windsor Locks, Connecticut, pictorial postmarks of the 1830s. Shown are two of four distinct types of this marking. Fabricated in very exacting detail, they depict an early steamboat in the locks, presumably at Windsor Locks, on the Connecticut River, north of Hartford.

A review of the *American Stampless Cover Catalog* shows many postmarks with such characteristics. Americans have always had a desire to be different. Our early postmasters were no exception.

Stock postmarking devices

In a chapter contributed to that excellent compendium on 19th-century postmarks, Simpson's *U.S. Postal Markings, 1851-61*, Arthur Bond noted that "a very high percentage of the domestic mails received markings of the type hereinafter referred to as 'stock styles.'" Bond was referring to markings that were made by handstamps furnished to postmasters at government expense. These were furnished only to those post offices with a sufficient volume of mail to justify the expense. As I noted, I call these markings "G.I." or "Government Issue" handstamps.

The 1859 Postal Laws & Regulations, the last such issued until after the Civil War, said that post offices with gross receipts of over $1,000 per annum would be furnished with "circular marking and rating stamps of class No. 1." Those with gross receipts less than $1,000 but over $500 would receive class 2 markers. Offices with less than $500 but over $100 would get class 3 devices. Although that issue of Postal Laws & Regulations neglected to define the classes, it is known that class 1 referred to steel instruments. It is believed class 2 referred to brass or handstamps made of other metals, and class 3 represented devices of wood.

Figure 19. Two examples, both struck in red, of the Windsor Locks, Connecticut, pictorial postmark, possibly the most distinctive early handstamp of them all.

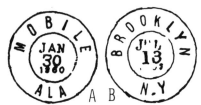

Figure 20. Stock or "G.I." postmark types of the 1860s.

Figure 21. A typical example of the new stock style of 1863.

The class 1 markings were usually uniform in shape; at least, they were apparently made to the same specifications, entering the 1860s with a style we call "small double circles." These markings (typical examples are A and B in Figure 20) were apparently specified to have a one-inch outer circle and a concentric inner circle one-half inch in diameter. Today, collectors describe these as 25- by 13-millimeter double circles, although the inner circles vary from 12mm to 15mm. Some years ago I was told that the earliest known use of the small double-circle style was at Mobile, Alabama, in late 1859, but tracing A in Figure 20 shows the earliest example I've seen to date, dated January 30, 1860.

During the summer and fall of 1863, a new stock type appeared. This had a similar but larger double-circle device, duplexed with a killer attached, so that the town datestamp could be applied and the stamp canceled with one strike of the marker.

Use of townmarks to cancel stamps was banned by U.S. Post Office Department edict after 1860. The new stock style of 1863, a typical example of which is shown in Figure 21, came in two sizes: with outer circles of 1 1/8 and 1 3/16 inches, and inner circles, respectively, of 9/16 and 5/8 inch. Today, we call these 28mm- by 14mm and 30mm- by 15 1/2mm double circles, duplexed with target killers. Some vary slightly from those dimensions.

Even the stock-type class 1 markings show considerable variation at times. While it is probable that most of these were furnished by the government, which contracted for them in quantities as postmasters requested them, I think some may have been made for postmasters locally or to order. It is likely that most of the class 2 and class 3 markings were ordered from the manufacturers and shipped directly to the postmasters, under contract arrangements with the Post Office Department.

Figure 22 shows a cover sent from Lockport, Illinois, in July 1862, bearing a marking similar to the stock small double circle, except for minor differences that suggest it wasn't furnished by the contract supplier. The marking, a tracing of which is shown in Figure 23, has the normal 25mm outer circle, but the inner circle is 14+mm. This is larger than normal, and the spacing of the letters is somewhat wider than normal. However, the characters in the date slots provide the unusual appearance. They are of a different and somewhat smaller type than was used in other stock markings. In fact, the year

Figure 22. The Lockport, Illinois, marking on this cover was probably meant to imitate the stock small double-circle type of the early 1860s, but there are small differences that indicate it was made privately.

date is so very small and delicate that I was unable to make a tracing that fairly represents it. The marking is struck in red. The accompanying killer, canceling the stamp and struck in black, is somewhat like the target killers then used — except that it has a fancy star in the center (Figure 24).

Under the Postal Laws & Regulations of 1859, as established by a law of 1854, postmasters' compensation was based upon the amount of postage received each quarter, per the following schedule (with compensation capped at $500 per quarter):

60 percent of the first $100
50 percent of the next $300
40 percent of the next $2,000
15 percent of all over $2,400

From the records of postmasters' compensation in the U.S. Register of 1861 and 1863, two postmasters at Lockport shared $562.19 in the fiscal year ending June 30, 1861. The amounts still due the government totaled $1,185.75.

In 1863, Lockport Postmaster Charles D. Holcomb's compensation, plus the amount due the government, totaled over $1,500. So there was no doubt that Lockport was entitled to class 1 postmarking devices. I have also seen small double-circle postmarks from Lockport that are slightly different from the example shown here, but resemble other stock types. We may theorize that the government didn't furnish enough instruments, so the Lockport postmaster had at least one additional town datestamp made up, to imitate the G.I. type.

As the Civil War drew to a close, the government went to still another style of stock marking — a small single circle, as shown on the cover in Figure 25. The Figure 25 marking is from Benton, Dakota Territory, an ephemeral town on the Union Pacific Railroad, where it crosses the North Platte River. The Benton post office was established on June 29, 1868, to service the workers who were building the Union Pacific. It was closed on October 16, 1868. Construction had moved on — and so had the people. In the meantime, the stock townmark was issued, but by the time the Figure 25 cover was mailed, the townmark should have read Wyoming Territory instead of Dakota. The area had been transferred. Some of the small single-circle markings of the era were duplexed, as with the marking shown in Figure 26. Others, like

Figure 23. This "G.I." postmark has the normal 25-millimeter outer circle, but the inner circle is 14+mm.

Figure 24. The killer is somewhat like the target killer, except that it has a fancy star in the center.

Figure 25. Mailed from Benton, Dakota Territory, in 1868, this cover bears a stock-type postmark that was obsolete almost before it was placed in use. The town of Benton had been transferred to Wyoming Territory a month before — and the town itself vanished soon afterward.

Figure 26. This small single-circle marking was joined with the killer canceler in what is called a duplex marking.

the Benton marking on the cover in Figure 24, were not. So despite being "stock" styles, there were many variations.

Patent canceling devices

The term "patent cancel" usually implies a method of canceling stamps in which the surface of the stamp is cut into or scraped away by the canceling device. Yet, considering the many patents granted in the last century for all kinds of postmarking devices and special essays intended to prevent reuse of stamps, it's difficult to understand why the term "patent" should be restricted to cancels provided by one type of instrument.

Duplexed canceling devices are a type of handstamp that combines two postmarking functions into one instrument. Figure 27 shows a typical duplex handstamper of the late 1880s, from an advertisement in one of the post office papers of the times. This type of handstamper has a history dating back before postage stamps, when the canceling portion contained a rate-marking imprint.

After the use of postage stamps became prevalent in 1851 because of that year's rate reduction (3¢ prepaid as against 5¢ unpaid), the combination of town datestamp and canceling device gradually came into use. But many post offices simply used the town datestamp to cancel the stamps.

However, this practice was discouraged by regulations. The cause was twofold. First, the dates in the town datestamps didn't show clearly when struck across the design of the stamp. This was the reason given for the regulation of 1859 requiring a separate device to cancel the stamps. Postmarks with clear dates were considered a legal necessity in establishing dates of mailing. The other reason was that the townmarks often didn't cancel the stamps effectively.

As the use of postage stamps increased and became a legal requirement on domestic mails (on January 1, 1856), the Post Office became very apprehensive that large numbers of postage stamps were being cleaned and reused. Obviously, a lightly canceled postage stamp was far easier to clean and reuse than was a heavily inked example. In 1859, Marcus P. Norton of Troy, New York, patented a duplex-style handstamp that was intended to solve the problem. It was used experimentally at Troy for three months starting in May 1859. A portion of one of the three recorded covers with that marking, used on June (abbreviated "JE") 2, 1859, is shown as Figure 28. Later in this chapter, I will explain other features of this handstamp, including its lazy year date.

The Norton patent described a "blotter" attached to one side of the town datestamp, with sharp edges projecting "to cut and stain the postage stamps." This feature was somewhat subordinate in the patent to the concept of the duplex design. Norton's attempt to sell his product to the Post Office Department for general use was very well-timed because of the Department's concern about the reuse of cleaned stamps. The feature of Norton's patent — the "blotter" that cut the surface of the stamp so that the canceling ink would penetrate well and be more difficult to remove — obviously had much appeal.

Whether the Norton patent is where the Post Office Department officials got the idea is questionable, but for many years thereafter, they were obsessed with the concept of cutting into the paper of the stamps to get better penetration of canceling inks. Although in his annual report for 1863, Postmaster General Montgomery Blair (Lin-

Figure 27. A duplex handstamper.

coln's postmaster general) noted that it wasn't believed "the Department ever suffered any considerable loss from the use of washed or restored stamps," the Post Office Department continued to experiment with ideas of stamp design, culminating with the use of the patent of Charles F. Steel for the grilled postage stamps of 1867 on into the early 1870s. The basic idea of grilling was to break the fibers of the paper and thus permit canceling inks to penetrate better. Stamps so canceled were considered impossible to clean without removing portions of the design.

In the meantime, postmasters at offices around the country tried special canceling devices of their own, using the same idea. Figure 29 shows a typical such effort used at Albany, New York, in the 1860s. As a matter of fact, this design, also used at other offices, may well be the most obvious of the patent cancels. The Albany device was arranged with a "cork" duplexed with the Albany town datestamp, probably arranged somewhat like the handstamper in Figure 27. The "cork" contained a small metal tube or cutting die in its center, arranged to cut a circular chunk out of the stamp as well as to let the ink penetrate. If the stamp were removed from the cover, it would come away as two pieces, or so it was intended. Similar devices were used at Buffalo, Rochester and other cities.

Figure 30 shows a cover sent from Philadelphia with a somewhat different type of patent cancel killing the stamp. This patent killer, also duplexed with the town datestamp, consisted of a set of cutting blades arranged as a grid. The blades were supposed to cut the surface of the stamp. For the two covers shown, the Albany device worked as

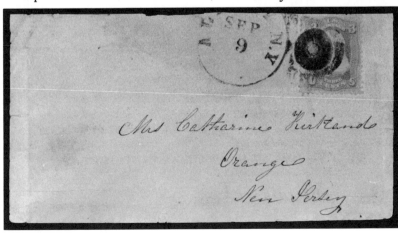

Figure 29. The well-known Albany patent duplexed handstamp of the 1860s, on a cover to Orange, New Jersey. The circular die has cut a small, neat hole into the stamp.

**Figure 30. A cover with the Philadel-
phia patent duplex handstamp. The
killer portion of the duplex device
had cutting blades, intended to cut
into the surface of the stamp.**

intended, cutting well into the stamp. The Philadelphia killer shows
no sign at all of any cutting into the stamp surface.

It is probable that the duplexed devices weren't as effective as
separate canceling handstamps specifically intended to cut into the
stamps, but the time-saving advantage of the duplex would be lost if
a separate canceling handstamp had to be used. Many small offices
continued to use separate handstamps to cancel during this period.

All the designs intended to cut into the stamps had similar
problems, which ultimately led to their being discarded. For one thing,
they could damage the contents of the letters. This was pointed out by
Postmaster General Blair in his discussion of these instruments in
1863. He also noted a second problem — that the canceling devices
dulled rapidly and would no longer cut after a short period of use. Also,
the thin cutting edges didn't carry much ink.

Looking at the Albany and Philadelphia types in Figures 29 and
30, it doesn't seem that their cutting edges could be sharpened very
easily. In the case of the Philadelphia patent killer, the thin blades
carried very little ink, so they would neither cut nor heavily cancel
soon after being placed in service.

The late Fred Schmalzriedt of Detroit collected patent cancels
both on and off cover and probably had one of the greatest collections
of these ever formed. His listing of these, which appears in Volume I
of Delf Norona' *Cyclopedia of United States Postmarks and Postal
History* (reprinted by Quarterman Publications, Lawrence, Massachusetts, in 1975) covers 25 pages of text and listings. He probably
listed a good many cancels as patent killers that were never intended
to cut into the stamps. However, most of those that were so intended
are included. He also added a term to our philatelic vocabulary. The
term "patent cancel" or "killer" means to us a type of cancel intended
to penetrate the surface of the stamp by cutting or scraping, even
though most of these weren't the subject of patents, and the patents
including such usually have other claims considered more important
by their inventors.

Beginnings of duplex handstamps

As previously stated, a duplex handstamp is a postmarking
device made to apply two separate markings at one stroke. In the

1830s in the United States, town datestamps had rate wheels attached to imprint both town and rate marks simultaneously. These datestamps were made under a patent granted to A. White of Templeton, Massachusetts, February 27, 1830. Neither the patent number nor the details have survived. A later style of duplex handstamp, still much used today, combined the town datestamp with a killer. The datestamp provided a record of posting, and the killer obliterated the stamp, both in one stroke.

Figures 31, 33, 34 and 35 show several tracings of duplex markings from the early 1859-62 period of the later style. Obviously, no canceling devices were needed in the United States prior to the use of postage stamps in the 1840s. When the 1847 stamps were introduced, separate handstamps, such as the New York square grids, were used by some towns. But most towns soon were using their own datestamps to cancel stamps to avoid having to apply marks with two different instruments by two separate strokes.

Until the 1851 issue appeared with a rate structure that encouraged prepayment of postage, few letters actually bore stamps. The prepaid rate was 3¢ for letters weighing one-half ounce carried less than 3,000 miles. The collect rate was 5¢.

Using separate cancelers was not a lot of work as long as there was not a lot of mail. But when the use of stamps became popular in the 1850s, with their use compulsory in 1856, postmarks used to cancel stamps became a focus of much attention in the U.S. Post Office Department. Ever since stamps were first used, the Post Office Department had required that printing inks be used to cancel them. Gradually the Post Office Department pressured postmasters to use separate instruments for canceling. This was caused by two problems: Townmarks were often unreadable when used to cancel stamps, and stamps often were so faintly canceled that the Post Office eventually became paranoid about stamps being washed and reused.

As previously mentioned, in 1859 Marcus P. Norton of Troy, New York, obtained Post Office Department permission to test for three months an experimental handstamp developed by him. The tests were run at Troy, New York, and I have record of three surviving covers with the marking.

A tracing of the marking from one of these covers is shown in Figure 31. A portion of the actual cover is shown as Figure 28 on page 19. The marking is dated JE (June) 2, 1859, and is on an embossed stamped envelope. Another example, dated May 24, 1859, cancels an 1857 U.S. 3¢ stamp, and the third example is also on a Nesbitt envelope. The markings are distinguished by large letters between two large concentric circles. The dates have two-letter abbreviations and a two-digit year date lying on its side. This is known as the lazy year date.

These characteristics stemmed from what was to have been the main feature of Norton's device. Figure 32 shows a drawing of the device, adapted from his patent drawing. The device had rotatable wheels with the numbers and letters of the date on them arranged like a mechanical automobile odometer. The device also included an attached blotter, as Norton termed it, with sharp cutters to mark and dig into the stamp and cause the canceling ink to penetrate.

A patent application was granted Norton on August 9, 1859, but only for his blotter "attached to or connected with the main part of any canceling device," as the patent stated. This wording was to cause

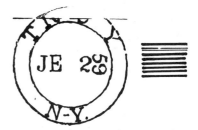

Figure 31. An early U.S. duplex post-mark with the lazy year date.

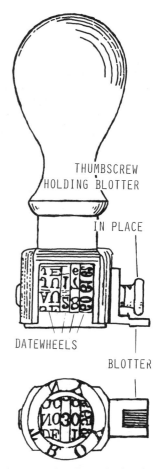

Figure 32. The first duplex hand-stamper developed by Marcus P. Norton, based on drawings of his patent of August 9, 1859. A thumbscrew holds the blotter, or killer, to the main body of the handstamp.

21

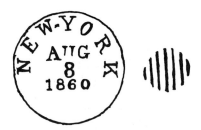

Figure 33. The earliest New York duplex postmark.

Figure 34. The earliest Cleveland duplex postmark.

Figure 35. This marking has closely spaced vertical lines in an open circle for the blotter.

Norton much agony in later years. Norton's claim for the rotatable, easy-setting date wheels was denied.

Although Norton had devised a workable idea made very applicable a few years later by a new regulation ordered by Postmaster General Joseph Holt, unfortunately his patented design was flawed. It was too fragile for hard use, and it is probable that the cutter blades of the blotter, when sharp, cut into letters and damaged them, although they didn't stay sharp long. Apparently Norton's original device was never used again after the three-month test at Troy.

On July 23, 1860, Postmaster General Holt absolutely banned use of town datestamps to cancel stamps, requiring instead that a "distinct canceler" be used. All post offices were thus required to use two different instruments and separate strokes to postmark letters and cancel stamps. In large post offices, this required additional clerks and more instruments.

Soon, New York Postmaster John A. Dix and Cleveland Postmaster Benjamin Harrington did the obvious. They attached stamp-canceling devices to their town datestampers so that again letters could be postmarked and stamps canceled with one stroke. The earliest of these New York duplexes, recorded by Bond, is August 8, 1860, shown in Figure 33. Thomas F. Allen recorded the earliest such Cleveland duplex as August 17, 1860, shown in Figure 34.

Dix exulted in his solution to the problem and wrote to the Post Office Department. He was mortified when promptly informed that his idea was in conflict with Norton's patent. The matter was apparently soon resolved, for then at least, by giving Norton a contract to furnish 10 of his patented devices to Dix. These markings had closely spaced vertical lines in an open circle for the blotter. The latest use known to me, January 30, 1862, on two different carrier covers, is shown in a tracing in Figure 35.

The Post Office Department standardized duplex markings in the 1860s, but it could never make any long-lasting agreement with Norton. He apparently always asked for all the thousands of dollars his devices saved. In addition, the U.S. Supreme Court finally determined that the words "attached to . . . the main part" (of a marking device) didn't really describe Norton's blotter. For example, the handstamper shown in Figure 36 (courtesy of Don Johnstone) isn't much like the device described by Norton's patent, although it actually bears the 1859 Norton patent number. The handstamper in Figure 36 has its cancel and postmark sections solidly attached to a crossbar rather than with a thumbscrew as in the original design.

Some writers believe that Norton's patents were defeated by technicalities. Of course, that's what patents are all about. Interestingly, Norton himself was a patent attorney and attempted by a wave of successive patents to rectify the defect of his earlier claims.

Duplexed cancelers with fancy designs

Figure 37 shows one of a lot of postal cards, all addressed to the Alton Agricultural Works of Alton, Illinois, just across the Mississippi River from St. Louis. This card is Scott UX5. Some of the other Alton cards are the later UX7, which had the legend "Nothing but the address can be placed on this side," rather than "Write the address . . ." as on the card in Figure 37. Scott UX5 was issued in late 1875; UX7 appeared in 1881. This helps date cards that have no year dates in either postmark or message.

The postmark on the card in Figure 37 is one of several in the lot bearing dated postmarks, usually duplexed with a star or other fancy killers of similar appearance. Since the addressee was a manufacturer of agricultural machinery, most of the cards are from small towns in rural areas.

Prior to the Congressional appropriations act of May 4, 1882, postmasters of fourth-class post offices had to buy much of their office equipment, including letter scales, postmarking and canceling devices, and ink pads. Consequently, many of the small offices, defined at that time (by Section 100 of the Postal Laws and Regulations of 1879) as fourth-class offices when the postmaster's annual compensation was under $1,000, used manuscript postmarks. If the volume of mail warranted the expense, some purchased postmarking devices from suppliers. The first-, second- and third-class offices, with postmasters appointed by the president, were furnished such equipment. These postmasters were on salary, periodically readjusted to reflect the business done at their offices. Their postmarks usually resembled those of other post offices of similar size.

Compensation for the fourth-class postmasters, who were appointed by the postmasters general, was the sum of box rents, the value of stamps canceled and the proceeds from the sale of wastepaper, including "dead" or unclaimed newspapers. The act of May 4, 1882, allowed up to $5 per fourth-class post office for letter scales and postmarking instruments. The total appropriation was $35,000. In 1883, 44,798 of the 46,893 U.S. post offices were fourth-class offices. A bit of arithmetic shows that a $35,000 appropriation, allocated at $5 per office, didn't go very far. In recognition of the size of the appropriation, the announcements said that such expenditures would be approved first come first served, as long as the appropriation lasted. I think this law greatly stimulated the manufacture of postmarking devices. Far more manuscript markings seem to exist on covers from the 1870s than after 1882.

While some specialists believe the new devices of the early 1880s were acquired through the Post Office Department supply office, it is obvious that most of them were simply purchased from suppliers and charged as an expense.

The *U.S. Postal Guides*, sent to postmasters throughout the country, show a greatly increased number of advertisements from

Figure 36. This handstamper from the late 1860s bears Norton's 1859 patent number. It is not much like the device described by the patent.

Figure 37. A shaded star in purple, duplexed with an 1879 postmark from Assumption, Illinois. See A in Figure 39 for a tracing.

Figure 38. A duplex-style flange post-marking and canceling device, advertised by the F.P. Hammond Company of Aurora, Illinois, in the *U.S. Postal Guide* for January 1881.

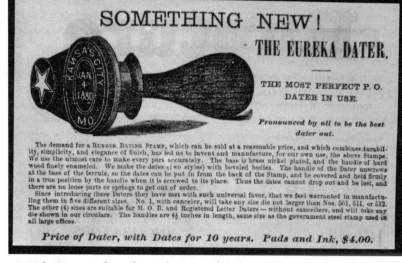

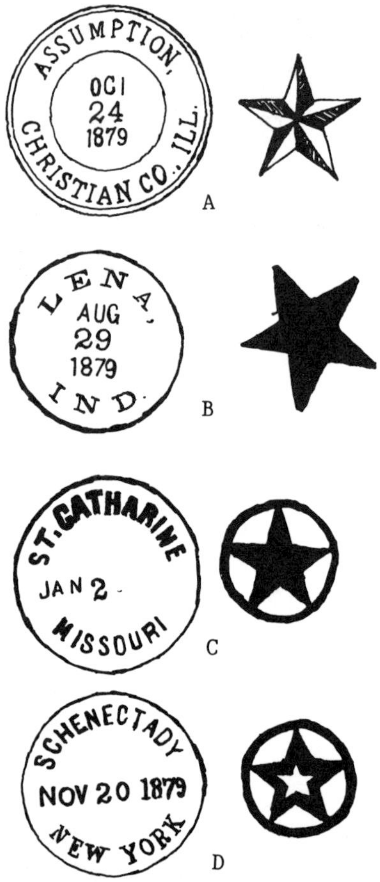

Figure 39. Duplexed star cancelers of 1879-81, probably furnished by Hammond, on postal cards addressed to a manufacturer of agricultural equipment at Alton, Illinois.

manufacturers of marking devices after 1882. Figure 38 shows part of a two-page advertisement from F.P. Hammond & Company of Aurora, Illinois, in the *Guide* for January 1881. This was before the fourth-class offices could charge such purchases as an office expense. It was one of only two such ads in that issue. Hammond was obviously doing some business prior to the "bonanza" of 1882.

The device in the ad in Figure 38 is a conventional duplex postmarking device with a Kansas City postmark and a star killer. Figure 39 shows (as A) the postmark on the card in Figure 37 and three other duplexed markings with star killers. These are representative of the 10 or 15 cards with similar postmarks using stars as killers in the group of Alton cards under discussion.

This raises a few questions of interest. Was the star killer shown in the Figure 38 advertisement actually used from Kansas City? And since many of these instruments were furnished by the same manufacturer, were exactly similar star cancels used at other towns? None of the 10 or so star killers in the Alton lot was alike. Yet it seems logical that a manufacturer would furnish a uniform product.

In listings of fancy cancels, usually the town of use is paramount. If many duplicates of each killer type were furnished to various towns, then identifying the sources of killers on off-cover stamps (or covers with illegible postmarks) becomes a problem.

Another aspect of interest is that most of these postmarks used colored inks, despite a regulation of that period (section 202, page 671, January 1883 *Guide*) that "the Postmaster General insists that . . . black ink be used for postmarking." Since an ink supply was usually part of a purchase of postmarking devices (in Figure 38), it would seem that various shades of purple, ranging from magenta to a near violet, were sold with the devices and frequently used.

Fourth-class post office postmarks, 1880-85

Figure 40 shows both sides of a U.S. postal card (Scott UX5) used in 1879 to convey an advertisement to a postmaster for a patent postmarking tool. As previously stated, prior to 1883, U.S. fourth-class offices — those with less than $1,000 annual revenue — had to furnish their own postmarking devices. In the early 1880s, these were bought from private parties. Manufacturers of such devices (Figure

24

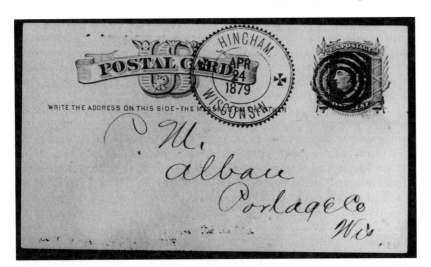

Figure 40. A U.S. 1875 1¢ Liberty postal card, with a magnificent strike of the elaborate Hingham, Wisconsin, town datestamp. The reverse of the card shows an advertisement of the Rubber Stamp Works for a new patented postmarking device, aimed at postmasters of fourth-class offices who had to buy their own postmarking devices.

40 is just one example) found them to be good business. Respecting the device shown on the card in Figure 40, the six different imprints mounted on one wheel would seem to be ideal for a postmaster operating a compact, one-man office, often in a store.

The address side of the postal card, shown in Figure 40, bears a perfect strike of a fancy-toothed Hingham, Wisconsin, postmark, which leads me to the assumption that the proprietor of the Rubber Stamp Works, the advertiser, was also the postmaster or at least had furnished the Hingham postmaster with his deluxe postmark, a tracing of which is shown in Figure 41.

The *U.S. Official Postal Guide* for January 1883, which announced the new benevolence to the fourth-class offices, also (under section 976) remarked:

"The use of a rubber stamp is a violation of the law. The Post Office Department furnished metal postmarking stamps and requires postage stamps to be canceled with black printing ink, which cannot be used with a rubber stamp."

Thus, while the *Postal Guide* noted in one section that "metal stamps" had already been furnished, it is obvious from the terms of the announcement that the project had just started for the fourth-class post offices.

Figure 41. A fancy-toothed marking from Hingham, Wisconsin.

Figure 42. This marking from Clifford, Ohio, probably was struck from a rubber datestamp.

Figure 43. These markings are from daters made of other materials other than rubber.

This chapter is based on the following *Linn's* columns: G.I. town datestamps, April 9, 1984; stock postmarking devices, July 27, 1987; patent canceling devices, July 23, 1984; beginnings of duplex handstamps, September 24, 1990; fancy duplexed cancelers; fourth-class post office postmarkings, February 15, 1988.

Apparently, the project stemmed from the Post Office Department's objecting to the inks used with rubber stamps. The ink usually furnished by the rubber-stamp suppliers was an aniline base that could easily be washed from the stamp. Postmasters avoided using the black printer's ink, evidently because it damaged or clogged their privately owned postmarking devices.

Despite the published sections in the *Postal Guides*, rubber postmarking stamps continued to be used for some time. Apparently someone developed a black ink that wouldn't wash off but could be used with rubber postmarking devices. It wasn't long before the Post Office Department was furnishing small offices with rubber town datestamps. The *Postal Guides* of the early 1880s carry a large number of advertisements of suppliers of town datestamps and other postmarking tools, with many illustrations of the postmarks they produced. Most of these seem fairly standard from supplier to supplier. Different suppliers even illustrated the same fancy cancel or postmark ornamentation. Markers continued to be advertised as made from rubber. This leads me to suspect that the advertisers bought outfits, including molds in which the designs were formed, from the same manufacturers.

However, not all suppliers advertised in the *Postal Guides*. For example, I found none for the Rubber Stamp Works, which produced the Figure 40 ad. And while most of the handstampers used at fourth-class offices in the early 1880s were obviously furnished by well-known suppliers, there are major exceptions to the standard patterns. The markings shown in Figures 41 and 42 illustrate various aspects of this idea. The Hingham, Wisconsin, marking in Figure 41 contains ornate embellishments and a style of cogged outer rim not evident in any of the *Postal Guide* ads. This was obviously a deluxe product of someone in the business — probably the Rubber Stamp Works of Hingham. The shape and arrangement of the Hingham marking is quite conventional.

The Clifford, O. marking in Figure 42, traced from a cover bearing a 3¢ green Bank Note stamp, is also conventional in arrangement, including the fancy negative star killer. But it contains ornate borders and ornamentation that I haven't seen in any advertisement. The star killer is obviously duplexed with the circular datestamp.

The Galena, Ohio, dated townmark (the top tracing in Figure 43) is something else. Although of a conventional size, and fairly well-spaced and arranged, it shows the year date split into "18" and "84," surrounding the "O" for Ohio. It seems probable this device was made by someone who had the equipment but was unaccustomed to making postmarking devices. The marking is struck in magenta on a 3¢ Bank Note cover. The Genoa, Illinois, marking (the bottom tracing in Figure 43, is probably homemade. It isn't symmetrical, nor is it duplexed with a cork killer.

I think a decision was made about 1883 to supply all the post offices with standardized postmarking devices to get rid of inadequate devices that sometimes produced illegible postmarks and were often struck in inks that could be cleaned from stamps. Prior to the 1880s, the post office had promulgated no regulations about the style of datestamps, only how they were used. Beginning in the 1880s, the post office began establishing standard styles for use throughout the country. The only way to accomplish this was for all such instruments to be furnished by the Post Office Department.

Chapter 3

Machine Cancels

Introduction to collecting machine cancels

Machine cancel collecting can be both rewarding and frustrating. The reward comes from collections such as will be discussed here. The frustration can come from attempting to cover too broad a field, making a coherent and comprehensive collection nearly impossible.

Figure 44 shows a cover from Columbus, Ohio, with an interesting corner card and a machine postmark that doesn't much resemble the machine postmarks used today. This cover, and some others with similar markings, led Arthur Bond to send me a compendium authored by Eugene Funk and himself, so that I was able to identify and group portions of my Columbus postal history collection into a collection of Columbus machine postmarks.

Machine cancels are an enormous subject, with a vast supply of inexpensive covers. Selecting a field to collect should include consideration of a number of aspects. *Machine Cancel Forum*, a periodical for machine cancel collectors, has touched upon many of the possibilities. This publication, originated by John McGee some years ago, is now the periodical of the Machine Cancel Society. This society deals not only with machine cancels but the machines that produced them. *Machine Cancel Forum* provides new and current information and also updates the series of handbooks on markings of various manufacturer's canceling machines, published by the society and others.

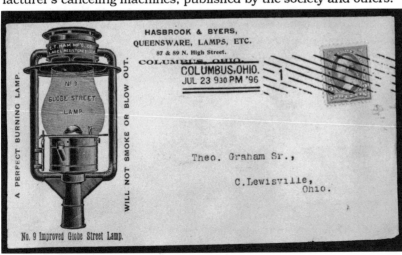

Figure 44. An illustrated cover from Columbus, Ohio, sent in July 1896, as indicated by the Barry machine cancel strike.

Russell F. Hanmer's *A Collector's Guide to U.S. Machine Post-marks, 1871-1925*, is a 188-page compendium covering the markings of all different U.S. canceling machines, so that most markings can be identified. Published by David G. Phillips Publishing Company, this is available from both the publisher and literature dealers.

There are many ways to collect machine cancels, but specialization is essential to maintain interest. The question is, how to select a field of interest? Most American and many foreign machine markings have been cataloged by towns of use and types. Many of these are listed by Hanmer. For collecting in any depth, a catalog of what exists is the first prerequisite. Collecting may be done by manufacturer. In fact, the classification of markings usually starts with and always includes the name of the machine manufacturer.

Canceling machine postmarks are usually classified and cataloged according to the different types of town postmarks or "dials," and to the different killers used to cancel the stamps. To illustrate this, recourse to Hanmer's compendium shows that the marking on the cover in Figure 44 was applied by a Barry machine. Barry machine cancels appeared on the scene in 1894 and eventually were used in at least 156 post offices in 138 different cities. Further details about Barry machine cancels may be found in Reg Morris and Robert J. Payne's three-volume set of handbooks, *The Barry Story*, published by the authors. Barry machine markings exist with three basic dial types — straightline, oval and circular. With these were used a dozen different styles of killers of straight or wavy-line bar arrangements.

While most of the killers could be used with any of the styles of dies, not all possible combinations have been seen. There also were several one-of-a-kind types or combinations, such as the Toledo, Ohio, slogan on the cover shown in Figure 45. This has an extra oval in the bars advertising the Ohio Centennial Exposition scheduled for 1902-03, which was never held because of a depression.

While not all the killer dials are known with each and every type of killer (dials and killers were usually individual pieces so that each, in theory, could be used with any of the matching components), the possible combinations, provided by 156 post offices over more than 10 years, offer ample opportunity for forming a considerable collection that hangs together well.

There are other machine manufacturers, such as International and American, with far greater volume of markings. And, of course,

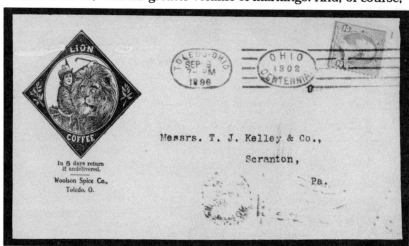

Figure 45. A special type of Barry machine cancel, with an extra oval in the killer bars to advertise an exposition.

Figure 46. At left are straight-line Barry machine cancels used at Columbus, Ohio. At right are oval-type Barry machine cancels. Variations in type are shown.

Figure 47. Earliest known U.S. machine cancels, produced at Pittsburgh by a machine of unknown make in 1871.

it is possible to impose further limitations. Machine cancels can be an important segment of a collection or a handbook about the markings used in geographic areas, such as states or cities.

I collect just Columbus machine markings. Figure 46 on the previous page shows Barry machine types used in Columbus, as traced from my covers. Rather than dwell on the details of these markings, I have given the types of each, per the *The Barry Story*. The Columbus listing isn't necessarily complete, and not all the possible combinations were used in Columbus. Figure 46 shows the straight-lines and the oval styles that were used in Columbus.

Figure 46 also shows variations in some of the types, such as the oval marking with a seven-bar killer sometimes having the top bar either very faint or entirely missing so that it is mistaken for the rare type 0-6(1) with six bars. It may be noted, too, that there are three tracings of the oval markings with five wavy lines, type 0-9(1). Each of the first two listings represents a separate phase of usage, and the third example shows use of a new and different oval dial.

The real point of all this detail, however, is that collectors may collect as deeply or shallowly as they wish. There are many different ways to use the information available in the machine cancel field.

Experimental machine cancels

Machine cancel collecting also can take many different forms. It can be classic or modern, highly specialized or part of a larger postal history collection. Unlike many postal history subjects that are now long gone, we can still receive new styles of machine cancels in our daily mail. New developments in mail-processing equipment will continue to produce much that is collectible.

Machine cancels are mostly collected on full covers. A few areas, such as flag cancels, with an enormous amount of material available, have been collected on 2- by 4-inch cutout corners to save space.

Most specialists collect machine cancels by manufacturer. Others, including myself, collect machine cancels as part of other postal history interests (such as my hometown). Still others maintain a "type" collection of markings produced by machines from as many different manufacturers as can be acquired. Such collections display the development of canceling machines as a postal history subject, without delving into the minor variations of the cancels.

Figure 48. A Groth-Constantine machine cancel applied in 1893 during one of the test periods of this machine at New York.

Hundreds of patents for postmarking devices have been granted by the U.S., British and other patent offices in the 19th and 20th centuries. Examples of markings produced by most of the patented devices have never been recorded. Conversely, the earliest recognized U.S. machine postmarks (see Figure 47), used with two or more different killers in Pittsburgh in the early 1870s, have never been identified with a manufacturer's patent, although these markings have been the subject of considerable speculation, linking them to a few patents of that period. The Pittsburgh markings were probably produced by an experimental canceling machine on which no patent was ever granted. Making a trial run in a post office before patents were granted was unusual in the 19th century. It was almost never done after 1880.

Collectors find markings of experimental or pilot-model rapid-canceling machines extremely interesting. It can take a protracted search through patent records and post office reports to work out details of just whose machine produced a given marking, particularly when a machine was in service only a few days or weeks. For example, Figure 48 shows a cover with a New York City Groth-Constantine machine marking, applied on June 22, 1893. One or more of these machines may have been in use intermittently from 1890 through 1895, but the markings are rare.

Figure 49 shows a photo of a six-station machine believed to be a Groth-Constantine machine, as illustrated in Marshall Cushing's *Story of Our Post Office Department*, published by Thayer & Company in Boston in 1892. Figure 50 shows two diagrams from Groth's series of patents issued in the early 1890s. The drawing at the left shows his machine, as depicted in his patent of January 7, 1890. The drawing at right shows a revised canceling head, part of his patent granted in 1892. In between, the machine had been tested, rejected and redesigned — leading to the last of three patents. It was again being operated, presumably as a test, as late as May 1895. Such was the normal pattern of experimental canceling machine uses, which were usually conducted at a post office near the inventor's home or at Washington, D.C., or if the hometown tests looked promising, at both.

Some markings, while known to be machine cancels, are the subject of differences of opinion as to whose machines produced them. Figure 51 shows such a marking, felt by many to be the product of a Meyers machine when used at New York, or a Palmer and Clark machine when used at Washington. Others feel that it is simply a

Figure 49. The Groth-Constantine six-station rapid-canceling machine.

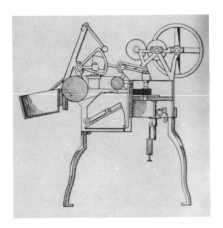
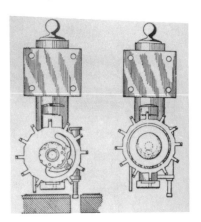

Figure 50. Drawings from the patents of William Groth, upon which the rapid-canceling machine shown in Figure 49 was based.

Figure 51. A postal card with a post-mark believed to have been applied by a Palmer & Clark experimental machine. Very little is known about the machine or the marking.

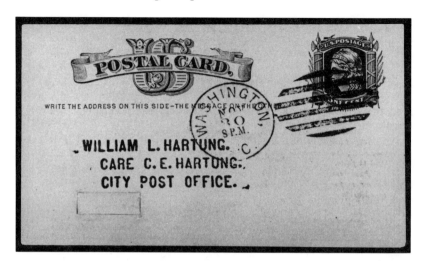

handstamp, similar to the mute-barred ovals used at many cities, with the oval rotated 90 degrees. Obviously, a great deal of research remains to be done. New data shows up about the old machines, and as new equipment goes into service, new markings also need to be recognized and documented.

The Machine Cancel Society, formed from the Flag Cancel Society membership plus the subscriber list of *Machine Cancel Forum* only a few years ago, has grown rapidly. There are several reasons for this surge in interest. First is the subject itself. In many cases, machine cancels are so sharply and cleanly struck that constant minute varieties, or products of different look-alike dies, can be readily detected and collected. Such markings share many attributes encountered in traditional stamp collecting — including first and last days of use and flyspeck aspects. Second, machine cancels are an important part of many other postal history subjects, as noted previously. The owners of such collections are finding that knowledge of machine cancels helps them properly describe their material.

Interest in this field, as with most others, is enhanced by documentation, which in machine cancel collecting is constantly growing. I have mentioned Russ Hanmer's work, *A Collector's Guide to U.S. Machine Cancels, 1871-1925*. This is the only reference I know that reviews the entire machine cancel field up to 1925. Several handbooks covering the machine cancels of individual manufacturers have been compiled and have been published by either the authors or the Machine Cancel Society.

This brings us to what is probably the major reason for the growing interest in machine and flag cancels — the continued improvement in *Machine Cancel Forum*, the quarterly publication of the Machine Cancel Society. The society has appointed 10 specialists to head 15 study groups covering the various makes of machines and the cancels they produce. Each issue of the society publication includes reports from some of these groups, plus a column on machine cancels in general. Thus, the publication appeals not only to specialists, but to those, such as myself, who have a more general interest in machine cancels.

It's my opinion that this field offers much more to those wishing to get in on the ground floor in a field of high postal history interest than do the well-established fields we all cherish. This is because a large variety of collectible items are still available at low cost, and because finds can still be made of covers that research will eventually show to have rare cancels.

Flag cancels an inexpensive collection

The cover in Figure 52 bears a Canton, New York, weather report backstamp shown as an inset in the illustration. It also features the Boston "involute" double-year-dated flag cancellation. The flag marking on the cover in Figure 52 is fully as unusual as the weather report marking.

The late J. David Baker, one of our premier postal history collectors, used to marvel over the number of classic covers with a distinguishing feature that had collectors agog — but which also had other unusual facets, equally rare and interesting, not recognized by those bedazzled by the first peculiarity. The cover shown in Figure 52 is a good example. It was offered at a price determined by the weather report backstamp. The beautiful flag cancel wasn't noted at all.

Before discussing this item in detail, let's review some background information about flag cancels and the collecting of them. The key reference in the field is Frederick Langford's *Standard Flag Cancel Encyclopedia*, the third and latest edition of which was published in 1976. The data given here is taken from that publication. Langford notes that flag cancels, in common with most other machine cancels, have two components: the dial section, which gives the post office name and the date, and the killer die intended to cancel the stamps. It wasn't unusual for either component part to be paired off with more than one style of the mating portion.

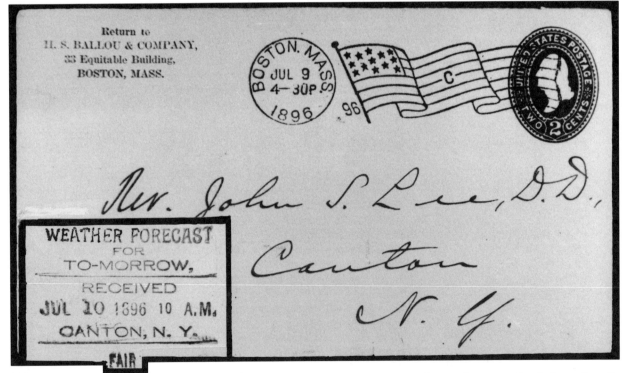

Figure 52. This cover's most apparent desirable feature is the Canton, New York, weather report backstamp (inset). However, the Boston flag cancel, dated July 9, 1896, is actually the earliest known use of the beautiful involute-style American flag machine cancel.

Figure 53. The earliest type of flag cancel, used first at Boston on October 31, 1894.

The first flag cancels were applied at Boston on October 31, 1894, by a rapid-canceling machine made by the American Postal Machine Company of that city. A tracing of the marking is shown in Figure 53. The marking was applied in November 1894.

American Postal Machines grew rapidly from there. By World War I, their machines were in use in most of the cities and towns in the United States. Langford, who bases his work upon the Post Office Department official records of the dates and placements of machines, states that by the time the last machines were phased out, at the end of the 1930s, more than 3,000 towns and cities had produced more than 7,000 varieties of flag cancellations. Of these, 6,891 varieties were produced by American Postal equipment. The few hundred more were imitations by other companies' machines.

Langford defines flag cancels as a design "with a waved, outlined area attached to a clearly defined staff," used for invalidating stamps. If it doesn't have a staff, the design has to have other features, such as a field of stars, to be called a flag cancel. He remarks that a flag cancel made by an American Postal machine can be "anything that looks like a flag," but that a cancel produced by any other manufacturer's equipment must "look very much like a flag" to be called such. This was because the flag cancel was American Postal's product and really no one else's.

The *Flag Cancel Encyclopedia* is based upon a cataloging system developed and copyrighted by Langford in which the dials bear letter designations. The canceling dies, which contain the flag designs, are identified by a chart designating staff and halyard details vertically and arrangements of stars and stripes horizontally.

For example, the cancellation on the cover shown in Figure 52 (a tracing is shown in Figure 54) has a type D dial with the post office name (Boston, Mass.) at the top and the year date (1896) in full at the bottom. The flag is involute (in folds) style — in Langford's system, a "40's" horizontal column type. It has a staff but no halyard, which is designated a 3 in his vertical column. So the flag design is a type 43 under Langford's system. The entire marking is listed as a D-43 type from Boston.

The distinguishing feature of the use on the cover shown in Figure 52 is that with the year date "96" at the base of the flagstaff, there are two year dates in the marking. The marking wasn't used in

Figure 54. The first involute flag postmark, as it appears on the cover shown as Figure 52.

34

this combination very long. The cover shown is the earliest date of use presently recorded, but the latest date seen for this combination of dial and killer was just five days later: July 13, 1896.

On July 16, 1896, the same involute flag killer appeared with a different dial that reads "Boston" at the top and "Mass" at the bottom, and the "96" year date (which was actually attached to the dial) still appearing at the base of the flagstaff. July 9, 1896, the date of use of the cover shown is also the earliest date of use recorded for any of the beautiful involute flag designs.

Referring to Figures 53, 54 and 55, it may be seen that two styles of arrangements were used for the stars in the fields of the flags. The earliest type marking (tracing in Figure 53) has what is termed an ovate arrangement. This was used at several cities and towns in the early versions of flag cancels. Most of the later types used the spread field of stars, as shown in Figures 54 and 55. The tracing in Figure 55 shows Langford's type B-14(1) used at Columbus, Ohio, in 1900. This is typical of the normal run of flag cancels of later days. The (1) in the designation refers to the number included within the lines of the flag, normally a machine number. Letters were sometimes used in this space.

Figure 55. A more common style of flag cancel, used at many post offices; here from Columbus, Ohio, on January 25, 1900.

The field of flag cancel collecting offers a great deal of pleasure to the collector interested in postal history and covers who doesn't want to spend much money. Most covers are obtainable for a few dollars. Even rarities, when they can be found, are not beyond the financial reach of most collectors. Due to the very large volume of markings available, flag cancel collecting is best handled within a specialized or limited collection — such as collecting only one style of flag or specializing in the cancels of a single city, town or area.

Flag cancel collecting really can't be done satisfactorily without a catalog, and the Langford *Standard Flag Cancel Encyclopedia* fills the bill very nicely. The fact that it was published in 1976 doesn't mean that it's outdated. Langford has provided occasional supplements to add the few new items appearing from time to time. He has left few, if any, stones unturned in this field. I doubt that any catalog has ever been so complete in terms of listing all material that can exist. Langford based his works on the records of when and where the machines were used. In three editions, his data has attained a very high level of completeness and, I imagine, accuracy.

The Flag Cancel Society, which flourished for many years, became part of the Machine Cancel Society when the group was formed. In each issue, *Machine Cancel Forum*, published by MCS, contains a section devoted to flag cancels. This recognizes the fact that flag cancels are a very important and widely collected specialty in the machine cancel field.

Figure 56. This 4¢ stamp was issued in 1960 to commemorate the opening of the First Automated Post Office in Providence, Rhode Island.

Intelex markings

Figure 56 shows the 1960 U.S. commemorative stamp, Scott 1164, portraying an architect's sketch of the new post office then being built at Providence, Rhode Island. The stamp is captioned "First automated post office in the United States." A total of 458,237 first-day covers were created for the Automated Post Office stamp.

In *Machine Cancel Forum* for October 1975, Eugene M. Funk illustrated an example of a Providence marking used in January 1961; a similar Washington, D.C., marking from October 1959; a Pawtucket, Rhode Island, example dated March 11, 1964; and a "U.S. Postal Service R.I. 028" marking from August 1973. These were the only U.S. cities then recorded as using this style marking.

Funk identified the markings as those of an Intelex machine, installed by Intelex Systems Inc., a subsidiary of International Telephone and Telegraph Company. According to Funk, the machine was designed and constructed by Standard Elektrik A.G. of West Berlin. The machine was capable of handling 25,000 letters an hour.

Funk wrote: "The mail is brought into the post office and placed into the culler, which removes packages and large flat pieces and stacks letters and cards into batches. These batches are placed in the facer-canceler by hand. The letters move past electronic scanners which reject envelopes without stamps and turn over those with stamps at the top. At the end of the lines all envelopes have stamps at the bottom, on the leading edge on one line, the trailing edge on the other. Two canceling dies apply the postmarks, and the envelopes emerge in two properly faced stacks." Funk had no further information to offer, although he did also illustrate examples of German and Italian uses of Intelex canceling machine markings.

Intelex machine cancels were used at Providence, Rhode Island, and Washington, D.C. Pawtucket, Rhode Island, cancels also were applied at Providence on mail received from there for processing. Intelex markings reading "U.S. Postal Service" with no town name also exist.

The Washington Intelex machine cancel, illustrated by Funk and traced here as Figure 57, is dated October 19, 1959, a year and a day before the first-day ceremony of the Automated Post Office stamp. Obviously, testing and pilot work was going on at Washington as well as at Providence.

I'm a retired engineer. Many years ago, I was involved in designing hardware that ultimately was used in some types of package-sorting machines. So I probably have more interest in this subject than most collectors. As a designer of machinery, I often get a chuckle out of the use of the word "automation." I wonder if Edgar Allan Poe was responsible for this word. In his story, *Maelzel's Chess Player*, Poe called an imaginative chess-playing robot an "automaton." Back in the 1960s, "automation" was a much-used word. Many people were concerned that their jobs would be taken over by machines. Even then, however, the machines that replaced 100 people required about as many of higher skills to keep them running.

Providence markings were applied in the so-called fully automated post office at Providence, Rhode Island. The stamp shown in Figure 56 celebrated the post office going on line.

Figure 58 shows a first-day cover with a block of four of the stamp, an appropriate cachet and the first-day cancel. My January 29, 1990, column in *Linn's* showed tracings of the Intelex Providence

Figure 57. This Intelex machine cancel is from 1959 from the U.S. Postal Service's Washington laboratory.

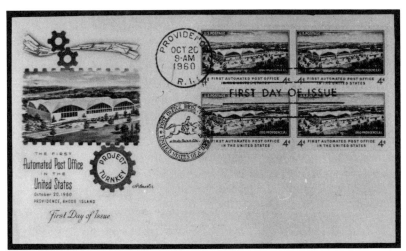

Figure 58. Shown is a first-day cover of the First Automated Post Office stamp of 1960, with a conventional commemorative U.S. Postal Service first-day cancel.

and Washington markings, but it is obvious from Figure 58 that the first-day cancel applied to that cover was not an Intelex machine marking. Figure 59 shows tracings of the first-day cancels together with an Intelex marking applied December 1960 for comparison. Without having seen any First Automated Post Office first-day covers, in my January 29 column, I speculated whether they had cancels applied by the new Intelex machines at the Providence automated post office.

Soon after I wrote that column, I acquired two first-day covers with different cachets. Both had the conventional style of first-day cancel used on first-day covers at that time. Retired ITT employee Robert B. Spear sent a tear sheet showing the new post office, equipment inside and the new stamp. The latter two illustrations were in color. The tear sheet probably came from an ITT publication published around the time the automated post office went into

Figure 59. The upper marking is the official first-day cancel applied when the new Automated Post Office stamp was issued. The lower marking is an Intelex machine cancel.

operation.

A reader who was making an in-depth study of the automated equipment sent the best response but asked that his name not be used. He stated that the first day of use of the Intelex canceler at Providence, Rhode Island, was November 30, 1960. He wrote: "If someone offers you an FDC of Scott 1164 with a Turnkey Post Office Intelex cancel, it is a fake. The Intelex cancels from Washington, D.C., were made, not in any regular post office, but in the postal lab. Intelex cancels from Pawtucket (and other cities) were actually made at Providence, not the city in the cancel."

His response seems quite authoritative and explains why the Washington cancel in Figure 57 is dated in October 1959, a year and a day before the Providence stamps were issued, fitting the period of a laboratory test program quite well.

The Pawtucket, Rhode Island, and U.S. Postal Service, R.I., Intelex markings applied at Providence might be considered forerunners to the application of cancels at centralized mail facilities today.

Canceling a cover with the name of the town where it was mailed (Pawtucket) but applying the cancel in a different city (Providence) is a twist of today's procedures at centralized mail facilities. Today's markings often show where letters were postmarked rather than where they were mailed. When they were postmarked also often lags behind when they were mailed.

Apparently, the Providence Intelex machines were used on regional mail only after the early 1960s, when peak mail loads brought them into use. The latest use I know of is a U.S. Postal Service, R.I., cancel from February 1973. Funk recorded it in 1975.

This chapter is based on the following *Linn's* **columns: collecting machine cancels, February 10, 1986; experimental machine cancels, May 30, 1988; flag cancels, October 7, 1985; Intelex markings, January 29 and May 28, 1990.**

Chapter 4

Special Rate Services

Drop letters

The earliest mention of drop letters in our postal laws was in the act of 1794, when the postage on such letters was set at 1¢ per letter, rather than being assessed by number of sheets or by weight. The drop payment was thus a fee, rather than a rate. Of course, the distance such letters were carried was nil.

The term "drop letter" stems from those years when everyone had to go to the post office to send or pick up mail. Such letters were dropped at a post office for the addressee to pick them up at the same office. They were never transmitted between post offices. The early Postal Laws & Regulations sometimes referred to these as "box letters."

Until the act of February 1861, drop letters could be prepaid or collect, although as of April 1, 1855, other domestic mails were required to be prepaid. Starting January 1, 1856, they were supposed to be prepaid by postage stamps. The Postal Laws & Regulations were unclear about prepayment of drop letters until the regulations of 1857, section 77, which clearly stated: "Prepayment on drop letters is optional." This was continued in the 1859 PL&R. But the act of

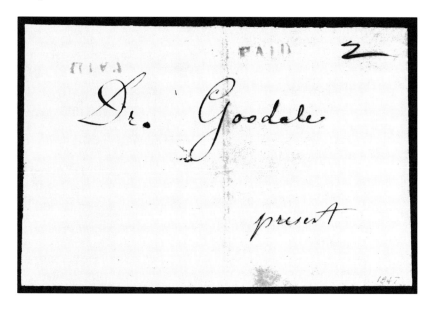

Figure 60. Without the dateline of the enclosed letter ("Columbus, Jan. 26th, 1847") neither the origin nor the year of this cover would be known. There is no town datestamp. The only postal markings are the two red "PAID" handstamps and the manuscript "2" — indicating the letter was a drop letter from the period 1845-51.

Figure 61. Mailed as a drop letter at Circleville, Ohio, this cover bears a complete set of postal markings and the town name included in the address. Probably fewer than half the drop letters mailed in the early 19th century show complete markings and a full address.

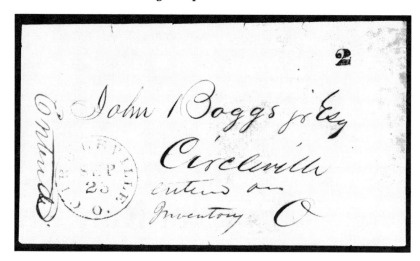

February 1861, section 14, required that drop letters be prepaid by postage stamps.

Since drop letters didn't go to other post offices, they were often treated casually by postal clerks in terms of postmarks. At times, they were treated with equal informality by mailers, as may be seen from the cover in Figure 60. The only markings on this cover are two red "PAID" handstamps and a black manuscript "2." The address is simply "Dr. Goodale, present."

Luckily when I spied this cover in a dealer's stock, I recognized the name of Dr. Goodale as that of an early Columbus, Ohio, personage. Both a street and a park are named after him. So I bought it for my Columbus collection. The content confirmed not only the Columbus usage, but also the date, January 1847, proving the cover was sent during the period (July 1, 1845 to July 1, 1851) when the drop-letter fee was 2¢. This was one of only two eras between 1794 and 1863 when the drop-letter fee was more then 1¢. The other period was 1815-16 when the fee presumably was 1 1/2¢, during the short time when all rates were increased by 50 percent to help pay for the War of 1812.

Prior to the requirement that postage be prepaid by stamps, it was usually more convenient to send letters collect. To send a prepaid letter, one had to take it to a counter and pay postage in cash. A collect letter could be mailed in the slot in a post office wall, even if the office wasn't open. To pick up one's mail, a call at the counter was necessary. The clerk had to sort through the accumulation filed alphabetically. Collecting postage in cash didn't delay this process much longer. Thus, when drop letters were delivered, collect postage often wasn't marked. And, except in the large cities, town datestamps were often omitted.

Figure 61 shows a drop letter with all the trimmings required by law. The cover was mailed at Circleville, Ohio and postmarked there on September 25 (circa 1850). A "2" handstamp in matching blue indicates postage was collect.

It wasn't until after 1855, when prepayment on domestic mails was required, that the term "Due" began to be used in handstamps. Prior to that, letters sent postage due were the norm, and the exceptions were marked "paid."

Figures 62 and 63 show styles of handstamps that may be found

A   B

Figure 62. Markings found on drop letters without townmarks. The stock-type marking A was used at Athens, Ohio. The "DROP 2" is a well-known marking from Mobile, Alabama.

on drop letters. Those in Figure 62 were probably used for nothing else. The New York markings in Figure 63 were traced from printed circulars. They probably occur not only on drop and circular letters, but also on carrier letters around 1850. Marking A in Figure 62 was probably a stock marking used by many post offices. This one is the only marking on a cover addressed to a Miss Frances at Athens, Ohio. Since the envelope was sealed and, according to the PL&R, circular-rate letters could not be sealed, the cover from which marking A is traced was probably sent as a prepaid drop letter.

Marking B in Figure 62 is the only marking on a cover addressed to Mobile, Alabama, in 1849, during the period when drop letters were charged 2¢ postage. This handstamp, applied at Mobile in red, contains the word "drop." If the content of this folded letter weren't present, it could be taken for a letter originating in Mobile.

Actually, the enclosed letter is datelined "Dayton (Alabama) May 28, 1849." The letter explains the usage. The sender, writing to her sister, remarks ". . . not knowing how long you would remain in Mobile . . . and as Mrs. Curry goes today, I will send a letter over direct and not by the circuitous mail route."

Dayton is in Marengo County, well north of Mobile. On the map, the "circuitous mail route" isn't obvious. During the 19th century, people knew their mail routes as well as we know our way home today. Thus the writer decided to send a bootleg letter, mailed at Mobile to save time. How many of us today would carry a letter for a friend to mail in a distant city, just to save time in mail transmission?

Circular rates create confusion

One of the problems in 19th-century cover collecting is determining the kind of usage a cover represents when different usages took the same postage rate. This is particularly true of covers at less than the normal letter rate. Such covers often have a minimum of markings. Carrier covers for local delivery, drop letters and circulars have frequently required the same rate.

A "circular" has been defined as a printed notice intended for mass distribution. In the U.S. Postal Laws & Regulations of 1825 and 1832, the U.S. Post Office Department carefully excluded circulars from any "concession" postal rates. Circulars were to be charged full letter-mail rates. Circulars were classified with advertising handbills. Magazines, newspapers and pamphlets — which received concessionary rates — were carefully defined to exclude printed matter that was purely advertising.

Figure 63. These New York City markings are found on drop letters, circulars and carrier letters.

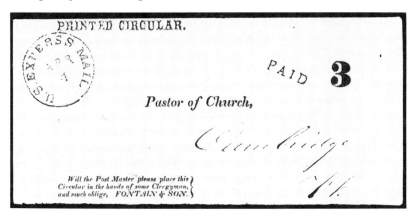

Figure 64. A circular sent under the act of 1847. The 3¢ postage was required to have been prepaid. The circular had to be mailed unsealed.

41

Figure 65. Markings from circular mail from New York City in the 1840s and 1850s.

The PL&R of 1843 still specifically required circulars to be rated as letters. But in 1845, Congress enacted our first circular rate. Approved March 3, 1845, the act stated: "All printed or lithographed circulars or handbills, or advertisements . . . printed on quarto post or single cap paper . . . folded, directed and unsealed, shall be charged with postage at the rate of two cents for each sheet and no more, whatever be the distance the same may be sent." The new law included the size of the paper as a limitation, because the word "sheet" could have referred to a very large sheet of paper, folded or refolded after printing and sent as one sheet.

The act had an important omission. It didn't require that the circulars be prepaid. Most mail at that time was sent unpaid, with postage collected from recipients. It is presumed that many of the circulars sent under the new law were sent both unpaid and sealed, despite the law, which required they be unsealed. Thus, it was possible to send letters (legally subject to higher postal rates) as circulars for only 2¢ each. Then as now, there was considerable resistance to receiving "junk" mail — particularly when it was sent collect. And, sealed or not, the circular rate of 2¢ identified such letters as circulars. Probably many were refused and masses sent to the Dead Letter Office in Washington.

Congress took prompt action. An act approved March 3, 1847, not only raised the circular rate to 3¢ but required that circulars be prepaid and sent unsealed. Figure 64 shows a circular sent under the revised law. It contains a printed letter with an advertisement datelined at Washington City, March 27, 1847. The letter offers to pastors a "Consumption Remedy" gratuitously for the "POOR." The legend printed on the face of the cover makes clear the rate of the cover, addressed to Vermont. Just how the cover received the "U.S. EXPRESS MAIL/Apr. 4" marking, with matching "PAID" of the Albany-Buffalo route agent, is anyone's guess. It seems reasonable to think that the cover was missent.

Tracings A and B in Figure 65 show markings taken from a folded circular letter sent from New York to Grooverville, Georgia. The date is unknown. The printed content offers "domestic goods" (yard cloth and yarn) to "Country Merchants" but gives no clue of the year. The cover has a black "CIRCULAR/PAID" handstamp (A in Figure 65) and a red New York postmark of "Feb. 4/PAID 2 Cts" — a type used in the late 1840s and into the 1850s. This rate is correct for a circular on February 4 in 1845-47, but it also is correct for a different circular rate in effect in 1851.

The table in Figure 66 shows U.S. circular rates, 1845-1925. As may be noted, changes were frequent and at times drastic. The revised postage act effective July 1, 1851, continued a reform pattern by lowering postal rates for prepaid letters. Circular rates also were lowered, but placed on a sliding scale according to distance. For a circular weighing less than one ounce, sent more than 500 miles but less than 1,500, postage was 2¢. The cover bearing the markings traced in Figure 65, addressed to Georgia from New York, also fits that category.

Tracings C through F in Figure 65 show more markings used on circulars sent from New York City circa 1847-56, mostly on undated covers. C was used during the 1847-51 period, when the circular rate was 3¢. D was from a cover sent in 1850. It has no rate indication whatsoever, but this was also during the 3¢ period. E and F are from a circular sent in March 1847 at the 2¢ rate but prepaid.

The complicated distance and weight circular rates established July 1, 1851, caused many misrated covers. Only 14 months later, effective September 30, 1852, the circular rates were again changed. The new rate called for 1¢ for each circular not exceeding three ounces, prepaid, sent anywhere in the United States. An additional 1¢ was required for each ounce over the three-ounce limit. As before, circulars were required to be sent unsealed.

The rates effective July 1, 1851, were set up on a weight-distance basis, much like today's parcel post. As may be seen in the table in Figure 66, the rates for circulars (and also books, pamphlets, etc.) as of July 1, 1851, were on a rather complex zoned basis. The section of the laws setting this up required that such material "must be prepaid by weight." The law included "unsealed circulars," but listed several other types of printed matter such as "transient newspapers, handbills, pamphlets, periodicals, magazines, books and every other description of printed matter." However, the paragraph following this noted that "when printed matter gets mailed not prepaid, double the above rates" (citing the table) were to be charged the recipient. Eli Bowen's *U.S. Postal Guide of 1851* was even more ambiguous, stating, "Upon all other (than periodicals) matter, as handbills, book, pamphlets, etc. . . . the postage must be prepaid, otherwise the party addressed must pay double the rates of postage imposed by this act."

Date	Rate	Basis
[1]March 3, 1845	2¢	per sheet, quarto or single cap paper, unsealed[2] (Larger sheet circulars rated as magazines at 2 1/2¢ per ounce)
[1]March 3, 1847	3¢	each, not exceeding one sheet, unsealed, prepayment required
July 1, 1851	1¢	per ounce, sent not over 500 miles, unsealed, prepaid[3]
	2¢	per ounce, sent over 500 miles, not over 1,500, prepaid[3]
	3¢	per ounce, sent over 1,500 miles, not over 2,500, prepaid[3]
	4¢	per ounce, sent over 2,500 miles, not over 3,500, prepaid[3]
	5¢	per ounce, sent over 3,500 miles, prepaid
Sept. 30, 1852	1¢	per unsealed circular, not exceeding 3 ounces in weight, prepaid, sent to any part of United States; 1¢ each additional ounce
July 1, 1863	2¢	each, three or up to three unsealed circulars. No extra charge for imprinted "card" on envelope or wrapper. Postage must be prepaid by stamps. Classified as third-class mail
[1]June 8, 1872	1¢	per two ounces; or 1¢ each, if by carrier
[1]March 3, 1875	1¢	per ounce or 1¢ each if by local carrier
[1]March 3, 1879	1¢	per 2 ounces
April 15, 1925	1 1/2¢	per 2 ounces

[1] Date approved; all other dates are effective dates. Effective dates came soon after approval. For example, the rates established by the act approved March 3, 1847, were announced to postmaster in a bulletin dated March 12, 1847.

[2] Prepayment of circulars was not specifically required by this law.

[3] Although circulars were clearly required to be prepaid by this law, a later provision of the same law rather ambiguously noted that if unpaid, postage on such printed matter was to be doubled.

Figure 66. U.S. circular rates, 1845-1925.

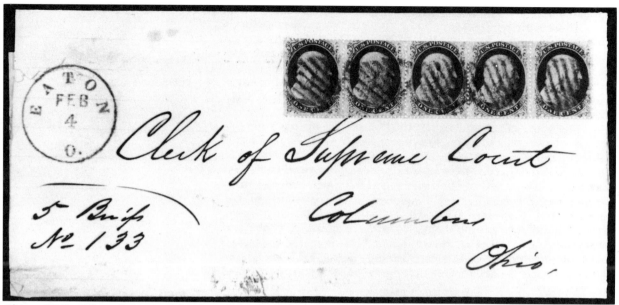

Figure 67. Sent from Eaton to Columbus, Ohio, in the late 1850s, this large cover contained five printed legal briefs rated at 1¢ each, for a total of 5¢ postage. Each of the briefs could have weighed as much as three ounces, as postage was per circular of that weight or less.

The complex act was in effect only from July 1, 1851, until September 30, 1852, and circular or other covers resulting from it are scarce. I have never seen an unpaid circular with double postage collected, sent under the PL&R previously outlined.

Figure 67 shows an interesting example of the rate that went into effect on September 30, 1852. This cover was sent from Eaton, Ohio, to Columbus to the Supreme Court of the State of Ohio. It contained five printed legal briefs, presumably printed for an appeal. Since the rate was per item, total postage was 5¢, prepaid by a strip of five of the type V 1¢ stamp of 1857. The briefs could have weighed up to three ounces each, for a total of almost a pound sent for 5¢!

The key in detecting circular-rate usages, all sent after early 1845, is that such circulars were required to be sent unsealed. Circulars often were sent huge distances, and were only occasionally mailed locally. Most carrier covers with 1¢ postage, as well as 1¢ drop letters, were sealed.

Book and newspaper rates

Circulars are the most common form of collectible printed matter mailed at lower than first-class rates. Newspapers also were sent through the mails in huge volumes during the 19th century, but newspapers have left us very little collectible material. As mailed by most publishers, they were sent without postal markings. True, newspaper stamps were issued and used, but those issued in the years right after the Civil War were used only for bundles of newspapers, in rather special circumstances. And the newspaper stamps of later years were applied to receipt forms for bulk postage payments. They never left the post offices (except as trash) legally.

The use of newspaper stamps was discussed in my column in *Linn's* for December 12, 1983, with a follow-up in the issue of May 7, 1984. As those columns explained, newspaper stamps never were applied to single newspapers mailed by publishers in bulk.

There is one type of newspaper mailing that has provided us with collectible covers. This is what the Postal Laws & Regulations call "transient" newspaper mailings, defined as newspapers not sent from the office of publication. What this really means is that such newspapers were sent by individuals and were enclosed in addressed wrappers with postage prepaid. These bear postal markings. Transient newspaper or periodical rates were first established by the act approved March 3, 1847. This set the rate for newspapers "not sent from or by the office of publication" at 3¢ each. Such mailings had to be enclosed in open-ended wrappers.

Figure 68 shows such a wrapper, sent in the 1860s, at a time when the rate for transient newspapers was 1¢ for the first three ounces and another cent for each ounce or fraction thereafter. Addressed to the Chief Justice of the Ohio Supreme Court, the wrapper, which apparently enclosed a paper of some sort, was mailed at Hamilton, Ohio. The postmark date is December 15, apparently 1861 or 1862. These year dates are established by the issue dates of the 1861 stamps and the change in transient printed-matter rates to 2¢ or more, effective July 1, 1863.

Transient-matter rates varied at 1¢ or 2¢ or more through the years. The distinguishing characteristic is that such mail had to be enclosed in open-ended wrappers, so that postal people could make sure no written matter was enclosed. It was permissible to underline or indicate specific paragraphs or items in writing, but enclosing other written matter, such as letters, required full letter rates.

Figure 69 shows another example of a wrapper of sorts used to mail printed matter. The wrapper is prepaid with postage stamps. This large item contained what was evidently a small book. It was sent from some unknown post office in the mid-1860s. Prior to July 1, 1851, bound books were usually sent by express mails, mainly because the postal laws set up rates only for unbound books and limited their weight to three and, later, four pounds. This was apparently done with the idea that heavy packages would damage the letter mail with which they might be intermixed. Also, heavy packages were inconvenient for post riders. Exceptions were made at times for

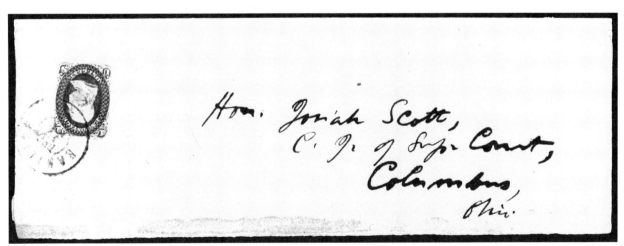

Figure 68. An open-ended wrapper, which enclosed "transient" printed matter in the early 1860s. This was mailed at Hamilton, Ohio, and addressed to the chief justice of the Ohio Supreme Court at Columbus.

heavier bound books sent by or by authority of Congress.

Bound books were first considered mailable matter in 1851 and were rated by weight and distance carried, as were circulars. As an example, a book weighing three pounds mailed over 500 but not exceeding 2,500 miles would have required postage prepaid (after 1852) of $1.44.

In 1863, a book rate of 4¢ for each four ounces weight was established, and this rate continued until 1872. This is the rate of the large wrapper shown in Figure 69. The rate is marked in the upper left corner as "Bk 4 p 4," which translates, "Book rate 4¢ per four ounces." Thus, this book wrapper enclosed a small book weighing more than four ounces but less than eight ounces. Postage was paid by a 5¢ brown stamp of 1863 plus a 3¢ 1861 stamp in a pale shade characteristic of those issued from 1865 to 1867. The stamps are canceled with a black cork. As is still the case today for some printed matter, no town datestamp was provided.

Linn's editor-publisher Michael Laurence has provided me with a photo of a much higher rated book wrapper, shown in Figure 70 in a folded state so that it can be mounted on an album page. Unfolded, it is about the size of *Linn's*, which explains why the survival rate on wrappers containing books is very low.

The wrapper in Figure 70 has 44¢ in 1869 stamps — a pair of 10¢ and a 24¢, prepaying the book rate for a music book weighing between 40 and 44 ounces, sent from Boston to Schoharie, New York, on January 8, 1870. The rate was 4¢ per four ounces, so the 44¢ in stamps paid an 11-times rate.

Collectors like high values on cover, and items such as the wrapper in Figure 70 show why they are scarce in exhibitable form. It takes a large cover to warrant a high rate, and few large covers such as this have been preserved. How many more large covers with high-value stamps have been recorded used for domestic postal rates?

Figure 71 shows still another type of printed-matter mailing that can be collected. This cover, an envelope addressed to New London,

Figure 69. A large wrapper used to mail a book, at the rate of 4¢ for each four ounces, for a total of 8¢, as noted on the wrapper.

Figure 70. A pair of 10¢ 1869 plus a 24¢ 1869, paying a 44¢ book rate (11 times the 4¢-per-four-ounce rate) on a music book sent from Boston to upstate New York in 1870.

Connecticut, has a black handstamp "PRE-PAID/QUARTERLY/PHILA/PA." The envelope has no indication of either date or rate. Covers with similar markings lacking dates and rates, but indicating quarterly prepayment of postage, are occasionally seen from other cities. These covers enclosed small periodicals upon which postage was prepaid quarterly, on a bulk basis, under the postal laws effective July 1, 1863. Since they have no rate indication, none of these quarterly prepaid covers will ever carry stamps. Very few of these have content or any indication of content. A November 24, 1984, auction conducted by Richard Frajola offered a pretty all-over gray lithographed cover of "E. Butterick, Reporter of Fashions" marked "Prepaid quarterly at New York." It was Frajola who first indicated to me the exact usage of covers with these markings.

None of the items shown here is common, yet all were undoubtedly sent in large quantities. However, the larger the item and the poorer the quality and attractiveness of the paper, the less the likelihood was of an item being saved. The same applies to our junk mail today. Perhaps some of our modern junk mail will become tomorrow's rarities.

Earliest U.S. registered mail covers

The sale of Barbara Mueller's collection of early U.S. registered covers by Christie's/Robson Lowe of New York in 1984 demonstrated

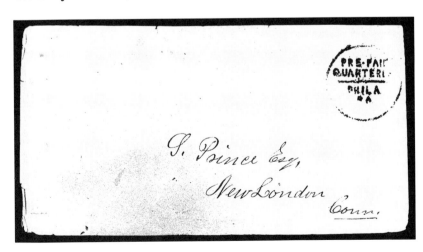

Figure 71. A manila envelope postmarked in black, "PRE-PAID QUARTERLY," from Philadelphia. Without any indication of date or rate, such markings appear upon enclosures of small periodicals sent after July 1, 1863.

47

a strong interest in the field of U.S. registered mail covers, if the prices attained are any criteria. Mueller's collection contained large numbers of landmark pieces in the U.S. classic registry field. She had explored her subject thoroughly. There are few if any facits in the evolution of the U.S. registry system where she could not show significant covers.

She has also authored articles that are the basic references on our U.S. registry system. These are, in the *Twenty-First American Philatelic Congress Book* (1955), "U.S. Registry Fees, 1855-1955" and, in the 29th book of the same series (1963), "United States Pre-Registry Systems." The first of these articles pretty much laid to rest a controversy that had been going on for some time as to whether the U.S. registry fee of 5¢, in effect when the system was first launched in 1855, was paid by postage stamps or by cash. As Mueller aptly demonstrated in her article of 1955, fees were paid in cash until after the fee was raised to 20¢ in 1867. The fact that one or a few postmasters used stamps in error to pay the fee in 1856 has about the same postal history significance as when a letter mailed today with a Christmas seal "paying" postage slips through undetected.

Although England's fee registry system had been in operation since 1841, and many U.S. post offices had been exchanging registered letter mails unofficially since the mid-1840s, the official U.S. registry system wasn't established until July 1, 1855. This was one of several important changes made in U.S. postal procedures during that era, the most important of which was requiring the prepayment of all U.S. domestic letter mails as of April 1, 1855, and requiring that prepayment be done by stamps as of January 1, 1856. The regulations establishing the registry system were written in the midst of this and were worded simply to require "the payment of a registration fee of five cents" on each registered letter.

When the postmaster general issued his edict that letter postage was to be prepaid by stamps, nothing apparently was said about fees, such as registry and "ship" and "way" fees. (Fees are per letter; postage is by weight or other factors.) In any case, the registry fees continued to be paid in cash, except for a few recorded instances, such as two covers sent from Albany, New York, in (probably) 1856 bearing the new 5¢ Jefferson stamps evidently paying the registry fee.

Despite the fact the 5¢ fee had been in effect nearly a year before the stamps appeared, some philatelic experts of the past claimed that the purpose of the stamp was payment of the registry fee, rather than for letters sent in British "open" mails to destinations abroad, and other more obvious uses.

The waybill forms of the period were designed to accommodate cash payments of the registry fee. The two uses from Albany are just about the only examples of U.S. registry fees prepaid by stamps that have been recorded prior to 1867. These were obviously a postmaster's misconception, or as Stanley B. Ashbrook suggested, they were applied by a sender in ignorance rather than at the post office. I imagine that other registered covers from Albany exist where the fee wasn't prepaid by stamps.

It was not until 1867, that prepayment of the registry fee with stamps was required. Figure 72 shows a cover sent from New York to Sumter, South Carolina, with the registry fee paid by stamps in December 1867. The fee at the time was 20¢. Mailed at New York by a commercial firm, the cover bears a "New York/Registered" marking

Figure 72. About six months after stamps were first used to pay registry fees, this cover was registered at New York, per the special postmark, on December 5, 1867, and sent to Sumter, South Carolina. The eight 3¢ 1861 stamps paid the 20¢ registration fee and overpaid the regular 3¢ postage by 1¢.

of December 5, 1867, and a registry number, in pen. The postage of 24¢ overpaid the combined registry fee and 3¢ regular postage by a penny.

The new regulations of 1867 required other important changes, in addition to the registry fee being prepaid by stamps. Registered letters were to be sent between post offices in official envelopes, and paperwork was revised. Announcements were made in the February, April and May 1867 issues of *U.S. Mail & Post Office Assistant*, the monthly semiofficial newspaper on post office affairs. Referring to the payment of the fees previously, the May article remarked: ". . . it will be well to be prepared to act under the new regulations so that when the postmasters begin to register letters according to their provisions, they will be sure to remember:

"1. That the registry fee is to be prepaid in stamps instead of money as heretofore. This applies to all registry fees — the twenty cent fee on letters to any part of the United States, England, Ireland, Scotland, Wales, or the Island of Jamaica, or the five cent fee on letters to Canada and Germany."

The 20¢ fee was apparently considered rather stiff, which may account for the fact that few covers are known showing that fee. The fee was reduced to 15¢ effective January 1, 1869. The 20¢ fee had actually been in effect since July 1, 1863, but prepayment by stamps only commenced on June 1, 1867.

The earliest cover with registry prepaid by stamps is dated July 3, 1867. The cover was recorded by Donald MacGregor, who specialized in early registered covers. Thus, from the early registry periods, no covers of the 5¢ fee era should have been prepaid with stamps, and stamps were not required until almost four years of the 20¢ registry fee period had passed. Thus, such covers can only exist correctly used with stamps prepaying the 20¢ registry fee, from June 1867 through the end of 1868.

The 15¢ fee was in effect from January 1, 1869 through December 31, 1873. From January 1, 1874 until June 30, 1875, the fee was 8¢. Not many covers from this period with this early version of the 8¢ registry fee can be found. On July 1, 1875, the fee was raised to 10¢, which lasted until it was again made 8¢ on January 1, 1893.

The table in Figure 73 shows the various registry rates through June 30, 1932, when the registry fees were well on their way to becoming the multifee, multivalue service structure we have today. The table shows the services given as well as the fees.

Figure 74 shows one of the more interesting aspects of the U.S. registry system of the early 20th century. This cover, which bears multicolored illustrations of monkey wrenches, front and back, was sent from Worcester to Fitchburg, Massachusetts, in 1913. It shows an example of the 10¢ registration stamp of 1911 to cover the fee for that service. This stamp was issued as an experiment in the hope it would provide faster processing of registered mail at the mailing office and better recognition of registered mail at other offices. The stamp, a 10¢ value in ultramarine, could only be used to prepay the registry fee and was in use until supplies ran out. The postmaster general ordered that no more printings be issued after May 1913.

Evidently the experiment wasn't a success — probably, we are told, because too many senders thought the stamp meant the registered letter need not be presented at the post office counter for the paperwork. Rather, letters bearing the stamp were simply dropped in mailboxes, which didn't achieve the senders' intent.

This is only one of many interesting and singular aspects of the U.S. registry system that distinguish its covers from other usages.

Beginning of U.S. special delivery

Special delivery of U.S. letter mail was established effective October 1, 1885. At first it was available only in towns with free carrier delivery service or towns with a population or 4,000 or more people. The post offices in those towns and cities were designated "special delivery offices" by the postmaster general in a list included with the circular that announced and described the service. A fee of 10¢, required to be prepaid with a new special delivery stamp printed in a larger-than-normal format, was required for the service. This was in

Period	Registry Fee*	Paid By	Features
July 1, 1855-June 30, 1863	5¢	cash	Registration with receipt, only. No indemnity.
July 1, 1863-May 31, 1867	20¢	cash	Registration, with return receipt. No indemnity.
June 1, 1867-Dec. 31, 1868	20¢	stamps	Same
Jan. 1, 1869-Dec. 31, 1873	15¢	stamps	Same
Jan. 1, 1874-June 30, 1875	8¢	stamps	Same
July 1, 1875-Dec. 31, 1892	10¢	stamps	Same
Jan. 1, 1893-Oct. 31, 1909	8¢	stamps	Same, with indemnity to $10; and to $25 in 1902.
Nov. 1, 1909-Nov. 30, 1911	10¢	stamps	Same, with indemnity to $50.
Dec. 1, 1911-March 21, 1923	10¢	stamps	Same (regular or special registry stamp)
April 1, 1923-April 14, 1925	10¢/20¢	stamps	Same, except dual fee for $25 or $50 indemnity.
April 15, 1925-June 30, 1928	15¢/20¢	stamps	Same, except fee raised to 15¢ for $25. indemnity. 3¢ charge for return receipt.
July 1, 1928-June 30, 1932	15¢ to $1	stamps	Same, except graduated multi-ranges of indemnities and fees.

* Fees were on a per-letter basis, in addition to the regular postage.

Figure 73. U.S. domestic registry fees and services, 1855-1932.

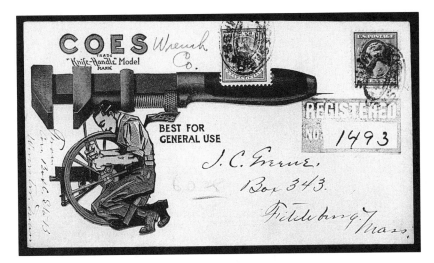

Figure 74. A multicolor illustrated cover advertising monkey wrenches on front and back shows use of the special 10¢ registration stamp of 1911, which could only be used to prepay registry fees. It was mailed from Worcester to Fitchburg, Massachusetts, in 1913, as indicated by the "registered" backstamps.

addition to the regular postage. This same special-delivery-size stamp was again used for the Columbian issue of 1892 and has come down to us today as a frequently used standard size for commemoratives and special stamp issues.

Special delivery was available to addresses within the "carrier limit" (area covered by free delivery carriers) of the cities with carrier service. For cities with populations of more than 4,000 without carrier service, special delivery was available to addresses within one mile of the post office. Special delivery was provided from 7 a.m. until midnight. Service was even available on Sundays, for letters received from other cities when the receiving post office had Sunday hours.

The first special delivery service of 1885 required that records be kept of letters delivered, together with times of delivery and notations about undeliverable letters. "Delivery books" were maintained by the messengers (boys over 12 were employed). Signatures were demanded of recipients upon delivery. Thus, the early special delivery service included many of the features of registered mails. However, there was no numbering done in the sending offices.

Figure 75 shows a special delivery letter sent on March 12, 1886 — six months after the service was initiated. The cover is addressed to a street address in Columbus, Ohio, and is backstamped as being received there at 5 p.m. March 13. A Mt. Vernon, Ohio, backstamp dated 11 a.m., March 13, also was applied.

This cover illustrates several interesting facets of the first special delivery system. Jelloway, Ohio, located in Knox County, of which Mt. Vernon is the county seat, was and is a village with far fewer than the 4,000 souls required to qualify it a special delivery office. While letters could be sent from there to be delivered in larger cities by special delivery, neither special delivery nor free carrier service was available in villages such as Jelloway. Delivery of mail had to wait for the addressee to call at the post office to pick it up.

In addition to the Jelloway manuscript postmark, the cover in Figure 75 bears a manuscript number (number 982), which was applied at Columbus, where the letter was delivered. This number shouldn't be confused with similar numbers on registered letters. It is the special delivery number under which the letter was entered in the messenger's delivery book, kept in the Columbus post office.

The 2¢ red brown stamp of 1883 paid the regular postage. The

Figure 75. An early special delivery letter, sent from Jelloway, Ohio, to Columbus on March 12, 1886. The number on the cover is a special delivery record number, required for the first years of special delivery service in the United States.

special delivery fee was prepaid by a copy of the first special delivery stamp, shown at the top in Figure 76. This stamp bears the legend "secures immediate delivery at a special delivery office." By "immediate delivery" was meant delivery as soon as the special delivery letters were sorted out of the incoming mail. The Scott U.S. specialized catalog lists the first day of use of the first special delivery stamp as October 1, 1885. This was the first day the special delivery service was in effect. However, at least one cover is known where the stamp was correctly used on September 30, 1885. This letter was mailed from a small New York town to Boston, the day before the service was to begin. It was duly delivered in Boston on the first day of the service.

That cover and the one shown in Figure 75 demonstrate that while special delivery service was available in only 555 post offices designated as special delivery offices, instructions for the new service had to be issued to all. And the new special delivery stamps had to be stocked by all, since no other stamps could legally be accepted to prepay special delivery fees. Since the special delivery stamps were usable only for that service and couldn't be used for regular postage or registry fee payment, small post offices had to maintain stocks of stamps for which they may not have had much demand.

An additional problem for fourth-class post offices, which received commissions on stamps canceled, was that no commissions were paid them on special delivery stamps canceled. This was because the fees for delivery, collected by sales of the stamps, were credited to the post offices delivering the letters. The special delivery messengers were paid from the funds thus accumulated. Fortunately, the system worked well from the beginning, although as with any new and novel enterprise, some adjustments had to be made. But, since the system filled a need, it became popular as soon as it was extended to all post offices instead of just selected offices.

An order issued August 10, 1886, extended the service to all post offices in the United States and Territories effective October 1, 1886 — the first anniversary of special delivery service. The announcement also extended the service to other classes of mail.

The announcement noted that the stamp legend "secures immediate delivery at a special delivery office" would be changed to "secures immediate delivery at any post office." Otherwise, the design would remain the same. Actually, this change wasn't made until late 1888. The first special delivery stamps specifying delivery at a "special delivery office" remained in use long after the need for the special wording had passed.

From a postal history standpoint, use of the first stamps can thus be divided into the first year, when the wording was applicable; a second period, 1886-88, when the stamps had to be used but the wording didn't apply; and a third period, when stamps with more appropriate wording were available.

Figure 76 shows at the bottom a stamp with the revised wording. The basic design carried through a temporary color change to orange from blue to avoid confusion with the 1¢ Columbian issue, and on into the first Bureau issue period, when lines added under "TEN" and "CENTS" were the most prominent change. Other slight changes were made in the basic design when the wording was changed and again when the Bureau of Engraving and Printing took over the printing of the stamps. But the basic design showing the running messenger continued to be used until the Bureau finally gave him wheels, by providing a new design with the messenger on a bicycle in 1902.

The running messenger stamps have two interesting aspects seldom noted by collectors. The first issues may be considered as classic-period stamps, since they were printed by the American Bank Note Company of New York, just as were the classic Bank Note issues. The other aspect is that these stamps, to provide easy recognition, were created in a large rectangular shape not used previously on letter mails in the United States. The size and shape was called the "special delivery" format. The term was used by the Post Office Department for many years to describe upcoming commemorative issues.

The basic reference on the special delivery service is a good one, written by Henry M. Gobie, who was a career Post Office Department employee in the special delivery service. Gobie's book, *The Speedy, A History of the United States Special Delivery Service*, was published in 1976. It is now out of print, but still available at reasonable cost from most dealers in philatelic literature. "The Speedy" in Gobie's title refers to the term by which special delivery letters were known by those handling them. His book offers many other such insights.

He also covers the laws and regulations and the production of the stamps in fine detail. Most of the data used in this chapter came either from his book or the *Postal Guides* of 1885-87.

1913 U.S. parcel post system

Although fourth-class mail for parcels up to four pounds was established as early as 1879, the parcel post system, much as we know it today, was established by an act of Congress of August 24, 1912. Under the 1879 provisions, fourth-class mail covered all matter "not embraced in the first-, second- or third-class . . ." up to a four-pound limit. Rates were 1¢ per ounce "or fraction, thereof," which produced a maximum rate of 64¢ for fourth-class mail sent anywhere in the U.S. postal system.

The new system, which went into effect on January 1, 1913, permitted packages up to 11 pounds, with the largest dimension limited to 3 1/2 feet. Length plus girth was limited to six feet. The instructions noted "a shorter parcel may be thicker; thus, if it measures no more than three feet in length it may measure as much as three feet in girth

Figure 76. Stamps of the first basic design of U.S. special delivery issues, showing the change in the wording from "secures immediate delivery at a special delivery office" (top) to "secures immediate delivery at any post office" (bottom).

	First pound	Each additional pound
Local mail	5¢	1¢
First zone (other than local)	5¢	3¢
Second zone	6¢	4¢
Third zone.....................................	7¢	5¢
Fourth zone	8¢	6¢
Fifth zone	9¢	7¢
Sixth zone	10¢	9¢
Seventh zone.................................	11¢	10¢
Eighth zone	12¢	12¢

Figure 77. U.S. parcel post rates effective January 1, 1913.

around its thickest part. Measurements will be made by means of a six-foot tape furnished to postmasters by the Department. So much of the tape as is not used in measuring the length is the measure of the maximum girth permissible."

Rates were based on eight zones based upon the distance the parcel was sent, plus a local zone. The local zone was simply the zone of service of the post office of mailing. In addition, rates increased with weight, although not proportionally. In a manner of speaking, the parcel post system reverted to the zoned postage charges used in the earlier days of our postal system.

The use of parcel post zones still prevails today, the main differences being in rates and allowable sizes. The table in Figure 77 shows the rates, as set up by the act of 1912. The table furnished with the 1913 instructions showed the postage applicable for each weight to each zone. Thus, mailing a four-pound package eight zones required 12¢ for the first pound and 12¢ for each additional pound or 48¢ postage. The same package could be sent seven zones for 11¢ plus three times 10¢ or 41¢.

Just as with the introduction of the special delivery system more than 20 years earlier, the post office issued special stamps exclusively for parcel post mailings. Regular stamps could not be used. The apparent purpose was to clearly isolate the revenue from the new system. The new stamps, issued in values from 1¢ to $1 for postage and from 1¢ to 25¢ for postage due, were in large size with distinctive designs (Figure 78). All the parcel post postage stamps were red and the dues green. This distinguished them from other stamps readily enough, but didn't make values easy to separate. Despite their drawbacks, the new stamps meant that the cost of the parcel post system could be evaluated against its revenue.

Apparently, the results of the first six months were satisfactory with respect to public acceptance and from a financial standpoint — of greatest interest to the Post Office Department. As always in a new system, there were some problems, mostly because of the large increases in stocks of stamps that window clerks had to have. Also the uniform color for all values made distinguishing them difficult.

The requirement that only parcel post stamps be used for that service was dropped after six months. Although insurance and registration had not been part of the original program enacted by

Figure 78. Representative U.S. parcel post stamps of 1913. The 20¢ postage issue, top, was the first government postage stamp to show an airplane. All of the postage stamp series were printed in carmine shades, and all due stamps in green.

Congress, insurance was added before the law went into effect. At first, registration was barred for parcel post, but parcels eventually could be registered by paying first-class postage plus registration. In essence, this simply meant the weight limit for parcel post could be extended to first-class mail by adding registration, although such mail still received parcel post handling. This situation continues in one form or another today. Weight limits also were raised so that within a year, they were 50 pounds for nearer zones and 20 pounds for the more distant zones.

The problem in collecting parcel post as postal history is to define just what "on cover" means relative to catalog listings. For uses after the first six months, one must also decide whether the parcel post stamps were really used to prepay parcel post rates.

Figure 79 shows both sides of a mailing tag used to mail a package. The tag, with 28¢ postage prepaid by a 25¢ parcel post stamp and a 3¢ regular issue, was mailed from Leetonia, Ohio, to Illinois in 1914. The 28¢ postage represents postage on a 12-pound package sent to the third zone under new rates effective January 1, 1914. Rates were then reduced for the third through eighth zones (third-zone parcel post postage was 6¢ for the first and 2¢ for each subsequent pound). Weight limits were increased to 50 pounds for the first two zones and 20 pounds for those beyond the second zone.

Considering the postal history aspects of the parcel post system, the first six months are distinctive. That was the period when only parcel post stamps could be used, and the stamps could be used for no other purpose. Thus, for parcel post use during this period, covers

Figure 79. Both sides of a mailing tag used to send a parcel post package from Ohio to Illinois in 1915. The 28¢ postage, prepaid by a 25¢ parcel post stamp and a 3¢ regular Washington head, probably carried 12 pounds three zones.

Figure 80. A mailing label from a small parcel sent from Salinas to San Francisco, California, circa 1918. Three cents postage was prepaid, while 3¢ due was represented by a 1¢ regular due stamp and a 2¢ parcel postage due stamp.

This chapter is based on the following *Linn's* columns: drop letters, January 26, 1989; circular rates, January 28 and November 4, 1985; book and newspaper rates, February 4, and November 4, 1985; registered mail, April 16, 1984; special delivery, January 6, 1986; parcel post, October 20, 1986. Special thanks to Lowell Cooper for loaning me the circular on page 41 and to William Michael, Milton Adair and others for providing photocopies and other information from their collections. The data in the parcel post section was taken mostly from official publications with interpretation from Henry Gobie's *U.S. Parcel Post*. Also thanks to Warren Bower, Harold Gallup, Daniel S. Pagter, Charles Wright and many others for contributions and useful comments on the parcel post section.

bearing high values can seldom (if ever) be found, other than in the form of tags, as shown in Figure 79. After June 30, 1913, high-value parcel post usages can be found on covers, just like any other regular-issue high values.

Although insurance was available on parcels from the beginning of parcel post, insurance fees were a uniform 10¢ for up to a maximum insurable value of $5. The fee was lowered to 5¢ after six months' operation so that insurance fees didn't much enhance the need for high-value parcel post stamps while they were in use. After the increase in allowable weight, effective January 1, 1914, high-value stamps were more frequently required, even though some of the zone rates decreased. But, by this time, most of the high-value stamps used on packages were regular issues, not parcel post stamps.

Figure 80 shows a parcel post postage due stamp used on what appears to be a mailing label from a large cover or small package, sent in 1918 or 1919. At first, the parcel post due stamps, like their red counterparts, were meant to be used only on parcel post packages. The main use for the due stamps was on parcels sent from foreign countries with due postage collect. Use of the due stamps during the early days (or later, for that matter) is rare.

The label in Figure 80 shows 3¢ postage prepaid and 3¢ due on a mailing from Salinas to San Francisco, California. In this case, although the stamp use is rare, the use of the 2¢ parcel post due in combination with the regular 1¢ postage due demonstrates well that the parcel post stamps had lost their meaning.

No printings of the parcel post stamps were made after 1913, and some remainders were destroyed in 1921. Nonetheless, I recollect buying a few loose values (including some dues) from a small post office around 1935. While the dues weren't supposed to be sold to the public, neither myself nor (apparently) the postmaster of this small fourth-class office knew that. I wonder what else he had in that dusty stamp drawer.

Chapter 5

Delivering the Mails

Prepaid and due stamps

An article by Fred Boughner in the August 25, 1986, issue of *Linn's* concerning the discontinuance of U.S. postage due stamps, aroused a good deal of irritation among those who collect such. One comment that seemed to rankle — at least on *Linn's* Readers' Opinions page — was the observation that there were only about as many postage due specialists as there have been U.S. due stamps issued, around 104 of them. While this is possibly true — who knows? — there are many fields of collecting with far less participation. In fact, many collectors, including myself, prefer fields in which nobody else collects. There's more opportunity for research and less competition for the goodies.

Another statement in Boughner's article that didn't sit well was his comment that most collectors regard postage due stamps as "little more than labels." Let's look at this from a postal historical viewpoint, carrying it beyond Boughner's observation that "everything seems to come full circle" and that the current method of handling due letters is "the way it was done in the mid-19th century."

Much of the present controversy seems based on semantics. Just what is a "stamp" or a "label" and what did these terms mean in the past? Sheets of the world's first adhesive postage stamp, the British Penny Black issued in 1840, bore a marginal inscription that is of interest here. It read: *"Price 1d Per Label. 1/- Per Row of 12. £1 Per Sheet. Place the labels ABOVE the address and towards the RIGHT HAND SIDE of the letter. In Wetting the Back, be careful not to remove the Cement."*

Why were the first adhesive postage stamps called labels by the British General Post Office? Because the word "stamp" was already in use, meaning the rate stamps and postmarks struck on letters. After the use of adhesive stamps became compulsory, these adhesive stamps soon assumed the name of the "stamps" they replaced. The term "stamp" has thus carried over into modern times, creating a need for the word "cancel" (or as the British term it, "obliteration") to describe the means of showing that an adhesive stamp has been used and its value expended.

In modern times, the term "cancel" also is changing to include all postmarks, whether they cancel anything or not. I believe such changes render our language less precise and therefore less useful in

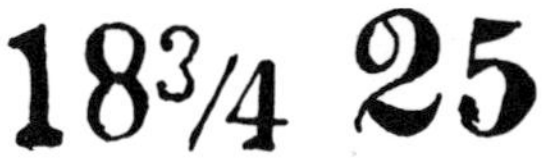

18¾ 25

Figure 81. These handstamped rating markings are postage due "stamps" that date before 1845.

conveying meaning. But observers were probably equally dismayed when the first British adhesive labels were called stamps. The British terminology was used in the United States prior to the issuance of adhesive postage stamps. Early U.S. rate marks were all "due stamps" unless the word "PAID" was specifically included.

Figures 81, 83 and 84 show tracings of a few U.S. rating stamps used before and after the introduction of the first U.S. adhesive in 1847. Handstamped rate stamps were the exception, rather than the rule, prior to the use of postage stamps in the United States. Most rates, even at large city post offices, were applied in manuscript prior to 1845 because of a complex rate structure that created a multiplicity of rates. On July 1, 1847, U.S. rates were simplified to a two-step distance structure: 5¢ for under 300 miles and 10¢ for single letters sent further. This simplification created a demand for rating handstamps. The rate stamps shown in Figure 81 date from before 1845.

The cover in Figure 82 illustrates use of an early duplex handstamp with a rate wheel attached to the town datestamper. The wheel could be turned to produce any of the five single-letter rates then current (presumably), although I have seen none with a 12 1/2¢ rate.

Figure 83 shows examples of Roman and Arabic numeral handstamps for the 5¢-10¢ rate era of 1845-51. A spelled-out "FIVE/Cts" is also shown. Prior to 1851, all these markings were automatically considered to be postage due markings — unless they were accompanied by the word "PAID," which showed the letter was an exception to the rule.

On July 1, 1851, the rates were reduced by 40 percent on prepaid mail, and the break in distance was increased from 300 to 3,000 miles. The basic rates of 5¢ and 10¢ for letters sent unpaid remained the same. Letters without stamps were still considered unpaid unless marked PAID — a practice that continued until prepayment of all domestic mail became compulsory in 1855.

The tracings in Figure 84 show two examples of the "PAID 3" rating stamps used during 1851-55. Most are not that fancy. Only

Figure 82. Shown here is a combination or duplex postmark with town dater and postage due rate applied with one blow, used from Wiscasset, Maine, in the 1830s. The "6" date was on a wheel attached to the postmarking device.

after prepayment by stamps became compulsory did the use of handstamped postal rates include the word "due." Even then, the practice of using rate stamps meaning "due" without saying so continued on incoming foreign mail for many years.

In the 1860s and 1870s, the need for due markings (other than low values) diminished rapidly. When due postage had to be charged, amounts could vary widely. As the old due handstampers disappeared from the scene, manuscript markings came back into use on due letters at odd rates. This inconvenience was resolved by the issuance of the first U.S. adhesive postage due stamps in 1879. These were issued in a range of values from 1¢ to 50¢. They proved convenient, and eliminated mistakes caused by indecipherable manuscript rates.

Figure 85 shows an early use of postage due stamps on a ship letter sent into Charleston, South Carolina, around 1880. Postage on ship letters after July 1, 1863, and for many years thereafter, was double the domestic rate when postage was unpaid. Thus the pair of 3¢ first-issue postage due stamps collected a two-times-3¢ rate on a single-weight ship letter brought into the Charleston post office on October 6, 1881.

The cover was marked "Due 6" and "ship" in Charleston and sent, via New York City (per an October 8 backstamp) to Orange Valley, New Jersey. That post office applied the pair of 3¢ postage due stamps and canceled them with a blue postmark, duplexed with a star killer dated Oct. 8/81.

Use of adhesive due stamps was a convenience 100 years ago. Other methods of collecting due postage have appeared. As outlined

Figure 83. Examples of Roman and Arabic numeral handstamps for the 5¢-10¢ rate era of 1845-51.

Figure 84. Examples of the "PAID 3" rating stamps used during 1851-55.

Figure 85. A pair of U.S. first-issue postage due adhesive stamps, used to collect a 6¢ ship-letter rate at Orange Valley, New Jersey, on a cover that entered the mails at Charleston, South Carolina.

in Boughner's article, regulations that require at least partial prepayment of postage have greatly reduced the number of postage due amounts collected. Until 1986, just as in the years before the issuance of adhesive postage stamps, both due or prepaid "stamps" were used to collect postage.

'Advertised' markings

As used on the cover shown in Figure 86, the marking "ADVERTISED" refers to a process used by the U.S. Post Office Department, as early as the 1790s, in its efforts to deliver mail to the proper addressee. The Figure 86 cover, from 1886, is a rather late example of one of the oldest processes in the post office, a system that endured, without much change, for many decades.

Until well into the second half of the 19th century, most letters were picked up at the post office. Today, we call this general delivery. But prior to the beginning of free carrier service in the larger cities in 1863 (and free delivery in rural areas around the turn of the century), stopping at the post office was how most Americans got their mail. Thus, before post office delivery service, letters would be directed simply to "John Doe, New York City." Especially in larger cities, a street number or business name was sometimes added, just to help identify the addressee when he called for his mail.

Prior to the 1850s, a very high proportion of letters was sent with postage collect. Thus, addressees would ask for their mail by identifying themselves at the counter or window. The postal clerk would check through his accumulated letters, usually filed or pigeonholed alphabetically. He would select those that fit the inquiry and then show them to the presumed addressee for confirmation. Upon agreeing which letters were for him, postage would be totaled. Payment was required by law (although postmasters could establish charge accounts at their own risk) before the letters were turned over.

This was the time and place where the Post Office Department received its revenue. When you think about it, payment on delivery was a reasonable way to assure delivery in what was sometimes a fairly primitive system. But letters for which no one had called were a liability for the system, unless the addressee could be found to pay the collect postage.

Figure 86. A local letter, franked with a 2¢ Bank Note red brown of 1883 and advertised at Cincinnati, Ohio, in 1886 — because it had an incorrect address.

As early as the Postal Laws & Regulations of 1794 (which is the earliest such document I have), a comprehensive law was on the books outlining the process of advertising letters. An even longer section under "regulations" explained the process in detail. Briefly, letters that had not been called for were to be listed alphabetically. The list was to be published in a local newspaper — in 1794, for "three consecutive weeks," doubtless referring to a weekly newspaper. Letters picked up as a result of being advertised had the "expense of publication" — in later years, usually not to exceed 2¢ per letter — added to the collect postage. The marking "ADVERTISED" was added to the cover to explain the additional charge.

If there were no local newspapers available, a not uncommon situation for many 19th-century small-town post offices, duplicate lists of the undelivered letters were to be made up and posted, not only in the post office, but at other locations where people gathered — stores, banks, taverns and meeting halls.

"Advertised" letters automatically divide themselves into two basic categories: those that were picked up because of the advertising, and those that were not. The process for those that were picked up remained relatively simple and didn't change much over the years, as is demonstrated by the cover shown in Figure 86.

Mailed at Cincinnati on July 26, the Figure 86 cover is addressed to a lady at "11 Brown St., City." A penciled note on the back reads, "Not Knowen (sic!) Dir. 60/no such number," indicating the address was incorrect. Hence, on July 28, 1886, the letter was turned over to the General Delivery section of the Cincinnati post office (bottom marking in Figure 87) and on July 31, it was advertised (top marking in Figure 87).

Since there are no other markings on the cover, and since it was found as part of a correspondence addressed to the same person, she presumably picked it up as a result of the advertisement — paying 1¢ for the privilege, under sections 447 and 448 of the PL&R of 1879.

The process of handling letters that weren't called for was somewhat more complex, since they had to be sent to the Dead Letter Office. There, if the content was deemed worth preserving, an attempt was made to return them to the sender.

Figure 88 shows such a cover, mailed at Mansfield Centre, Connecticut, on October 8, 1861, addressed to Edward Cosgrove, at Columbus, Ohio.

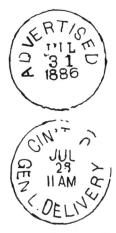

Figure 87. Markings applied to the cover in Figure 86, relating to its being advertised.

Figure 88. A patriotic cover, franked with a 3¢ 1857 stamp and advertised at Columbus, Ohio, in 1861. Not being claimed, the cover was sent to the Dead Letter Office, whence it was returned to the sender.

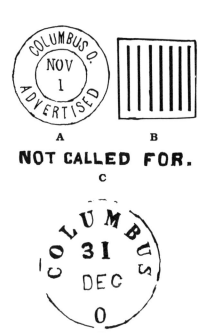

Figure 89. Markings on the cover shown in Figure 88.

The year is suggested by the patriotic envelope and the use of the 3¢ 1857 stamp, which wasn't acceptable for postage after 1861. Cosgrove had not called for his mail by the end of October, as a blue "Columbus/Advertised/Nov 1" handstamp (A in Figure 89) was applied to both front and back. By the end of December, 60 days later, the cover was still unclaimed, so the "advertised" marking on the front was canceled by a blue Columbus grid (B in Figure 89) and additional backstamps C and D ("NOT CALLED FOR" and Columbus datestamp) were applied in black.

The cover was then sent to the Dead Letter Office with other accumulated unclaimed mail. There, it was opened. Apparently having valuable content, it was returned (under separate cover) to the originating postmaster at Mansfield Centre, Connecticut, for him to attempt to locate the sender. Evidently, this was done since, otherwise, the cover would have been returned to the DLO again, this time to be destroyed, per the postal laws of the time. When receiving the returned letter from the DLO, the sender was charged the accumulated postage on the letter, including the 1¢ advertising fee.

Fees for advertising varied and also took some odd quirks. Postmasters were required to advertise in the local newspaper with the "largest circulation," then a subject of considerable controversy, but the postmaster was required to make the selection.

Dead Letter Office prior to the Civil War

The operations of the U.S. Dead Letter Office have always been obscure and perhaps even somewhat mysterious to most collectors. The DLO is the place where letters found undeliverable or unmailable (because of lack of postage or an incomplete address) are sent periodically by postmasters. At the DLO, such letters are opened and, if appropriate, returned to their senders.

Prior to 1825, letters without value, such as circulars, were sold as waste paper. In later years, they were incinerated.

Prior to the Civil War, except in larger cities, all mail had to be picked up at the post office. If a letter remained for a period without being called for (the period varied with the size of the post office), it was advertised in the newspapers. If the letter still wasn't called for after advertising in newspapers or posting in the post office, it was sent to the DLO. Accumulated letters were sent at least every three months. In the larger post offices, they were sent as often as weekly.

At the DLO, the accumulation from each office was checked

Figure 90. Franked by Third Auditor of the Treasury Peter Hagner in 1833 to an elusive Captain Delafield of the U.S. Army engineers, this cover was returned to Hagner's office eight months later from the Dead Letter Office at Washington.

against the accompanying letter bill and then sent to an opening room. There, under supervision, unclaimed letters were opened at a high speed by a few clerks who did nothing else. Letters containing valuables (such as money, jewelry, checks, notes or other legal documents) were saved and recorded. Until about 1860, all other letters were destroyed.

Under the laws governing the postal system, the only people permitted to open letters addressed to others were the designated people in the DLO. No postmasters or, for that matter, the postmaster general, had that privilege.

By reading the enclosures and notifying the postmasters of the addressing or sending offices, an attempt was made to deliver letters and valuables, either to the addressee or the sender. If such efforts weren't successful, valuables were identified and kept on file for some years, against the possibility of being claimed. Thus, surviving covers with evidence of having been sent to the DLO are those that were ultimately delivered to the addressee or returned (in later years, by the "Return Letter Office") to the sender. All others were destroyed. Varying rates of collect postage were charged on such returned letters, depending on current regulations and the value of the enclosures.

Figure 90 shows a cover returned in 1834 to Peter Hagner, third auditor of the treasury, whose free-franking signature and title it bears. Hagner (Figure 91) was an extreme example of what might be called a career bureaucrat. Born in Philadelphia in 1772, he was appointed a clerk in the Treasury Department in 1793 and became assistant accountant of the War Department when that post was created in 1797. When the War Department accountants' posts were transferred in 1817 to the Treasury Department, Hagner became the first to fill the newly created post of third auditor of the treasury. This was really his old job with a new name. Hagner stayed in that job until his death in 1849. He was in office 56 years. This was unusual in posts where incumbents were normally evicted every time the party in power changed, if not more frequently. Perhaps Hagner's nickname, "Watchdog of the Treasury," had something to do with his tenure.

The cover in Figure 90 was sent from Washington August 29, 1833, to a Captain Richard Delafield (who was to become chief engineer of the U.S. Army in the Civil War) at Ft. Delaware, Delaware. He had apparently left, since the letter was then forwarded to Cumberland, Pennsylvania. When it reached Cumberland, the elusive Captain Delafield had apparently left for parts unknown. The letter ended up at the DLO. It was postmarked there (Figure 92) on April 5 of the following year, which was probably when it was returned unopened to Third Auditor Hagner. Opening of franked letters wasn't necessary since they had the sender's name on the outside.

Figure 93 shows a DLO marking taken from a cover free franked by Commissioner of Patents Thomas Eubanks on October 14, 1851. The cover wasn't returned to the patent office by the DLO until May 12, 1852, some seven months later. (Note that the name has been changed from General Post Office to full departmental status in the marking of 1852.)

Figure 94 shows a later version of the DLO markings. Sent from Penn Yan, New York, in September 1857, this cover is addressed to New York City. It was advertised there, presumably after it hadn't been picked up, but to no avail. The letter was thus sent to the DLO,

Figure 91. Peter Hagner, "Watchdog of the Treasury" for 56 years.

Figure 92. DLO marking that appears on the cover in Figure 90.

Figure 93. DLO marking taken from a cover free franked by Commissioner of Patents Thomas Eubanks on October 14, 1851.

opened there and returned, presumably to Penn Yan, on July 13, 1858. Such returns were made to the postmasters, with the name of the sender endorsed on an outer envelope. If the postmaster couldn't locate the sender, the letter would be returned to the DLO to be destroyed.

Covers with markings of the Dead Letter Offices are quite interesting. Their handling is in many cases far from obvious.

A DLO was always maintained in Washington during the period before the Civil War. In the 1850s, a similar office operated at San Francisco for a time. Other branch offices occasionally operated in other cities for a few years for one reason or another. Markings of those offices are recorded in Simpson's *U.S. Postal Markings, 1851-61*, published by the U.S. Philatelic Classics Society in 1979.

Only a few covers bearing the marks of the Dead Letter Offices at St. Louis, Philadelphia and San Francisco are known.

Forwarding rules evolved in 19th century

Today we expect letters to be forwarded promptly, with no further postal charge. This hasn't always been the case. By "forwarded" is meant mail sent to an individual at a specific address but redirected and remailed to the same person at another address, because the person has moved, whether permanently or temporarily.

Prior to 1867, additional postage was always charged in this situation, except when letters were "missent and forwarded" by post office error. In essence, when a letter was redirected and forwarded, other than because of post office error, it was rated as if it were a newly mailed letter. Previous unpaid postage (if any) was added to the postal charges for forwarding.

Figure 94. Sent from Penn Yan, New York, in September 1857, this cover was advertised in New York City. The addressee never called for his letter. It was sent to the DLO where it was opened and the addressee or sender identified.

Figure 95. Albany to Rochester and back in 1828. Postal charges are expressed here by adding the two components.

Figure 95 shows a typical forwarded cover from the stampless era. It was mailed at Albany, New York, to Rochester, New York, September 10, 1828, and then mailed back to Albany September 14.

The cover is addressed to the 19th-century merchant, congressman and railroad entrepreneur, Erastus Corning, who was the main cog in the formation of the New York Central Railroad. Corning, who then lived at Albany, evidently was on a trip, but had left Rochester by the time the Figure 95 cover reached there. Before he left Rochester, he either left forwarding instructions at the Rochester post office or had someone forward his mail for him.

The letter was originally sent with 18 3/4¢ postage due, the single-letter rate for 150-400 miles. At Rochester, the cover was struck with an oval town datestamp and a "FORWARDED" in red. A scribbled "18-3/4" was added below the similar Albany rate mark, and the two were totaled to show the 37 1/2¢ accumulated postage to be collected from Corning when he picked up his letter at Albany.

Postal rates were reduced in 1845 to 5¢ for single letters sent under 300 miles and 10¢ for such sent over 300 miles. This applied equally to letters sent prepaid or collect. In 1851, an incentive to prepay letters was introduced by reducing postage to 3¢ for prepaid letters sent under 3,000 miles and 6¢ for those sent further. Rates for unpaid letters continued at 5¢ and 10¢ but the distance break point was made 3,000 miles rather than 300. This change produced some interesting covers, such as that shown in Figure 5 on page 5.

This folded letter was mailed from Georgetown, D.C., to New York City on May 12, 1852, then forwarded back to Washington on May 20. The original postage was prepaid at Georgetown with a 3¢ 1851 stamp. But since the forwarding was on a due-postage basis, the cover was struck with a New York 5¢ due datestamp. Thus, comparing the covers shown here in Figure 95 and in Figure 5 on page 5, each was forwarded back practically to its point of origin. The postage on the cover of Figure 95 was the same both ways, but that on the cover shown in Figure 5 differed because the letter was prepaid one way and collect the other.

It should be recognized that letters were normally forwarded by instructions of the addressee, left at post offices or with associates. Since forwarding postage was almost invariably due, unless funds were left with post offices or there was a charge account available, letters weren't forwarded without a reasonable expectation of collecting the postage. The Post Office Department took a dim view of charge accounts, requiring the postmaster to be accountable for any postages not collected. By 1842, regulations required that instructions to forward letters be made in writing, to be kept on file at that post office.

In 1855, prepayment of domestic letters was made mandatory, but letters could still be forwarded collect, as is demonstrated by the cover shown in Figure 96. Originating at Springfield, Illinois, on October 31 (day-of-month date slug is inverted) 1864, this cover was addressed to an officer at Ottawa, Illinois. The postage was prepaid by a 3¢ 1861 stamp. The cover bears the printed corner card of the U.S. Mustering and Disbursing Office (of the Civil War Federal Army) and a written note, "If not called for within 10 days, PM will please return to this office." This could be considered a written instruction to forward, but the new postal act, effective July 1, 1863, contained a provision providing routine return of letters to mailers who endorse letters in this manner. Just as with forwarding, postage had to be paid on such returned letters, which were called "request" letters in the regulations.

The new act also contained a law and regulation regarding forwarding; the regulation being as follows: "In all cases where the party addressed leaves directions for the forwarding of his letters to another office, and in *all* (italics in the original document; this was an important change) cases where the postmaster has knowledge they will reach him if forwarded to another office (and no contrary directions being given), such letters should be immediately forwarded, charged with additional postage at the prepaid rates."

The original wording of the new act of 1863, as submitted to Congress, had called for letters to be forwarded without additional postage, but this benefit was rejected by Congress.

During the Civil War, letters could be forwarded free when addressed to soldiers who had moved in response to official orders. This caused such letters to be endorsed "Follow the Regiment," to remind postmasters of the free-forwarding provision. Free forwarding

Figure 96. From 1863 to 1866, letters requesting return if not called for would be returned (and charged) automatically as forwarded mail.

Figure 97. Mail taken from the post office, readdressed and then remailed required forwarding postage, even after forwarding was free. Here, forwarding postage was prepaid by a second 3¢ 1861 stamp.

wasn't granted to the general public until July 1, 1866. The 1866 regulation permitted forwarding only when addressees notified local postmasters in writing of a change of address.

The new act of 1866 also included free return of such "request" letters. Free forwarding still retained the important limitation that requests had to be in writing and filed with the postmasters, who were to foward the letters free with no further prompting. A letter taken out of a post office, readdressed and then remailed could not be forwarded without a new full rate of postage being paid.

Figure 97 shows an example, originally sent from St. Augustine, Florida, to Newburyport, Massachusetts, and then forwarded to Beverly, Massachusetts, in 1867. Under the law of 1866, this cover could have been forwarded without additional postage if the addressee had left a written instruction with the Newburyport postmaster to forward her mail to Beverly. As it was, someone called for the letter, readdressed it and remailed it at Newburyport. A second 3¢ 1861 stamp was placed just to the left of the original stamp, partially covering the St. Augustine postmark. The Newburyport postmaster canceled the stamp with a cork killer and for good measure placed a second strike on the original stamp.

It was not until the late 1870s that letters taken from the post office could be remailed without added postage, provided such letters were "promptly" returned for remailing. This is approximately the situation that still prevails today.

Rural Free Delivery

Figure 98 shows a pair of covers from a correspondence sent just after the turn of the century from one farm in Ohio to another located about 20 miles away. Both covers bear typical "R.F.D./CAMBRIDGE/ date/OHIO" markings with a numbered killer indicating they were postmarked on Route Number 1.

Most of us today will readily recognize the Rural Free Delivery usage, but our appreciation of this postal landmark probably doesn't go much further. By today's standards, mailing a newsy, gossipy letter to someone living fewer than 20 miles distant is about the same as mailing such a letter to someone living in the next block. Today, in both situations, people use the telephone. But in 1900, mail was about the only good way to communicate such news, and prior to the Rural Free Delivery system, mail communication was not easy for those living in rural areas.

Before Rural Free Delivery, people had to walk or hitch up a horse and drive at least a few miles to a post office to mail letters or to receive them. While each hamlet, it might seem, had its post office and general store, often the latter housed the former. "Going to town" to shop, pick up and send mail, and run similar errands was usually a weekly or fortnightly chore. It could consume a half day or more, and was not a particularly casual affair.

The advent of Rural Free Delivery changed rural life. The rural routes were put into operation in a big way by 1901, and a great many small town and village post offices were closed permanently in the process. In essence, the rural-route mail carrier became a traveling post office, performing just about all the functions the crossroads offices had performed. The major change was that RFD made the writing and receiving of letters easier for rural people than for those in towns without carrier service.

The contents of the two covers shown in Figure 98 are letters from a farm wife to a cousin. They are full of family news, gossip and trivia. Both are written in pencil and are casual in tone, like a telephone conversation. Such letters were rather like a visit between the country cousins. The letters may well have been their main source of entertainment. It is doubtful that such a correspondence would even have been thought of before Rural Free Delivery brought daily (except Sunday) mail pickup and delivery.

Although Postmaster General John Wanamaker had experimented with an RFD system on a limited basis in 1891, the first operation to have lasting impact was a pilot attempt in Jefferson County, West Virginia, starting in October 1896. This wasn't exactly a random selection; Jefferson County was the home area of then

Figure 98. A pair of covers from the same correspondence, transmitting gossipy, penciled letters from a farm wife to a cousin a few miles away. These covers bear two of the standard RFD postmarks. The "1" in the barred killers refers to the rural-route numbers of the Cambridge, Ohio, post office. Rural Free Delivery made such casual communication convenient for the first time in our history.

Postmaster General William Wilson. Apparently, no postal markings (other than the routine products of the three towns involved there) were used to indicate origin on those first rural postal routes.

For some years, there had been great political pressure from the agricultural states and farm groups, such as the Grange, for rural free delivery. The city free carrier delivery system was costing more than $11 million annually, and rural elements took a dim view of this situation, since they in no way benefited from the city services.

Congress passed a $40,000 appropriation in 1896, and RFD was under way. By October 1897, rural service had been established in 29 states over 44 different routes. However, prior to 1899, there were no postal markings reflecting RFD handling, so collectors have nothing to show for the years before that.

In April 1899, what was to lead to the first county-wide RFD system was started. This was the Carroll County, Maryland experimental postal wagon system. Although this system used postmarks, they weren't the standardized "R.F.D." type as on the covers in Figure 98. The experimental system was succeeded by an expanded county-wide system, commencing in December 1899 and fully achieved by mid-1900. This system, which eliminated the small country crossroads post office by replacing them with traveling wagons, was soon declared to be a success by the Post Office Department. However, later adjustments had to be made, as shall be discussed.

The Carroll County markings were of more conventional designs, but those used from April 1, 1899, all had the legends "wagon" and "R.F.D." included in the wording. The first provisional marking of the experimental system is shown as the left marking in Figure 99. Examples dated June 20, 1899, and September 20, 1899, are shown in the standard references with comments that the markings are rare. The center marking in Figure 99 was used on the second day of operation of the expanded pilot system in Carroll County, Maryland. The two markings at the right in Figure 99 are traced from the covers shown in Figure 98. They are in the more conventional styles issued by the Post Office Department after the RFD operations were extended nationally.

In December 1899, the Carroll County "County Wide" system started. The Carroll County system, which replaced the small county post offices with traveling wagons, was deemed a success. It was extended throughout the county by mid-1900.

More important to collectors today, it was ordered that as of August 1, 1900, stamps were to be canceled by the carriers on all mail

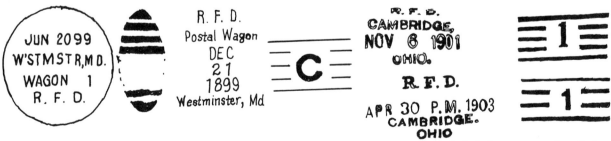

Figure 99. Handstamps associated with the establishment of the RFD routes and their later expansion. Left, a provisional handstamp used on the experimental Carroll County, Maryland, route in 1899; center, a marking used on the pilot Carroll County county-wide system; and right, the two different styles of handstamps used on the covers shown in Figure 98, both used on Route 1 of Cambridge, Ohio.

collected for later delivery along the same RFD routes. In addition, as is demonstrated by the cover shown in Figure 100, RFD carriers also provided the other services of a post office.

The cover shown in Figure 100, mailed on an RFD route out of Fillmore, New York, in February 1902, is a registered cover. Patrons could meet the carrier at their mailbox and buy stamps, register mail and — surprisingly — buy money orders. The carrier was permitted to accept cash with a money-order application and an unsealed envelope prepared for mailing the money order. When the carrier reached his postal facility, he bought the money order, inserted it in the envelope, sealed and mail it. The receipt for the transaction would be delivered back to the patron in the next day's mail.

The county-wide (a Post Office Department designation) RFD systems, which soon evolved to complete systems in 69 counties in 22 states, with nearly 2,600 routes, weren't all the RFD routes. There were many more individual routes in all parts of the United States. All used postmarks.

The standard government-issue markings were the types shown on the covers pictured here. They were applied with a small pocket handstamper with a lid. Some called these handstampers "pocket post offices." As long as the carriers were in a horse and buggy (see Figure 101) or spring wagon, there was ample time between stops to cancel stamps and postmark letters picked up on the route. A trained horse would usually go between stops without more than casual attention from the driver, so that hands were free to sort mail and postmark letters. When the automobiles came, they had to be driven. That took both hands and both feet!

According to Harold C. Richow's *Encyclopedia of R.F.D. Cancels*, the first of the government-furnished self-inking pocket handstamps were supplied to RFD mail carriers on August 1, 1900. Their purpose was to postmark letters picked up on the route and addressed to other patrons encountered later on the same route. By postmarking such letters after pickup, they could be delivered the same day and not have to be taken into the central post office for postmarking. Nonetheless, many letters bearing these distinctive markings are known addressed to other points.

The use of the RFD postal markings was officially discontinued as of July 1905, in that the Post Office Department quit supplying the handstamps. It didn't forbid the use of them. However, later regula-

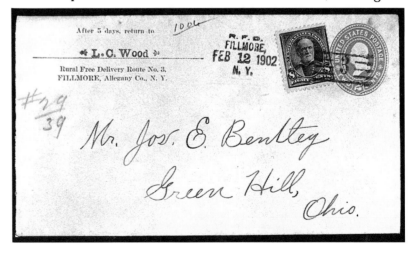

Figure 100. A letter given registry service on RFD Route 3 out of Fillmore, New York, in 1902. After 1899, patrons could purchase stamps, register letters and even buy money orders on the RFD routes.

tions simply required that stamps on letters for later delivery on the route were to be canceled with the indelible pencils supplied by the Post Office Department. These pencils had to be moistened to produce the really permanent, smeary purple manuscript markings found on covers picked up and then delivered along RFD routes in the early years of the 20th century. Use of the indelible pencil often was marked by purple marks on the lips of those using these government-furnished supplies.

There was much pride among the carriers. Many continued to postmark letters with their own devices, a number of which greatly differed in design from the styles supplied by the government.

Considerable literature exists on the subject of the RFD aspect of the Post Office operations. Professor Wayne E. Fuller, in his *R.F.D., The Changing Face of Rural America*, has handled the historical and social aspects quite well. This book was published by the Indiana University Press, Bloomington, Indiana, in 1964.

More to the point for collectors, Edith R. Doane traced the history and development of the Carroll County system and the county-wide systems that evolved from that in her book *County Wide Systems of R.F.D.* This book lists the county systems in detail, as to offices and numbers of routes, and also shows some of the markings. It is, however, a postal history handbook and not a catalog.

Harold C. Richow's *Encyclopedia of R.F.D. Cancels* is a large format, hardbound book of 282 pages. It illustrates more than 300 types of RFD markings and catalogs several thousand markings by post office, route and marking type. Updates of the catalog appear in the postal history magazine, *La Posta*.

I recommend all of these publications highly. One of the most frequent requests I get is "where can I learn more?" The answer is, in publications such as these.

Figure 101. A typical rural carrier's buggy, equipped with a working shelf dashboard, post for the reins and other niceties for the carrier's convenience. (From a contemporary advertisement)

This chapter is based on the following *Linn's* columns: prepaid and due stamps, November 24, 1986; "advertised" markings, March 2, 1987; Dead Letter Office, June 16, 1986; forwarding rules, November 25, 1985; rural free delivery, March 26, 1983, and December 1, 1986.

Chapter 6

Mobile Post Offices Markings

Early railroad markings

Those interested in the early types of U.S. route-agent markings applied "aboard the cars" (as the 19th-century term had it) are usually surprised to learn that these were first applied in upstate New York and New England, even though the first U.S. railroads were operated in South Carolina and out of Baltimore. Actually, the lines on which most of the early styles of markings were used in the late 1830s and into the 1840s were those westward from Boston through New York state and on to the Great Lakes.

Figure 102 shows tracings of a few of these markings, which were unlike the later circular markings that had the terminals of the routes included. These say "Rail Road," "R.R." or "Rail Road Car," without any dates, terminals or other indication of origin. Only covers having enclosed letters with appropriate heading or with docketing can be identified as to date and place of origin.

In Massachusetts, the first railroad in operation was the Boston and Worcester Railroad, completed between those cities in 1835. The Western Railroad, from Worcester to the New York state line, provided service to the Albany area by 1842. In New York state, the first line in operation was the Mohawk and Hudson Railroad in 1831, stretching just 16 miles from Albany to Schenectady. It was soon renamed the Albany and Schenectady. The Utica and Schenectady Railroad was operating in 1836.

The marking "Rail Road" in Old English type, as shown in Figure 102, was our earliest railway marking. It was applied on the Mohawk and Hudson Railroad in 1837. The earliest known cover, shown in Figure 103, is dated "1837/Nov. 2" by the docketing on the back flap of the New York Comptroller's Office. This docketing is also shown in Figure 103 in the section below the face of the cover. Another cover having the same marking contains a letter dated December 5, 1837, at Albany. Figure 104 shows a cover with a letter datelined at Utica on February 18, 1841. The cover bears a red circular "RAIL.ROAD" with an arc completing the circle below the words. (See the marking in Figure 102.) This marking was in use from 1838 until 1841, at least. It is one of the more common of these primitive types of railway postmarks. It also was in use between Schenectady and Utica, with a few covers reported from other locations.

It should be understood that the early railroads were built in

Figure 102. Early U.S. railroad route-agent markings. Several other types exist with similar wording.

72

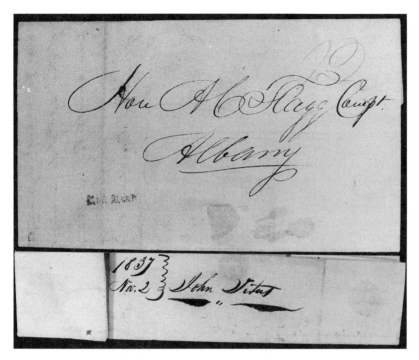

Figure 103. This cover, bearing the Old English-style handstamp "Rail Road," shown in Figure 102, and dated November 2, 1837, by a combination of content and docketing, is believed to be the earliest known cover with a U.S. railroad postal marking.

short sections, usually by different companies (although often with virtually the same backers) who secured separate charters from state legislatures to build the specific sections. The segments were soon consolidated. For example, by 1853 the five or more short lines making up the railroad between Albany and Buffalo were consolidated into the New York Central. The railroad equipment of the late 1830s and 1840s was primitive even by the standards of the often-depicted balloon-stack engines of the Civil War.

Figure 105 shows a cut of a train, taken from an advertisement in a Rochester newspaper in 1842, announcing that the last segment of railroad between Buffalo and Albany had been finished. It is interesting to consider just where the route agent operated "aboard the cars" on this train. His quarters were probably on a bench with passengers or expressmen — or perhaps in the car back of the engine with cotton bales to protect passengers in the event of a boiler

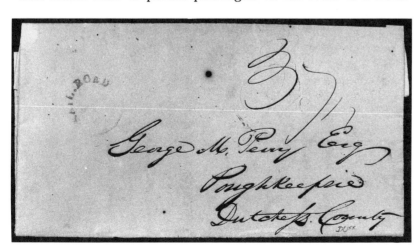

Figure 104. The early types of route-agent markings had neither dates nor origins. This particular "RAIL.ROAD" marking was used between Schenectady and Utica, 1838-41. The enclosed letter, headed Utica, is dated February 18, 1841.

73

Figure 105. An advertising cut showing a railroad train. The advertising cut was taken from a Rochester, New York, newspaper from the early 1840s. The engines didn't have cabs, which made it more convenient for the crew to jump when the boiler threatened to explode. The car behind the engine was loaded with cotton bales to protect the passengers from such explosions.

BUFFALO. ALBANY AND BOSTON RAILROAD.

explosion. Actually, it is not improbable that these early markings associated with railroads were applied at post offices where mail received en route was turned in by the route agents.

Figure 106 shows a cover with a red handstamp reading "RAIL ROAD CAR." The cover has an enclosed letter dated at Boston on September 17, 1841. This red marking is fairly common. It was used between 1841 and 1847 on the lines west from Boston to Albany, over the Boston and Worcester Railroad and the Western Railroad, from Worcester on west. A few later examples are known in black. The marking was succeeded by a more conventional circular "Boston & Albany R.R." marking by the late 1840s.

In considering such normal railroad markings, it should be recognized that it is the terminals that are mentioned, and not necessarily the name of the railroad. In fact, most of the early agents' routes covered the span of two or more railroads, which had names that might or might not agree with the terminals of the route.

Returning to the marking on the cover in Figure 106, most of these covers originated on the western portion of the route. This cover, datelined in its enclosed letter at Boston, is an exception. It must have been handed aboard the cars at the route's eastern terminal.

Carroll Chase and other pioneers in studying railroad covers had great difficulty working out where the markings originated, what lines were involved and when. They finally assigned markings to routes on the assumption that no route-agent marking could have been applied aboard the trains of a railroad line unless the line had a mail contract from the Post Office Department. While correct and logical, this approach has two huge loopholes (aside from locating and securing data about the contracts). The problems are that many of the lines with contracts didn't always have route agents aboard the cars, and not all of the route agents postmarked loose letters handed to them. The route agents' duties were primarily to care for the mailbags. On the smaller routes, with low volumes of mails, the route-agent

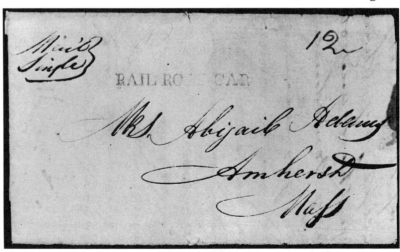

Figure 106. The marking on this cover, a red "RAIL ROAD CAR," was used on the lines between Boston and Albany, 1841-47. The enclosed letter is dated Boston, September 17, 1841.

duties were often assigned to train personnel who didn't have keys to the mailbags. Loose letters given to them were simply handed over, along with the mailbags, to the postal people at the end of the route.

The pioneer work on the early railroad route-agent markings was Charles W. Remele's *United States Railway Postmarks, 1837-1861*, published by the U.S. Philatelic Classics Society in 1958. Carroll Chase and William W. Hicks published earlier material on the early railroad routes, and all their works were based upon the mail contracts given to the railroad lines. The same was true of the all-encompassing *U.S. Transit Markings Catalog* of the Mobile Post Office Society, written by Charles L. Towle, and *Railroad Postmarks of the United States, 1861-66*, the work of Towle and Henry A. Meyer on later markings, also published by the USPCS (1968).

Use of the contract data, even with careful interpretation, has been known to produce incorrect conclusions at times. In just the last few years, John Kay, an indefatigable excavator of postal history data, has located and transcribed, from the Post Office Department records in the National Archives, the actual route-agent appointments, including dates and routes. Kay's data came from the journals for the Immediate Office of the Postmaster General, 1835-1861; rosters of special, route and local blank agents and stamp agents, and rosters of railway postal clerks, 1855-1897; and registers for star-route contracts, 1841-1855. This is a major breakthrough. It makes identifying specific route-agent markings far more positive because it places route agents aboard the cars at the correct places and times so that markings on covers can be correlated. In 1986, MPOS published another book by Towle, *U.S. Route and Station Agent Postmarks*. This replaces the Remele and other earlier works. This huge volume includes all known markings of route agents aboard trains, steamboats and steamships through circa 1887, which were gradually superseded by the RPO markings of later years. In addition, it includes station-agent markings and the actual names of the route agents on each route through 1861.

Towle's mobile post office catalogs

The catalogs by Charles L. Towle showing mobile post office markings occupy a lofty position in U.S. postal history. I believe that the catalogs are among the few postmark listings that show accurate tracings of each and every one of the thousands of postmarks they record. Towle's catalogs also provide detailed data on each page facing the page illustrating the postmarks. It's an extremely usable format. A great deal of labor went into its production.

At the time of his death, April 9, 1990, Towle had been working on a catalog of railway post office markings, a gigantic project involving thousands of postmarks. He completed much of the work. Fred MacDonald has assumed the editorship with help from Towle's wife, Betsy, John Kay and other members of the Mobile Post Office Society to finish the project. Figure 107 shows a photograph of Towle.

The first two sections of the new Towle catalog, *The United States Railway Post Office Postmark Catalog, 1864-1977*, are an eight-page introduction and 102 pages of catalog listings, including all RPO markings beginning with the letter A and part of the B group. The 102 pages list approximately 1,500 markings, with approximately 30 tracings per page and data on the facing page. Further sections will be mailed to MPOS members at the anticipated rate of three mailings per year until the catalog is completed. Eventually, the work will form

Figure 107. Charles L. Towle

Figure 108. A railroad post office cover mailed on the Columbus and Middleport Railroad, a typical local railroad line. It meandered from Columbus, Ohio, south through the rural countryside to Middleport, on the Ohio River.

three large books of about 300 pages each. They will be available as hardbound volumes. I conservatively estimate they'll have more than 13,000 listings.

RPO markings are those postmarks applied by clerks of post offices of the old Railway Mail Service of the Post Office Department. It was formally in existence from about 1882 until 1977, although a 20-year test period preceded the formal organization.

Data and tracings in the new RPO catalog are handled in exactly the same way as in Towle's existing works. Towle's *U.S. Route and Station Agent Postmarks*, a 477-page hardbound work in 8 1/2- by 11-inch format, covers markings applied by the RPO predecessors: the route agents who traveled aboard trains and steamboats, and the station agents who moonlighted as postmasters and used their ticket datestampers as postmarkers.

Towle's RPO postmark catalog lists only markings containing the words Railway Post Office or the abbreviation RPO, or those known to have been used by the Railway Mail Service.

The cover in Figure 108 has a June 6, 1885, postmark that reads "Cols. & Middleport/ R.P.O." The cover's contents show that it was mailed at Basil in Fairfield County, Ohio, in the RPO aboard a train of the Toledo and Ohio Central Railroad. The Columbus and Middleport line meandered across the southern Ohio countryside to the Ohio River. Middleport is located east of Portsmouth near Pomeroy.

This cover illustrates a process that went on for some years in the compilation of the RPO catalog by Towle. John Kay's archival research produced records leading to Kay's *Directory of Railway Post Offices, 1864-1977* (MPOS, 1985). It lists all known traveling post offices of what became the Railway Mail Service. These listings presented a problem, since no markings were known from many of the post offices. Towle, therefore, held up the publication of his so-called final version of the new catalog and published lists of those routes from which markings could exist, hoping that collectors would report covers they own.

The cover in Figure 108 was reported to Towle a few years ago. It is an example of a marking from a local line. Trains on local lines made frequent stops, and very little mail was deposited with their RPOs. Local trains were the extreme contrast to fast trains. Mostly, the locals were milk runs that wandered across the countryside picking up milk cans, egg crates and veal calves for market. A great many of the RPO listings from which no markings are known are from local lines. This is as it should be. The primary duty of an RPO was to sort mail and have it ready for distribution upon arrival. Schedules on many routes offered no advantage to mailing a letter aboard a train.

Figure 109 includes three tracings. The one marked A is the marking on the Figure 108 cover. The other two tracings are of markings applied by either a route agent or an RPO clerk aboard trains of the Illinois Midland Railroad, another road with many local lines. Towle's listing for the Figure 109 marking shown as B, taken from *U.S. Route and Station Agent Markings*, page 167, is "Illinois Midland, R491, RRA, Peoria-Terre Haute, IL, IN, 178." A second line reads, "716-A-1; PEO. & TERRE H. AGT., 24.5, blue, Banknote, 1887, III." Illinois Midland is the name of the railroad. R491 is a reference to the railroad's history in another MPOS work. RRA means that the marking is a railroad agent marking. The terminals and distance of the run are given, with coded data as explained in Towle's introduction. The second line provides Towle's catalog number and the wording, diameter in millimeters and color of the marking. Banknote means the period of U.S. stamp issues when the marking was used. The year of the recorded example, 1887, comes next. Finally, there's a rarity factor, a Roman numeral convertible to dollars.

The tracing shown as C in Figure 109 is another marking from the same Peoria-Terre Haute route. I can't provide catalog data, since it is a new RPO listing. I can say, though, that it is one of two examples used on this line in rural Illinois in an area centered around Decatur.

Both covers bear corner-card illustrations related to farming. One shows a wheat binder, the other a buggy.

As Towle remarked, the demarcation line between agent markings and RPO markings wasn't so much a matter of time. It was more a result of the gradual sophistication of the RPO system, with conversion of postmarks on smaller lines lagging well behind the actual details of organization or personnel aboard the trains.

Charley Towle was a longtime friend. From the beginning of our association, his work in organizing and compiling huge amounts of data ranked as exemplary. His works are huge — and so was he, not only physically but in ability. Although his new catalog will have to be finished by others, the path is well-established.

Station-agent markings

Collectors of covers with railway postmarks, like all collectors, tend to classify markings according to how they are worded rather than how they were used. Of course, in the absence of information as to how markings were used, it might be asked, "How else?" For many years, catalogs of railway postmarks separated "R.R.," "AGT.," "R.P.O." and station-agent markings, as if each represented a different postal usage. Actually, the first three were all applied by postal employees working mail aboard the cars.

Markings bearing both railroad and station name designations represented a different kind of usage. Figure 110 shows a cover with such a marking. It reads, "FROM CARBONDALE./ILL. C. R.R.," with a date of November 22, 1864, and a target killer tying a 3¢ 1861 stamp. (The "DUE 6" on the cover indicates the cover weighed more than half an ounce and was underpaid. Double the unpaid balance was charged on such letters during this era.)

The railroad connection — with the Illinois Central Railroad in

Figure 109. At top, a tracing of the marking on the railway post office cover in Figure 108. The other two tracings are of postmarks from the Illinois Midland Railroad route from Peoria, Illinois, to Terre Haute, Indiana. Tracings B and C show the transition from route-agent (AGT.) marking to RPO marking.

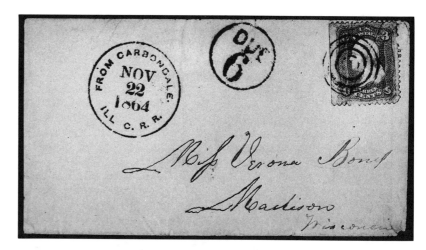

Figure 110. Cover mailed from Carbondale, Illinois, on the Illinois Central Railroad in November 1864. The "DUE 6" is double postage charged for the letter being overweight. Markings such as "from Carbondale" were applied by station agents doing double duty as postmasters at railroad depots.

this case — is obvious from the wording. The question was: Why and how were markings of this style used?

For many years, it was thought that the markings were from some sort of mobile mail agent associated with the railroad under an agreement between the railroad and the Post Office Department. Consequently, the markings were listed with the mobile post office markings of route agents aboard trains and boats, but no one really understood the usage.

In an article in the 33rd *Congress Book*, Towle reviewed the Baltimore & Ohio Railroad station markings. He suggested that the markings were simply a coincidence, in that they were applied by railroad station agents who were also postmasters, who had used their ticket datestamper as postmarking devices. Towle also went on to point out that of about 300 station markings known to him, 44 were B.&O. main-line and branch-line designations, 11 more were Illinois Central markings and no more than 10 existed with the designations of any other railroad line.

Figure 111 shows a typical B.&O. station-agent marking, used at Sir John's Run, Virginia (now West Virginia), on the B.&O. main line in February 1863. With the preponderance of the station markings being from the B.&O., research was concentrated on that line,

Figure 111. The B.&O. Railroad had more combination station agent-postmasters than any other railroad. This cover, franked by Edward Stabler, postmaster at Sandy Spring, Maryland, shows how a postmaster could frank mail from any office.

attempting to work out a reason for the station markings. This effort was hindered because most of the B.&O. records had been destroyed in a great fire in Baltimore in 1904.

In the *Chronicle of the U.S. Classic Issues* for May 1982, Towle reported a breakthrough. Denwood Kelly of Baltimore, one of America's finest postal historians, had located a publication pertinent to the subject while searching the archives of the Maryland Historical Society for an entirely different purpose. This book, the *Business Guide to the Baltimore & Ohio R.R., 1860*, listed station agent names. Recognizing the book contained information long sought by railway postal history researchers, Kelly relayed the data to them, as reported in the *Chronicle* by Towle.

Comparing the names of the station agents with the listings of postmasters in the towns on the B.&O., data that had long since been assembled by Towle, it was found that more than 40 percent of the station agents were also postmasters of their towns. No particular reason has been found to explain why this moonlighting was more prevalent on the B.&O. than other lines. Undoubtedly, the railway stations in small towns and villages would often have been an ideal location for the post office. Not only did most of the business of such towns revolve around the railroads, but meeting trains was a fine 19th-century recreational and social practice.

Such moonlighting was taken for granted in the last century. With the exception of the very largest offices, many U.S. postmasters were businessmen whose service as postmasters was simply a sideline to enhance business, secure an additional income or provide service to the community. The remaining 60 percent of the towns on the B.&O. apparently had separate post offices, away from the railroad depot, manned by postmasters who weren't station agents.

The cover shown in Figure 111 bears the postmaster's free frank of a man whose work has survived both in the form of interesting postmarks and on many documents important in American history. This was Edward G. Stabler (Figure 112), whose Quaker-dated postmarks of Sandy Spring, Maryland, have always been quite popular with collectors. Figure 113 shows a tracing of a Sandy Spring postmark. Stabler, according to the letter enclosed in the cover shown in Figure 111, was in Sir John's Run on business connected with the military guarding the railroad during the Civil War. As per regulations, the postmaster's frank "went with the person," so Stabler could frank his mail from anywhere in the country.

Stabler spoke in his letter that he "and the Colonel were . . . thinking of killing a wild cat or two, or half a dozen foxes, tomorrow." An interesting project for a peace-loving Quaker!

The attractive serifed Quaker-dated ("7 M° 27") markings, in which both month and day are designated numerically (since Quakers did not observe days of the week), were probably struck from an instrument manufactured by Stabler himself. His main profession was that of a seal cutter. The impressed seals applied to a great many government documents between the 1830s and the 1880s were made with seals and seal presses (like a notary's seal) made by Stabler. In 1850, he supplied the president of the United States with a seal. He is known to have supplied such seals to both houses of Congress and the State Department. Most other offices in Washington at one time or another used seals from dies and presses made by Stabler.

Stabler also served as postmaster of Sandy Spring (not on the

Figure 112. Edward G. Stabler

Figure 113. A typical Quaker-dated postmark of Sandy Spring, Maryland. This was struck from an instrument probably cut by Stabler himself. He was an important seal and die cutter of the 19th century.

Figure 114. "Collection & Distribution" wagon used at Washington, 1896-1901. The wagon was painted white with gold striping. This photo, one of two known of these wagons, was obtained by Robert A. Truax from the Smithsonian Institution.

B.&O. railroad) from 1830 until his death in 1883. At that time, he was said to have served the longest of any postmaster then living.

Returning to the station markings, these were applied by station agents serving as postmasters. Their ticket-dater instruments (usually with year dates, so people couldn't use year-old tickets) did double duty as postmarking devices. From a postal history standpoint, the markings with ticket datestamps on the covers shown in Figures 110 and 111 are of exactly the same category as Stabler's postmark illustrated in Figure 113. All are markings applied by postmasters engaged in another business that was their primary profession.

Collection and distribution wagons

Figure 114 shows one of the two horse-drawn collection and distribution mail wagons used by a few large cities between 1896 and 1904. These horse-drawn wagons were used to collect, sort, postmark (except in St. Louis, 1901-1904) and distribute mail in the same way as did their trolley-car counterparts — with one major exception. Being horse drawn, the routes weren't limited to where rails had been provided. But neither did horses move as fast as the trolleys where there wasn't traffic congestion. The wagons were equipped with tables and mail-sorting cases. From the photograph, it is obvious that the crew consisted of a driver and one or more clerks.

Of the four cities where the wagons were used, covers with the special postmarks applied aboard the wagons are known from three of them. Two of the cities used more than one type — possibly indicating that two clerks at times were required to process heavy volumes of mail. The two matching wagons were first placed in service in Washington and New York City on October 1, 1896.

Figure 115 shows a pair of covers postmarked aboard the New York wagon, the two postmarks being similar but slightly different. While the two New York postmarks have identical wording, differences in spacing of the letters indicate they are the product of two different handstampers. The easiest differences to note (see Figure 116) are that in one type the year date is always in the top of the logo's cluster,

Figure 115. Covers showing the two types of postmarks applied aboard New York's Collection & Distribution wagon, 1896-97. The markings, worded identically, differ by spacings of words and letters, and the "N." of "N.Y." of the type on the upper cover usually doesn't show in the postmarks.

and in the other it is always at the bottom. In addition, for those not sure that these are products of two different handstamps, the "Y" of "N.Y." lies under the "T" of "DISTRIBUTION" in one marking and under the "U" of that word in the other. The spacing between "DISTRIBU-TION" and the "1" of "No. 1" also differs in the two markings, and the "N." of "N.Y." usually doesn't show in one of them.

The New York wagon was moved to Buffalo as of August 2, 1897, so that the New York markings can only exist between October 1, 1896, and August 2 of the following year.

The third marking in Figure 116 shows the Buffalo "COLLECT'N & DIST'N" postmark traced from a cover addressed to Chicago. The wagon made nine trips per day in Buffalo, although markings showing the trip numbers are only known from eight of them. The wagon is said to have been placed in service at Buffalo the day after it was taken out of service at New York, so that the markings can exist with dates as early as August 3, 1897. That's a fast shuffle off to Buffalo, if true, but the Post Office Department was capable of swift and positive action in the gilded age.

The New York-Buffalo wagon was again moved, this time to St. Louis, terminating operations in Buffalo on June 30, 1899. It wasn't placed in service at St. Louis until in November 1899, and then apparently no letters were postmarked.

The second wagon, which is the wagon shown in Figure 114 (said to have been painted a glistening white with gold pin stripes), was placed in operation at Washington, D.C., on October 1, 1896. It also was moved to St. Louis in 1901. Thus, St. Louis was the only town to have had two wagons in operation at the same time. Paradoxically, while the other three cities using the wagons all had postmarks clearly indicating "Wagon No. 1" unnecessarily, St. Louis used no postmarks indicating service aboard the wagons.

The Washington wagon made as many as nine trips daily, and the wagon at New York had made as many as 14, but markings with trip numbers are not known for all trips. One of the Washington markings spells out the full "COLLECTION & DISTRIBUTION" legend, while the other has "COLLECT'N & DIST'N" in a manner very similar to the Buffalo wagon marking. (See Figure 116.) It does not appear that the Washington markings were used concurrently, but those in use at New York were used concurrently, judging from the tabulation shown in Figure 117. That table provides a listing of the markings, with Mobile Post Office Society catalog numbers, numbers of trips made daily, and earliest and latest recorded dates of use.

Figure 118 shows a cover with the abbreviated Washington-type marking on an overall-flag Spanish-American War patriotic cover.

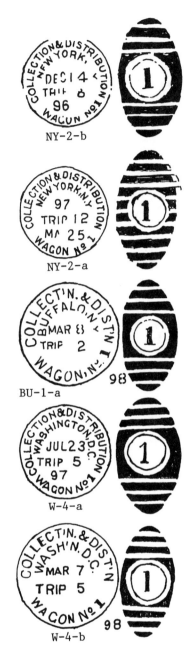

NY-2-b

NY-2-a

BU-1-a

W-4-a

W-4-b

Figure 116. Tracings of the five collection and distribution wagon postmarks so far recorded for Washington, New York and Buffalo.

Collection & Distribution Wagon Markings					
City	MPOS catalog number	Size circle (mm.)	Number of trips daily	Earliest date reported	Latest date reported
New York	NY-2-a	26	14	Dec. 8, 1896	Sept. 23, 1897
New York	NY-2-b	2	14	Dec. 2, 1896	May 13, 1897
Buffalo	BU-1-a	29	9	Nov. 11, 1897	May 29, 1899
Washington	WA-4-a	28 1/2	9	Oct. 8, 1896	Oct. 4, 1897
Washington	WA-4-b	29 1/2	9	Nov. 10, 1897	May 23, 1900

Figure 117. A tabulation of the collection and distribution wagon markings used from 1896 to 1900.

Figure 118. A Spanish-American War all-over flag patriotic in the traditional colors, with the "COLLECT'N & DIST'N/WAGON No. 1" marking from Trip 7, July 8, 1898. This is the most common of these markings.

This collection and distribution wagon marking is the most common style of the markings, regardless of what city was involved.

Figure 116 shows tracings of the five different collection and distribution wagon postmarks seen by me to date. All are duplexed with oval barred killers having a "1" in a circle in the center; all designate the wagon as "Wagon No. 1" (for that city); and all are known only in black. These are listed in *The United States Transit Markings Catalog*, Volumes II and III, published by the Mobile Post Office Society, and compiled by Charles L. Towle. The MPOS numbers are used in Figures 116 and 117. In 1986, MPOS published a 54-page monograph, *Collection and Distribution Wagons, 1896-1904*, by James H. Bruns. The monograph is about the wagons and includes a compilation of the trips and markings. It was edited by Warren F. Kimball, who also compiled the data on the markings.

Train wreck covers

Covers showing damage from wrecks of ships, planes or trains have always made fascinating postal history collectibles. Such covers are rarely found in pristine condition. In fact, the more damage a cover shows, the more it is appreciated.

Figure 119 shows an official envelope in which a letter, badly

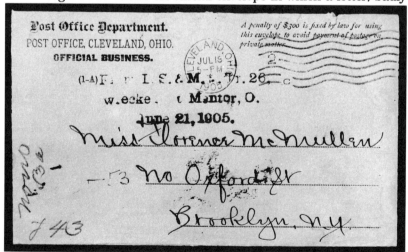

Figure 119. An official envelope from Cleveland containing the charred fragments of a cover damaged in a train wreck.

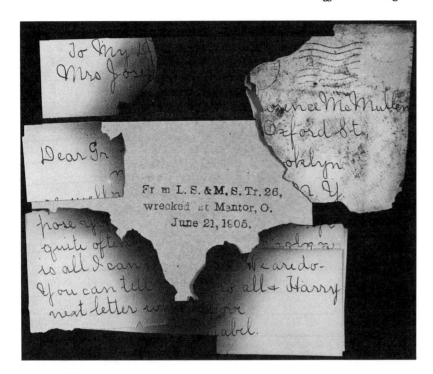

Figure 120. The charred remains of a letter damaged in the wreck of the *20th Century Limited*, running on the Lake Shore & Michigan Southern tracks, east of Cleveland, on June 21, 1905. About 15 people were killed and more than 20 injured in the wreck.

damaged by fire in a train wreck, was sent to the addressee. The remains are shown in Figure 120. Only fragments of the cover and content remain, but enough survived to enable the postal service to forward the charred remains to the addressee. The piece of envelope at upper right in Figure 120 contains enough information so that all but the title and street number of the addressee was determined. The missing facts were worked out subsequently, as may be noted from the official envelope.

Collecting such covers is greatly enhanced by details of the disasters in which the covers have been involved. The cover and charred letter shown in Figures 119 and 120 stem from the wreck of a famous train, the *20th Century Limited*, at Mentor, Ohio, east of Cleveland, on June 21, 1905. The train involved was similar to the one on the U.S. 2¢ Pan American stamp of 1901 (Figure 121).

According to the *New York Times* for June 22, 1905, the *Limited*, eastbound from Cleveland to New York City and running about 70 miles per hour, hit an open switch in front of the Mentor passenger station. It jumped the rails and crashed into a freight station across the tracks from the passenger station.

The accident happened about 10 p.m., so the buildings were apparently unoccupied. However, fire ensued. The baggage and mail car and two other cars of the five-car train were badly damaged and partially burned. About 15 of the crew and passengers were killed in the wreck or died soon after. Some 20 more of the 67 passengers and crew were injured. Considerable mail was salvaged and forwarded. Intact letters were forwarded with a label explaining the circumstances. Those not intact were enclosed in official envelopes, as is shown in Figures 119 and 120.

Shipwreck covers are comprehensively listed, for the whole world, in Major A.E. Hopkins' *A History of Wreck Covers*. The last edition was published by Robson Lowe of London around 1969. This

Figure 121. The fast express train, shown on this 2¢ Pan American Exposition stamp, was similar to the train whose wreck produced Figures 119 and 120.

Figure 122. This cover was probably damaged when its mailbag was run over by a train. The marking indicates the damage was caused by a Mackinaw & Richmond (Indiana) train on November 7, 1946.

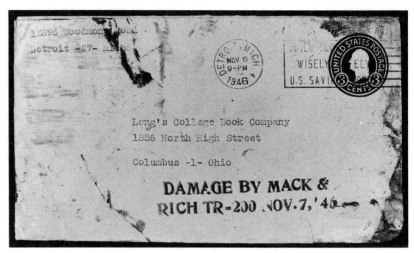

book is usually available from dealers in philatelic literature. Hopkins' book lists not only shipwreck covers but also airmail crash covers, railroad wreck covers and covers damaged by handling accidents and mistakes on board trains. Even covers with markings due to earthquakes and natural disasters are included.

Not all covers with markings pertaining to train damage were involved in wrecks. Figure 122 shows a cover whose dirt, grease stains and rumpling were probably caused when a mailbag got run over or was otherwise mistreated. Mailbags were transferred to moving trains by placing the bags on a standard alongside the track, with the bag loosely gripped above and below. A "pouch catcher arm," attached to the side of the mail car, plucked the suspended bags as the train passed. At the same time, bags of mail for that destination were thrown out the mail-car door. Sometimes the catcher arm didn't engage the bag accurately or bags were poorly thrown from the cars. The result was bags of mail getting under a train, going off viaducts into rivers or highways, or getting caught beneath station platforms.

The result, for collectors, was covers marked as shown in Figure 122. This marking didn't result from a train wreck, although it did stem from accident or human error connected with a mail train.

The Hopkins book contains listings of mishap covers of this nature. However, of seven covers I was able to examine, all bearing markings pertaining to U.S. train wrecks or mail mishaps connected with trains, the cover shown in Figures 119 and 120 was the only one listed. At present, I know of no compendium on damaged covers from train wrecks and accidents. One is being planned.

Seapost markings

The markings reading "seapost" (or a foreign-language version of the same idea), when found on transatlantic covers sent between 1891 and the early years of World War II, are souvenirs of the golden era of passenger steamships. Figure 123 shows a typical liner of the early days. Another marking that arrived on the scene in the 1890s, the marking "paquebot," fills out the same picture.

The difference in use between the two markings is that sea post office markings were applied at post offices aboard the liners, and paquebot markings were applied at shore post offices to letters received from vessels that had no post office aboard.

The seapost service was intended to accelerate letter mail in

Figure 123. One of the early Hamburg-American liners, which may or may not have had a sea post office, was the SS *President Grant*. This 18,000-ton ship had six masts. Even in fast steamers of the 1890s, a sail was available for emergency use.

transit across the Atlantic by having all the mails sorted and ready for immediate dispatch when the ship reached port. This way, mails didn't have to be processed at the port post office. Letters mailed aboard the ships were also accepted, postmarked and sorted into the proper bags. Mail also was accepted at shipside up until just before a ship sailed. A supplementary mail fee, usually an additional rate of postage, was normally charged for such service — at least in the United States.

The sorting en route by post office personnel was said to save up to a full day's transit time on letters coming into the United States.

However, the seapost idea wasn't an exclusive U.S. enterprise by any means. Germany, England and France, at least, provided similar facilities in close cooperation with the United States, starting in the

Figure 124. A 5¢ Grant stamp from the first Bureau series, tied by a seapost marking. The cover was mailed aboard the American Line steamer *St. Louis* in 1896.

Figure 125. Seapost markings applied, from top to bottom, aboard the steamers *St. Louis, Paris/Philadelphia* and *New York* of the American Line. The ship is indicated by the number in the barred oval.

Figure 126. The 10¢ Pan American stamp of 1901, showing the American Line steamer SS *St. Paul.*

1890s. For example, in some cases, a U.S. post office crew sorted mail on an eastbound trip so that the mail could be sent out immediately from the European port upon arrival, and a German, French or British postal crew sorted mail on the westbound trip, so that the mail would be ready for immediate dispatch when the ship reached its U.S. destination. The U.S. Post Office Department (and also, I assume, various European counterparts) made contracts with the transatlantic steamer lines for post office facilities to be installed aboard the liners.

Figure 124 shows an example of an early "UNITED STATES/ SEA P.O." marking on a cover mailed aboard the USMS (mail steamer) *St. Louis* on September 9, 1896. The marking is traced as A in Figure 125. A sister ship to the *St. Louis*, the SS *St. Paul*, is depicted on the 10¢ Pan American stamp of 1901, shown in Figure 126.

Each ship with a U.S. sea post office was assigned similar handstamping devices, with a different number in the barred oval killer section. The *St. Louis* had a number 3 in its handstamps and the *St. Paul* a number 4.

The ships assigned numbers 1 and 2 are the subject of a strange story regarding transatlantic mail-carrying contracts of the U.S. Post Office Department. The British Inman line of steamers, founded at Liverpool in 1850, had operated the first really successful line of transatlantic screw steamers in the face of the Cunard line's mail monopoly. Inman even succeeded in wringing a contract from the British Post Office, which it lost in 1887.

By 1892, the Inman line had become the "I.&I." (Inman and International line.) It had placed in service between New York and Liverpool the two largest (10,499 tons) and fastest (Queenstown, Ireland, to Sandy Hook, New Jersey, in under six days) liners in the world. But the line had no mail contract.

In September 1892, it was announced that the I.&I. line, reorganizing with a strong American branch, had a contract to carry U.S. mails between New York and Southampton, England. The two new large liners were to be transferred to American registry. A special act of Congress was required to make this legal. This activity produced the effect, illusionary to a degree, that U.S. mails were being carried by ships built and operated by an American company.

Part of the deal required that two matching American-built ships were to be provided by the line as soon as possible. These were the *St. Louis* and the *St. Paul*, placed in service in 1895. This new American Line was the first U.S.-owned steamship line of prestige — like Cunard and North German Lloyd — in the North Atlantic passenger business since the Collins line of the 1850s.

The interests of the United States had turned westward in the 1850s, and later the Civil War had virtually extinguished the U.S.-owned North Atlantic packet business. The new line, with sea post offices aboard its ships, was operating quite satisfactorily when the Spanish American War broke out.

Under the agreement of 1892, all four liners became U.S. Navy auxiliary cruisers. The *New York* was called the *USS Harvard* and the *Paris* became the *USS Yale*. The *St. Louis* and *St. Paul* retained their names, but when the liners resumed service in 1899, after being refitted, the *Paris/Yale* was renamed the *Philadelphia*.

The markings used aboard the ships, as noted previously, were similar except for the numbers in the killers, which were 1 for the *New York*, 2 for the *Paris/Philadelphia* and 3 and 4 for the *St. Louis* and St.

Figure 127. A cover with the seapost marking of the *New York* in 1916, only a short time before the seapost service was discontinued because of World War I. The cover was delivered ashore at Cherbourg and sent on to Havre, forwarded from there by diplomatic pouch to London, after receiving a British field censor marking. From London, the cover traveled in the British mails to Maidstone.

Paul, respectively.

Figure 127 shows a cover franked with a 5¢ Washington head stamp, near the end of the service of the American Line sea post offices, which were discontinued in March 1917, because of World War I. The Figure 127 cover, with the "U.S. SEA P.O." marking dated December 23, 1916, shows a 1 in the killer (C in Figure 125), indicating it was carried by the *New York*. The cover was evidently carried to Cherbourg, France, delivered to the British consul at Havre and then, after receiving a British field censor marking, forwarded back to England by British diplomatic pouch. It was then remailed at Maidstone.

I know of no complete literature on the subject of the transatlantic seapost markings. The United States also had seapost services to the Canal Zone and other ports not on the Atlantic. The best references I have on these markings are a series of articles by Robert S. Gordon in the *Seaposter* of the Maritime Postmark Society of the 1960s. A good, but short, review of the subject appeared in *Transit Postmark Collector*, for May-June 1982.

The transatlantic mail, the ships carrying it and the post offices on board are a large subject, but one well worth studying. While early examples of covers with sea post office markings are rare (most of the mail was carried in closed bags, of course), many philatelic examples exist from later years.

This chapter is based on the following *Linn's* columns: early railroad markings, July 2 and December 31, 1984; mobile post office catalogs, August 6, 1990; station-agent markings, August 8, 1983; collection and distribution wagons, June 4 and November 26, 1984, and March 31, 1986; train wreck covers, January 7, 1985; seapost markings, July 4, 1988.

Chapter 7

Ship Letters and Ocean Mail

Ship letter charges

"Ship letters" — a type of mail bearing the marking "SHIP" — have been around since the beginnings of mail service in the United States. The basic meaning of the marking is that the letter was turned in to the port post office by the master of a private ship upon its arrival. By "private ship" is meant a ship neither owned by the government nor having a mail-carrying contract or other government subsidy. For conveying such letters and turning them over to the post office at a port of arrival, ships' masters were (with a few exceptions) paid 2¢ per letter. Such may be still the case today. The ship-letter classification was still part of the postal law at least as late as the 1950s, but almost never was used in this century.

The 2¢ paid out per letter was called a ship fee since it didn't vary with either the weight of the letter or the distances it may have been carried before and after it entered the mail system. Until July 1, 1863, the 2¢ ship-letter fee was simply added to the regular postage for letters for delivery beyond the port of entry. (Those addressed to the port were charged a flat fee.) Ship letters could be mailed with postage collect even after domestic letters had to be sent prepaid.

Figure 128 shows a typical ship letter of the earlier period. Mailed at St. Mark, Florida, and addressed to Tallahassee, less than

Figure 128. Sent by private ship from an unknown origin in the Caribbean, this letter was mailed on January 24, 1840 (per docketing) from St. Mark, Florida, as a ship letter. The ship fee of 2¢ (explained by the marking "SHIP") and the regular postage of 6¢, for transmission under 30 miles, are shown as a sum on the cover — adding up to a total of 8¢ postage due.

30 miles away, the letter was charged a 2¢ ship-letter fee with 6¢ regular postage for a total of 8¢ due. The letter is docketed as having been sent in 1840; the origin is uncertain.

Figure 129 shows a ship letter mailed after July 1, 1863. At that time, postage on ship letters was changed to a simple calculation of double postage, whether prepaid or due. Thus, the additional postage required because of being a ship letter depended on the regular postage. The "ship" charge therefore changed, from a fee to a rate. The cover shown in Figure 129 originated in the Caribbean (as shown by the crossed-out "via Havana") sometime between 1879 and 1883. These dates are established by the fact the first U.S. postage due stamps, which this cover bears, were issued in 1879 and the first-class rate was reduced from 3¢ to 2¢ on October 1, 1883. Double postage was charged on this cover at the rate of twice 3¢, or 6¢ due. The cover was mailed at Charleston, South Carolina, on October 6 and sent on to New York, where it was backstamped on October 8, year not given. At Orange Valley, New Jersey, to which the cover is addressed, the pair of 3¢ 1879 due stamps were applied and canceled in blue with a circular datestamp of October 8, duplexed with a star killer.

So, prior to July 1, 1863, except at the port of entry, ship letters were charged 2¢ plus regular postage. After that date, double postage was charged for ship letters. But the ship captain's fee was always 2¢, except when no fee was paid at all, for reasons such as the ship not being of U.S. registration.

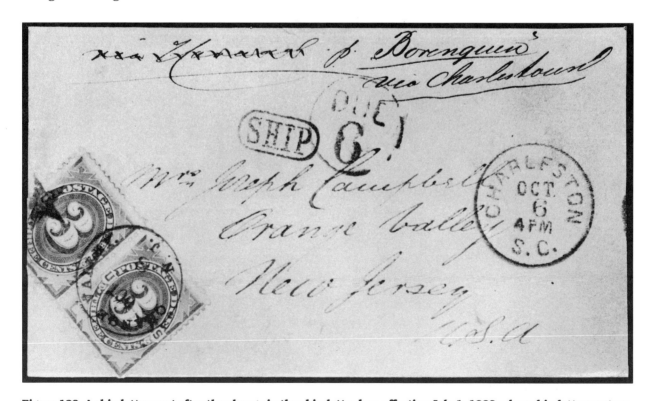

Figure 129. A ship letter sent after the change in the ship-letter law, effective July 1, 1863, when ship-letter postage was changed from a fee of 2¢ per letter to a rate of double postage, due or prepaid. This letter was brought from the Caribbean to Charleston, South Carolina, circa 1880, where it was mailed as a ship letter with double the regular 3¢ postage due, to Orange Valley, New Jersey. At that office, the pair of 3¢ first-issue postage due stamps was applied and canceled in blue with a circular datestamp of October 8, duplexed with a star killer.

Paquebot markings

Seapost markings were discussed in Chapter 6. These markings are found only on loose letters mailed at ship side or handed in at the post office aboard the ship at sea. The rest of the vast amounts of mail handled by the seapost offices reached the ship in mailbags, already postmarked at their point of origin. Most ships of the late 19th and early 20th centuries, ocean passenger liners or otherwise, had no sea post offices aboard. Any mail they handled was in locked bags. Such mails weren't sorted until they reached the post office at the port of arrival. Loose letters handed to pursers (or whoever was in charge of the mailbags aboard) had to be handled separately. When such letters were turned in to the post office at the port of arrival, they often bore uncanceled stamps of other nations, obviously not valid at the port of arrival under normal circumstances.

The marking "paquebot" (French for "packet boat") first came on the scene in the British empire in 1894 to cover this situation. The Universal Postal Union had possibly discussed the situation as early as 1891. Use by the British in 1894 showed the practicality of this method of handling.

In 1897, at the UPU Congress in Washington, D.C., the word "paquebot" was officially adopted for international use on mail received at ports from ships at sea. It wasn't necessarily used by all nations in quite the same way, and details of usage varied somewhat as the years passed, but it usually meant that letters bearing the marking had been received from a maritime source. In essence, it replaced the traditional ship markings of the 19th century, which normally were applied to explain a postage due charge that wouldn't otherwise be obvious.

Figure 130 shows an early example of a U.S. paquebot marking on a cover backstamped at Cincinnati on June 18, 1896. Per the corner card and a backstamp, the cover originated at Curacao, Dutch West Indies. When the *SS Valencia*, by which it was directed, reached New York, this unpaid letter received a purple "Paquebot/(N.Y.-2D DIV.)" handstamp and was marked for collection of 10¢ postage because the letter bore no stamps. The postage due stamp was applied at Cincinnati, which was the office that had to collect the postage and account for the stamps. It is interesting to note that this paquebot marking was used before the UPU Congress authorized it on international mails. Since the collect postage was solely a U.S.

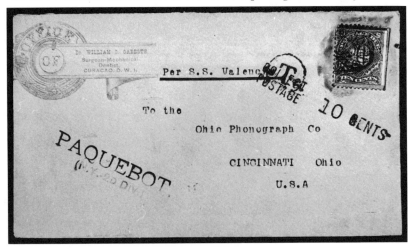

Figure 130. Originating at "Curacao, DWI," this cover was marked "T" there and sent aboard the steamer Valencia to be carried to New York. There, it received a "Paquebot/(N.Y.-2D DIV.)" marking and a "Collect/Postage 10 cents" handstamp before being sent along to Cincinnati. At Cincinnati, the postage due stamp was applied to collect the postage.

affair, the UPU aspects may not have been pertinent.

Many 20th-century paquebot markings are quite common, particularly on postcards, some of which have the additional attraction of depicting the ship on which the card was mailed. Such an item is shown (both sides) in Figure 131. The card bears the paquebot marking of Southampton, England, dated August 11, 1948, on the address side, at the top of the photo. The picture side, below, shows the *Queen Elizabeth*, flagship of the post-World War II Cunard-White Star passenger fleet. Completed as World War II was starting, the *Queen Elizabeth* served as a troop transport at first. I first crossed the Atlantic aboard the ship in that service. After the war, it was reconditioned and served 20 years, until air travel caused liners to be reduced to excursion and cruise service.

Figure 132 shows a cover with a Paris-St. Lazare "paquebots" marking of 1935, a different sort of usage of "paquebot" terminology, since it is on outgoing mail. The cover has a Paris return address on the back, and is addressed to Columbus, Ohio. The marking reads "PARIS-ST. LAZARE/*PAQUEBOTS*." This use of the word here, peculiar to the French postal system, was on outgoing steamship mail posted at the foreign mail section of, in this case, the Paris post office.

The references on paquebot markings focus on the sources and scarcity of the markings, rather than their usages. The compilers and collectors are apparently content with the knowledge that the markings have a maritime association. The compilers have shown little interest in the details and differences of the various types of paquebot markings as used by various countries. This is probably because paquebot markings were applied to covers brought into port by ships from all over, under a wide range of uses, so that the common aspect of maritime origin is enough.

The current basic reference on this subject is *Paquebot Cancel-*

Figure 132. Not all paquebot markings were used exactly for the same purposes, as suggested by this "Paris-St. Lazare/paquebots" machine cancel on a 1935 cover from Paris (as per return address on flap) to Columbus, Ohio.

This chapter is based on the following *Linn's* columns: ship letter charges, February 27, 1984; paquebot markings, July 18, 1988. Thanks to Warren Bower, Fred Schmitt, Edwin Dreschel, T.G. Hirschinger and many others who provided information for this chapter.

lations of the World, second edition, 1987, by Roger M. Hoskings. The standard reference for many years was M.A. Studd's *"Paquebot" and "Ship Letter" Cancellations of the World, 1894-1951,* published by Robson Lowe in 1953 and long out of print. An even earlier pamphlet on the subject was Philip Cockrill's *Ocean Mails,* published in the 1930s but reprinted since. More up-to-date, in terms of listing and markings, are several large tomes that have greatly expanded the listings. Most useful to U.S. collectors is *The Paquebot Marks of the Americas* by Gustav J. Lund, 192 pages in loose-leaf style, replete with tracings of paquebot markings accompanied by dates of use, rarity ratings and other data.

For years, collectors of paquebot markings have indulged in a practice that I don't recollect encountering previously. When a post office didn't use and, in fact, didn't have a paquebot-marking handstamp, collectors would have one made up and supply it. At the same time, they would create covers bearing the marking. When the particular post office did use its new instrument on incoming maritime mail, the previously made test covers then became collectible philatelic examples of the marking's use. In his 1959 work on paquebot markings, cited above, Studd deplored this practice, saying that "many of the cancellations which have been thus 'commercialized' in the past are now of little value, owing to abundant supply."

I think the test of time has proven Studd wrong. Most collectors can distinguish between philatelically inspired examples and those used because of genuine need. The fact also remains that without the philatelically inspired covers, many markings would be excessively rare or unknown to collectors. Thus, the philatelically created cover is an aid to the cataloger and researcher, in addition to making examples of the markings available to many more collectors.

I do feel, however, that manufacturing handstamps and making up covers anticipating an actual use on commercial mail does create a strong lack of respect for even those modern paquebot markings applied by government-created handstamps on mail received from cruise ships or other commercial or quasi-commercial uses.

Chapter 8

Foreign Mail Covers

U.S.-British treaty mails, 1848-1868

The basic United States-British mail treaty of 1848 remained in effect until it was revised in 1868. This field has an undeserved reputation for complexity and high prices, probably caused by two factors. First, high-value stamps were sometimes used to prepay international mail rates. Today's high prices for such covers reflect the esteem with which valuable stamps on cover are regarded, rather than the fact that such covers represent foreign mail uses. The great bulk of U.S. foreign-mail covers sent before 1868 were either unpaid or prepaid stampless covers, or bear low-denomination stamps of moderate value.

The reputation for complexity comes from specialists writing about covers showing unusual usages. But knowledge of a few facts will make clear the routine by which all but a small percentage of British treaty covers were handled.

Under the treaty, postage for a single letter between England and the United States was 1 shilling — or its U.S. equivalent of 24¢. Because each country paid certain steamer lines to carry mails across the Atlantic, the postage was broken down into segments comprised of each country's internal postage and the sea postage, as shown in the table in Figure 133. This was only for purposes of accounting between the countries. Postage had to be entirely prepaid or entirely collect at destination. Part payments were disregarded on letters between the two nations.

Figure 134 shows a typical cover, sent prepaid from Liverpool with a British 1/- stamp (Scott 5), canceled with that city's duplexed "spoon" marking (with its "466" killer) on July 7, 1854. The cover crossed the Atlantic on the Cunard steamer *Niagara* to Boston. The *Niagara* is shown in Figure 135. Boston acknowledged that the cover

Segment	British	U.S.
U.S. internal postage	2 1/2 pence	5 cents
Sea postage	8 pence	16 cents
British internal postage	1 1/2 pence	3 cents
Total	12 pence (1 shilling)	24 cents

Figure 133. Accounting of postage under U.S.-British mail treaty of 1848.

Figure 134. An 1854 treaty-mail cover from Liverpool to New Orleans. The 1-shilling British stamp prepaid the whole postage. The "5 cents" handstamp is not a due marking, but a credit marking of the accounting system between the two countries.

Figure 135. The steamer *Niagara*.

was prepaid by a handstamp reading "Boston Br(itish) Pkt (Packet)/ 24/Jul 20/PAID" and sent the cover on to New Orleans. The "5 cents" handstamp on the cover is not a due marking but a credit of 5¢ to the United States for the U.S. internal postage. This is all the United States got for handling this letter. The British kept their internal postage of 1 1/2 pence or 3¢. The British also kept the sea postage of 16¢ because the cost of transporting the letter across the Atlantic was borne under the British post office contract with the Cunard Line — thus the "Br. Pkt." of the Boston postmark. Each side always got its own internal postage, but the 16¢ sea postage belonged to the country that paid the steamer line to carry the mails.

On prepaid letters such as Figure 134, the originating country credited the other country, via handstamp, with its internal postage, plus (if appropriate) the sea postage. If the letter was sent unpaid, the originating country applied a debit handstamp to indicate how much was owed.

The cover in Figure 136 illustrates another facet of the treaty, one that particularly benefited the United States, even though England was undoubtedly glad to have the additional volume of paid mail that was generated. The treaty provided that each country could send

Figure 136. A cover from Brunswick, Maine, sent via Boston and England by British steamer lines to the west coast of Africa. The 33¢ postage, prepaid by U.S. stamps, covered all postage in the British mails. The crayon "28" is a credit marking to England, not a due charge.

94

Figure 137. Sent from Mormon Utah, this cover is addressed (in French) to a lady at the court of the czar at St. Petersburg, Russia. The 24¢ postage paid the 5¢ U.S. internal postage plus the sea postage by American packet, with 3¢ wasted. The remainder of the postage to carry the letter to St. Petesburg was collected at the destination.

letters, via the other, to nations with which the other country had mail treaties or arrangements. During the years before 1848, England had developed treaties with France and other countries in Europe and beyond for the exchange of mail. The U.S.-British treaty made these destinations available to the United States through a reliable and regular mail system in which postage could be prepaid to destination. In the rating of these covers, additional postage beyond England was substituted for the British internal charge.

The cover shown in Figure 136, bearing U.S. stamps of the perforated 1857 series, originated in Brunswick, Maine, in February 1861. It is addressed to an engineer aboard the *USS Mohican*, a Navy warship then patrolling for slave ships off the west coast of Africa. Postage, via England, was 33¢, consisting of the 5¢ U.S. internal rate and the 16¢ sea postage as per the Figure 133 table, plus an additional 12¢ (or 6d) to carry the letter by British mail steamer down the coast of Africa to St. Paul de Loando, as the principal port of Angola was then called. As noted, this 12¢ charge replaced the British internal postage.

The Boston post office, which placed the letter aboard a British Cunard steamer, marked a crayon "28" credit marking on the cover, thus giving the British post office both the sea postage of 16¢ and the 12¢ additional postage to carry the letter to West Africa. The United States, although collecting the 33¢ postage represented by the stamps, actually retained but 5¢ of it.

Figure 137 shows another aspect of how U.S. citizens could send mail via British mails via England to distant destinations. I can't imagine that many covers exist with a more contrasting origin and destination. The cover originated at Mormon Salt Lake City, Utah Territory, in November 1856. It's addressed to the court of the czar of Russia at St. Petersburg. The postage paid was 24¢ (represented by a right-margin pair of 12¢ imperforate Washingtons, Scott 17) at Salt Lake City.

The Figure 137 cover was sent under another provision of the treaty, the open-mail arrangement. The open-mail provision allowed letters to be sent from the United States to destinations beyond England with only a portion of the postage prepaid. Such letters could be sent either to a British steamer at a U.S. port for 5¢, or to a British

Figure 138. U.S. handstamps, all on the face of the Figure 137 cover. The "3" was voided by being smeared over in red.

Figure 139. Britsh and other hand-stamps on back of the Figure 137 cover. One Russian marking was too faint to trace.

port by an American steamer for 21¢. (In this latter case, the 16¢ sea postage would belong to the United States, since it paid the cost of carrying the letter across the Atlantic.) Such covers would then continue to their destinations beyond England as if they were unpaid covers that had originated in England. Appropriate due postage would have to be paid by the recipient.

The cover shown in Figure 137 was sent by "AM Pkt," as the handstamp applied at New York shows. Figure 138 shows a tracing of the handstamp. The cover had originated at Salt Lake City, Utah T(erritory), on November 1, 1856, so it was five months traveling from there (probably via the west coast and Panama, in winter) to New York. Although the cover has 24¢ postage prepaid by a pair of 12¢ stamps, of 1851, 3¢ of this was wasted since the open-mail rate was but 21¢. The New York exchange office marked a "3" on the cover as a credit for the British internal postage, but then smeared it with red ink to delete it as not applicable. Figure 138 also shows a tracing of this marking.

Thus, the letter was prepaid to the British frontier, but it was sent collect from there to Russia, as may be seen by the markings that appear in the tracings in Figure 139, and the various manuscript markings that include a "99(?)" on the back (not shown).

Had the letter gone by British packet, the postage would have been but the U.S. internal rate of 5¢. Open-mail postage had to be prepaid in the United States, however, as there was no mechanism to collect it from recipients abroad.

Note that this open-mail provision didn't apply to letters sent between only the United States and England. On those, all postage had to be prepaid or they would be treated as unpaid.

Many stampless covers survive from the 1850s, addressed to destinations abroad, showing a prepaid "5" marking in an era when domestic postage was just 3¢. These are all open-mail covers.

Cross-border covers

Prior to 1867, Canada consisted of several areas and provinces having their own administrations under the British crown. What was then Ontario and Quebec was at first called Upper and Lower Canada, referring to their positions relative to the flow of the St. Lawrence River. These later were changed to Canada West and Canada East.

Figure 140. A double cross-border cover, exchanged twice in transit from St. John, New Brunswick, to Toronto via Boston.

Sending mails across Canada between the provinces wasn't always easy. Figure 140 shows a cover originating at St. John, New Brunswick, on July 21, 1855 (per a docketing on the back) directed to Toronto, Canada West. At that time there were no railroads running from New Brunswick to Montreal and the west. A U.S.-operated steamer line provided service down the coast to Eastport and Portland, Maine, and on to Boston. These steamers carried route agents of the U.S. Post Office Department.

In July 1853, the New Brunswick postal administration arranged that these route agents would accept loose letters from the St. John post office, addressed to the United States or beyond. The St. John post office applied the "Province of New Brunswick" circular marking on the cover in Figure 140 before handing over the letter to the U.S. route agent aboard a steamer for carriage to Boston.

It should be noted that at this time, New Brunswick was a separate British colony, not part of Canada.

The U.S. route agent aboard the steamer applied his "U.S. EXPRESS MAIL/ST. JOHN" handstamp on July 23, 1855, and also his "10" handstamp to rate the letter as an unpaid letter to Canada from the United States under the U.S.-Canadian postal convention of 1851. Had this been done at an exchange office, the rate would have been expressed in Canadian money as due in Canada, but the arrangement was such that that provision apparently was not used. When the cover was turned over to the post office at Boston, the Boston British North American exchange desk applied its curved "U. STATES" and sent the cover by closed bag to Toronto. By 1855, most of the larger cities on each side away from the border exchange offices also exchanged mail by closed bag.

The markings on the cover, including the Toronto backstamp of July 26 and a "6" marking also applied there, indicating 6 pence postage to be collected, are shown with the tracings in Figure 141.

Under the U.S.-Canadian postal agreement then in effect, Boston exchanged closed mails (locked and sealed bags carried across international borders without being opened at intermediate offices) with Montreal and Toronto.

The U.S. route agent aboard the steamer, probably the *Eastern City* or *Admiral*, although we have no evidence which, applied a circular "U.S. EXPRESS MAIL/ST. JOHN/JUL 23" handstamp, and also a "10" due rating mark, indicating the collect postage in U.S. currency. I don't know how the local New Brunswick postage, if any, was accounted for, but I assume it was prepaid in cash. Or perhaps it was simply part of the postage to be collected by the separate Canadian postal administration.

Under the cross-border mail arrangements, which were between the United States and the separate provincial mail systems of New Brunswick and Canada, letters could be mailed either prepaid or collect, although in 1855, U.S. route agents were not supposed to accept cash for prepayment. Thus, letters mailed with them had to be either prepaid with stamps or sent collect. Partial payments were not recognized, and each postal administration retained all postage collected, with no complex accounting to adjust imbalances.

Thus, this cover passed from the New Brunswick colonial-mail administration to the United States and back to Canada, having crossed the border twice and been handled by three separate postal administrations, but only one rate was collected. By this route, it took

St. John, New Brunswick

St. John-Boston (U.S.) route agent

Boston Exchange Desk

6 pence due at Toronto

Figure 141. The markings on the Figure 140 cover.

Figure 142. From the U.S.-New Brunswick exchange office at Houlton, Maine, to Victoria Corner, New Brunswick. Postage of 10¢ was prepaid by U.S. 5¢, 2¢ and 3¢ stamps.

Figure 143. Backstamps from the Figure 142 cover, showing complete transit in one day.

but five days for a letter mailed in New Brunswick — with no rail connections to the western provinces — to arrive at its destination.

By proclamation on July 1, 1867, New Brunswick became part of the Confederation of Canada. Since the terms of the mail agreements between the British North American provinces and the United States were nearly identical for all provinces, Confederation had little effect upon the handling of covers. Canada did convert from shillings and pence to dollars and cents in 1859, and the other provinces did so concurrently or soon after.

Figure 142 shows a cover sent from Houlton, Maine, to "N.B./ Victoria Corner," a small town just across the border from Houlton in Carleton County, New Brunswick. The cover traveled less than 50 miles. Figure 143 shows the backstamps on the cover. These show that the cover, postmarked at Houlton on March 29, reached Woodstock, New Brunswick, the same day. The cover also was marked "W.O. VICTORIA" on that day. These markings demonstrate several features of the cross-border and New Brunswick mail systems. Houlton and Woodstock were a designated pair of exchange offices for mail crossing the border between New Brunswick and the United States. Letters processed by those offices were to have the country name and the correct postage handstamped by the exchange offices. At this time, postage was 10¢ whether prepaid or collect, in either the United States or New Brunswick.

The cover shown in Figure 142, with 10¢ postage made by a combination of 5¢, 3¢ and 2¢ stamps, is marked "PAID" and bears a curved "U. STATES" handstamp — also a faint manuscript "10." The backstamp "W.O. VICTORIA/N.B." demonstrates a feature peculiar to the operations of the New Brunswick and Nova Scotia postal administrations. The "W.O." means "Way Office." These were, in essence, branch offices established by larger town postmasters strictly on their own responsibility, as extensions of their own offices. The general postal administrations maintained no lists of way offices and considered the supervising post offices completely accountable for way offices they might establish. How long these were continued after consolidation of postal operations under Canadian administration, which occurred soon after the cover shown in Figure 142 was sent, I have no idea.

Figure 144 shows a cover with an interesting feature of the

Figure 144. Sent between Houlton, Maine, and Woodstock, New Brunswick, exchange offices, this cover required only 2¢ under a special cross-border rate.

cross-border exchange office arrangement. Letters between these offices, neither originating nor addressed beyond, had a "special exchange office rate" of 2¢. The cover shown in Figure 144, sent from Houlton, Maine, to its cross-border exchange office counterpart at Woodstock, New Brunswick, some 13 miles distant, needed only a 2¢ stamp.

Some collectors call these "ferriage" rate covers, although the term really isn't valid, as has been pointed out frequently by Susan M. McDonald, the authority on such mails. The problem is that there was a real ferriage rate, prior to the 1850s, which actually paid a ferry charge. That, however, is another story.

Beginnings of the Universal Postal Union

The organization that became the Universal Postal Union (UPU) was known as the General Postal Union (GPU) when it was first established. The Treaty of Bern, signed by 21 nations on October 9, 1874, established the GPU, which commenced operation July 1, 1875. Original members were Austria-Hungary, Belgium, Denmark, Egypt, Germany, Great Britain, Greece, Italy, Luxembourg, Montenegro, the Netherlands, Norway, Portugal, Romania, Russia, Serbia, Spain, Sweden, Switzerland, Turkey and the United States. Iceland and the Faroe Islands came in as part of Denmark, and various Spanish possessions were included as part of Spain.

Also included were Malta, as a British colonial affiliate; Madeira and the Azores, as part of Portugal; and Finland, as part of Russia. Poland was not mentioned, then being considered an integral part of Russia. Most of the rest of the familiar European countries signed.

Bulgaria and Albania were then under Turkish control, nominally at least. Other than Egypt, which was part of the British sphere of influence, the United States was the only independent nation outside Europe to be an original member.

France, although accepting the postal treaty provisions as of May 3, 1875, when the rest of the original members ratified the agreement, postponed bringing the provisions into force before January 1, 1876, even though the rest of the members placed them in effect on July 1, 1875. In addition, France insisted on transit rates on mails passing through France from one nation to another, which also was a problem for many of the other members of the new organization. It also was agreed that member countries could vary the basic international letter rate and that a surtax could be charged on letters being carried by sea more than 300 miles. Some of these provisions were transitory, but the reasons for them are still troublesome today in some instances.

The General Postal Union name was changed to today's Universal Postal Union at a conference at Paris in 1878. In his definitive article on the postal unions in the *American Philatelist* for March and April 1979, George E. Hargest remarked that the GPU and its successor UPU represent the first attempt among nations at worldwide cooperation to achieve a desired end. Hargest commented that this has been the only truly successful example of such an endeavor.

What did the GPU/UPU mean in terms of the covers we collect today? First, it meant cheap international postage. In U.S. money, the rate was 5¢ per single 1/2-ounce letter. This applied only to letters sent between member countries, and even then, because of the transit surtax and other deviations, there were many exceptions for years. Despite that, the GPU provided all its members with reductions in postage, sometimes substantial, on mail sent from one to another.

Figure 145 shows a cover sent from New Orleans to England under the U.S.-British postal arrangement that preceded the GPU. The rate between the United States and England had diminished dramatically in the late 1860s. From 1849 to 1867, the rate was 24¢. In 1868 and 1869, the rate was 12¢. From 1870 through mid-1875, when the GPU agreement went into effect, the rate was 6¢. This is demonstrated by the Figure 145 cover, franked with two 3¢ Bank Note stamps and posted on March 13, 1871.

The GPU arrangement eliminated postal treaties through which international postage on each letter was shared. Such treaties required an elaborate accounting system, including debit and credit markings on individual covers. Such items delight today's postal history collectors, but they required much clerical labor.

Underlying the GPU was the simple premise that every letter generates a reply. Individual accounting was eliminated. Under GPU regulations, all postage was retained by the country that collected it.

Figure 146 shows a cover sent to France from Los Angeles on December 30, 1875, with 9¢ postage prepaid by three 3¢ Continental

Figure 145. Sent from New Orleans to England in 1871, this cover — franked with a pair of 3¢ Bank Note stamps — bears the correct treaty-rate postage of 6¢.

Figure 146. Cover from Los Angeles to France, franked with three 3¢ Bank Note stamps on December 30, 1875. The treaty rate of 9¢, prepaid on this letter, was replaced by the General Postal Union rate of 5¢ just two days later.

Bank Note stamps. Although France is listed as a GPU signee and this cover was sent after the GPU rates went into effect on July 1, 1875, the rate is more than the GPU 5¢ rate. The reason is that, as previously mentioned, France signed with the proviso that it could delay putting the new provisions into effect until January 1, 1876.

France and the United States had a postal agreement, in effect August 1, 1874, by which U.S. rates to France were 9¢ per 1/2 ounce. This was still in effect when the Figure 146 cover was mailed, on the next-to-the-last day the old treaty prevailed. The sender could have waited two days and posted the letter for just 5¢.

The cover shown in Figure 147 illustrates another major benefit of the GPU. This cover was sent from Connecticut to England, addressed to a Mrs. D.D. Bishop, who evidently was traveling abroad. The cover was postmarked London on August 19, 1878. It was addressed in care of a forwarder, who placed the Monroe & Company forwarding label over the address, and remailed the letter to Paris. When the letter reached Monroe & Company at Paris, Mrs. Bishop had already gone on to Geneva. Monroe obligingly forwarded the letter in care of J.T. Bates & Company at Geneva, where it evidently caught up with the addressee.

Under the old postal treaty system, each successive forwarding would have required an added postal rate. Prior to free forwarding by

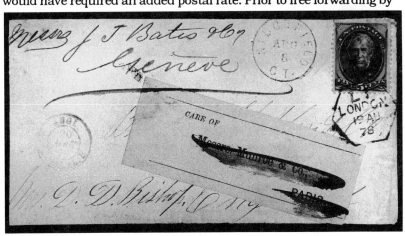

Figure 147. Sent from Connecticut with a 5¢ Taylor stamp in 1878, this cover was addressed to a traveler in care of an English forwarder. It was forwarded from London to Paris and on to Geneva, at no added charge.

the GPU, travelers often had to pay staggering amounts of collect postage to obtain forwarded letters. The GPU benefited users with lower rates and better service, and member countries with greatly simplified accounting.

It wasn't until the 1880s that the UPU became truly universal in the sense that most of the countries of the world were members. In fact, some nations didn't join until the 1890s. Today, international mails are handled as routinely as those from across town — and we give very little thought to how it all started.

Latin American airmail routes

Commercial air service for passengers and mail commenced in Europe soon after World War I. War surplus airplanes, mostly bombers or scout-observation types, were adapted for commercial uses. The later purely commercial designs evolved from these. Most of these early conversions were land planes with limited capacity to haul heavy loads long distances or at high speeds. However, such wasn't really necessary, since the distances between cities in Europe, although often crossing international boundaries, weren't very great. Thus, the European lines were reasonably successful.

Air travel was not only faster, but on some routes, such as across the English Channel, it eliminated the need to transfer from trains to boats and back again, with accompanying waits in terminals. The situation was different in the United States. Except in the eastern coastal areas, major cities were much farther apart. Even in the east, the early attempts at air service involved mail, but not passengers.

Truly commercial airlines carrying both mail and passengers didn't begin to develop in the United States until the late 1920s. This was also true of international operations from the United States to other countries. Although a few Foreign Air Mail (FAM) contracts were let by the Post Office Department as early as 1920, it was only after Juan Trippe established Pan American Airways, to operate in the Caribbean and Latin America, that meaningful airline service developed between the United States and foreign areas to the south.

The aircraft shown in Figure 148, a Sikorsky S-38 amphibian, was the key to that development. While airplanes are usually likened to birds, this one, with its conglomeration of struts and wires, was more like a bird cage. The lack of good airflow characteristics greatly cut down on speed, range and load-carrying capacity, as much of the fuel load was consumed pushing wires and struts through the air. Nonetheless, these craft answered a need.

In the 1920s, airmail routes in the Caribbean and Latin America could be established by island-hopping. Land planes could be used only after constructing airfields, neither easy nor inexpensive in the

Figure 148. The Sikorsky S-38 amphibian, used extensively by Pan American Airways on early Foreign Air Mail routes.

Figure 149. From Cuba, via FAM 4 to Miami, with 5 centavos Cuban postage prepaid by the Cuban stamp. From Miami to Colombia, with the required 30¢ U.S. postage paid by U.S. airmail stamps, via Cristobal, Canal Zone.

mountainous, heavily vegetated countries on the route. The use of land planes, where applicable, and the Sikorsky S-38 amphibians, where airports weren't available, produced a feasible system. The fact that there were several European-controlled airlines already in operation in South America created a cooperative attitude within the U.S. government, which encouraged U.S. airlines to compete, by offering Post Office FAM contracts to carry the mails to Latin America.

Trippe managed to secure an FAM contract to carry mails to Cuba from Key West in 1927. In 1928, he moved the U.S. terminal to Miami. By 1930, Pan American was the owner or co-owner of air services and routes from U.S. bases throughout the Caribbean and Latin America.

Figure 149 shows a cover that demonstrates how the FAM routes were used by foreign countries. The cover originated at Havana on March 9, 1930. It is addressed to "Officina del Correo Aereo, Apartado 293, (Scadta), BARRANQUILLA, COLOMBIA." It is probable that both the 5-centavo Cuban airmail stamp and the strip of three 10¢ U.S. airmail stamps were applied at Havana. From Havana, the cover was sent to Miami on a return flight of FAM 4 (probably by a Fokker trimotor) and, there, was postmarked and the U.S. stamps canceled — also on March 9.

The postal rate to Colombia at that time was 30¢ per 30 grams (stated in the April 1929 *Air-Mail Service* bulletin as equivalent to 2/3 ounce). This was paid by the U.S. airmail stamps. The 30¢ carried the letter to Barranquilla, Colombia, over U.S. FAM routes 5-6. The address shown was that of Scadta, the German-owned airline that then operated out of Colombia to points in South America. The bulletin remarked that if further forwarding was desired, such had to be prepaid with Colombian stamps.

The cover bears backstamps of the U.S. Post Office at Cristobal, Canal Zone, March 13, 1930, and (in purple) of the "Agencia Postal Nacional" at Barranquilla, March 18. Whether the cover contained another letter, prepaid for further transmission by Scadta, or simply a business letter, isn't known.

Trippe, as head of Pan American, signed numerous contracts with various Latin American nations to fly their mail to other destinations on Pan American planes traversing U.S. contract FAM routes. According to both his definitive biographies, Trippe turned over the

Figure 150. From the U.S. Military Aviation Mission at the U.S. Embassy in Quito, Ecuador, to Texas, via an FAM route in 1947. Is this cover commercial or philatelic?

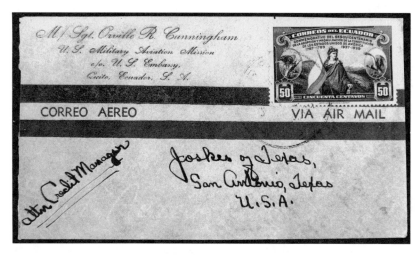

Figure 151. Stamps on back of cover shown in Figure 150.

This chapter is based on the following *Linn's* columns: U.S. British treaty mails, March 21, 1988; cross-border covers, February 24, 1986; beginnings of the UPU, November 13, 1989; Latin American airmail routes, January 20, 1986.

moneys received from contracts with other countries to the U.S. Post Office Department. But Pan American arrangements with other nations included many non-cash considerations, such as the rights to build airfields and facilities.

The postage charged on letters carried by Pan American out of those countries had no relation to U.S. airmail rates nor, it would seem, to surface-mail rates as established by the UPU. Thus, the U.S. airmail rate to Cuba at the time was 5¢, and apparently, the Cuban rate for letters the opposite direction was 5 centavos.

Figure 150 shows a cover from a member of the U.S. Military Aviation mission in Quito, Ecuador, sent to Texas in 1947. As of 1946, U.S. rates over the FAM route to any point in Latin America were 10¢, but the postage paid on this letter is 2 1/2 sucres, paid by the 50-centavo stamp on the front commemorating the U.S. Constitution, and a pair of the 1s of the same issue on the back, as shown in Figure 151. Although the stamps were issued in 1938, nine years before the letter was sent, the letter appears to be a commercial usage. Possibly the use of stamps commemorating the U.S. Constitution is connected with the fact the letter originated at the U.S. Embassy in Quito. Such mail could have been sent free if official, but not by air.

The cover illustrates the difficulty of figuring out the rates charged by the Latin American nations on mail sent over the FAM routes. Even excluding the possibility that the Figure 150 cover was a philatelic use and the 2 1/2s prepaid by the stamps was not necessarily the exact rate, the cover is puzzling. Postage on most groups of airmail covers sent from Latin America over FAM routes often doesn't fit any set pattern. There is also the possibility that the rates, presumably established to cover costs of Pan American service, changed frequently to adjust for inflation or other monetary factors. All this is speculative. But it does point out that the field of mail sent over the FAM routes under contracts between the originating countries and the carriers offers a marvelous opportunity for some interesting in-depth research.

Chapter 9

Carriers and Express Mails

City carrier covers to 1861

By "carrier" covers, collectors of postal history refer to a type of cover on which an extra fee was paid for local conveyance, usually to or from the U.S. post office. The distance such covers were carried was usually only a few miles. It was often less than a mile.

Figure 152 shows a typical carrier cover of the 1850s. The Blood's (1¢) "penny post" stamp paid the fee for the Blood's carrier to take the letter to the Philadelphia post office and place it in the government mails. The 3¢ U.S. 1851 stamp (Scott 11) paid the postage from Philadelphia to Alexandria, Virginia.

The traditional rate of a penny, stemming from similar English services, was defined by Blood as 1¢. Other carriers in the United States occasionally charged in the British sense, the British penny being equal to two U.S. cents.

In the postal laws of 1825 and 1836, where carriers were first mentioned in the sense used here, the local carriers were called "letter carriers." They were so referred to in the regulations until the elimination of the extra-fee carrier service. In large cities, this was generally on July 1, 1863. The term "letter carriers" was used to

Figure 152. Private carrier: Blood's local post, Scott 15L15, on a cover with the 3¢ U.S. 1851 stamp paying the postage from Philadelphia to Alexandria, Virginia. The Blood's local paid the fee of the private carrier for taking the letter to the post office.

distinguish the local carriers from the contract carriers of the mail sacks over the postal routes, who were called "mail carriers." We use the terms differently today.

However, it should be recognized that other than the service discussed here, which was available only in a few of the larger cities, there was no local carrier service. All postal transactions took place at the post office. While the larger cities were not nearly so vast geographically as they are today, some (such as New York or Philadelphia) required a considerable walk to go to the post office. In fact, such visits were often on horseback or by horse-drawn vehicles.

There were very few branch post offices in the earlier portions of the 19th century. In cities such as Washington, not called "the city of magnificent distances" for nothing, a trip to the post office took much longer than it does today.

Since businessmen couldn't spend time running such errands, they employed messengers or clerks for that purpose. It wasn't long until privately owned delivery services sprang up to handle this function. These private letter carriers not only carried letter mail to and from the U.S. post offices but also between points on their routes — for the same fee, usually 1¢ or 2¢ per letter.

The postal acts of 1825 and 1836 authorized government carriers to be appointed in the large cities where deemed useful, but authorized no salaries for the carriers. The official carriers were expected to be paid from the fees on the letters they carried to and from the post offices. Those fees were limited by the enactments to not more than 2¢ per letter.

The Post Office Department looked covetously at the private letter carrier business in the cities for some years. While letter mails were a government monopoly, the monopoly did not apply where the government did not offer mail service or operate routes. The act of March 3, 1851, made post roads of the streets and public roads of some cities. Thereafter, the post office could take over the carrier letter mails. However, this law didn't totally establish the postal monopoly, since the official carriers were to carry mails to and from the post office, and the successful private carriers had developed a large business in local mails that never passed through the U.S. post offices. The government found it hard to be competitive.

The U.S. Post Office Department had experimented for years

Figure 153. Semiofficial carrier: the Baltimore Government City Dispatch 1¢ stamp of 1857 (Scott 1LB8) paying the fee for carrying the letter to the Baltimore post office. The 3¢ 1857 stamp paid the postage from Baltimore to Philadelphia.

with local carrier services by appointing proprietors of local carrier services as official carriers. Figure 153 shows a cover illustrating this. This cover has a 1¢ black "U.S. Government City Dispatch" stamp of Baltimore, which paid the carrier's fee for taking the letter to the post office, and a 3¢ 1857 stamp, which carried the letter in the U.S. mails to Philadelphia. About the only difference between this and the cover in Figure 152 is that the carrier was officially appointed, which required that he be bonded. While he still collected his own fees, they usually were turned in to the post office to become part of a fund from which he was then paid.

The first of these semiofficial carrier services was the United States City Despatch Post in New York. This was set up by the New York Post Office arranging to take over the private Grieg's City Despatch Post as of August 16, 1842. Thus, the stamps of this carrier became the first official U.S. postage stamps. This was the start of a practice that went on for several years, by which the U.S. Post Office Department attempted to learn how to handle local carrier service.

In 1851, the Post Office Department brought out two stamps in rapid succession for local carrier use. These were Scott LO1 and LO2. LO1, which has a close resemblance to the regular 1¢ Franklin stamp of the time, was used but little. Figure 154 shows a cover with a copy of LO2 used at Washington, D.C. Here, the use was exactly the same as for the previous covers. The U.S. official carrier stamp paid the carrier fee, and the 3¢ 1851 stamp paid the postage in the U.S. mail to destination, which was Providence, Rhode Island.

So, while all three covers shown here represent the same postal usage, the differences are the degree of government involvement. The three covers thus depict the strong competitive tension between the private and government services, showing how private routes were gradually taken over by the government. The takeover really wasn't effective as long as the carrier's compensation was limited to fees from letters carried in and out of the post office.

While the carriers in many of the large cities were placed on salaries effective July 1, 1863, the change worked only in those cities. Meanwhile, private carrier service had been mostly eliminated by the extension of the postal monopoly, so that the rest of the country was a good many years obtaining door-to-door mail delivery.

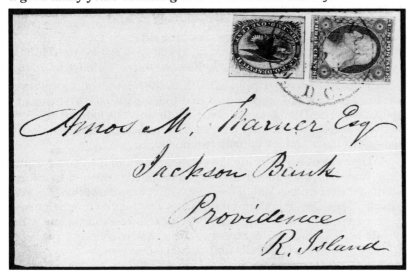

Figure 154. Government carrier: the U.S. official Eagle carrier stamp of 1851 paying the 1¢ local carrier fee to take this cover to the Washington, D.C., post office.

Figure 155. Typical U.S. EXPRESS MAIL postmarks used between 1842 and 1857 in the eastern United States. All are route-agent markings, some having been used aboard trains and others aboard steamboats.

Express Mail

The term Express Mail today means a special fast mail service, usually at a much higher rate than regular mails. It originated from the use of special couriers to carry military or government messages in previous centuries. The term was first employed by the U.S. Post Office Department in the War of 1812, but by then it already had been used by private enterprise to imply carriage of valuables, packages, and, when there seemed an opportunity, letter mails.

Figure 155 shows three examples of a large group of similar markings appearing on covers originating in the northeastern United States between 1842 and 1857. All read "Express Mail," usually with the name of a town included in the wording. These markings are artifacts of an early post office attempt to take over the seemingly lucrative express business being conducted by private enterprise aboard the burgeoning railroad and steamboat networks in the United States.

The earliest notice of the post office U.S. Express Mail service appeared in the Albany, New York, newspapers beginning July 19, 1842. It announced establishment of the U.S. Express Mail service between New York City and Buffalo, via Albany. Service between New York and Albany was by steamboat, with "route agents" or messengers (paid employees of the post office) aboard to handle the mails.

Figure 156 shows an early cover from this route, bearing a "U.S. EXPRESS MAIL/ALBANY/N.Y./MAY/3" marking in red. The "Albany" markings, as researched by the late Henry A. Meyer, were applied aboard southbound steamboats on the Hudson, between Albany and New York City.

Service between Albany and Buffalo was by railroad, over seven interconnecting lines. The newness of the system is illustrated by the fact that a 15-mile segment of the railroad (between Batavia and Darien in western New York state) wasn't completed until October 1842. Stagecoaches were used in the interim.

At about the same time the New York-Buffalo service was initiated, similar service between Boston and New York was announced. A third route, between Boston and St. John, New Brunswick, was in operation a few years later.

Specialists have been studying these markings for years and have recorded types with "Boston" or "N. York" in many varieties. It is probable that at least two varieties exist of each U.S. Express Mail marking. Even the rare "Albany" marking exists in two very similar varieties, showing slightly different spacing of words and letters. Some of the markings exist in a half dozen minor varieties or more.

With the frequent trips by more than one boat or train, each with a route agent aboard, every agent had to have his own instrument. Manufacturers of handstamps of the 1840s and '50s found it difficult to make duplicate marking devices identical. Small differences in spacing or letter shapes usually can be found.

The notices announcing the establishment of the routes made clear that the post office hired experienced expressmen as route agents for the Express Mail. The expressmen were permitted to carry parcels, packages and valuables for fees on their own behalf even while carrying the U.S. Express Mails. All this was to compete with private express mail routes already in operation in the same areas — and using the same railroads and steamboats.

Well-known names in the field were Harnden, Adams, Hawley,

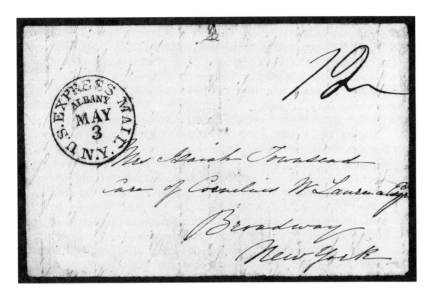

Figure 156. "U.S. EXPRESS MAIL/ ALBANY/N.Y." applied on a south-bound steamboat on the Hudson, between Albany and New York, in the early 1840s.

Wells (later, of Wells, Fargo), Livingston and Pomeroy.

Figure 157 illustrates a cover carried by Pomeroy's Letter Express from Utica to Troy, New York, in July 1844. Although the two stamps on this cover are listed in the Scott U.S. catalog as "locals" (117L3), the usage was anything but local. "Local" implies use within the bounds of a city. The Pomeroy stamps were used on letter mail between cities. They are really "Express Mail" or "Independent Mail" stamps, like the Pony Express stamps.

According to Elliott Perry, who did extensive research in this field, Pomeroy's Express line was established in 1841, with George E. Pomeroy as an important partner. By 1844, Pomeroy had left his original partners and started his own express service, for which he issued the Pomeroy's Express stamps.

Pomeroy and other express companies formed a network of mail carriers in competition with the Post Office Department from New York to the northeast and in upstate New York. They exchanged mail with one another, possibly handling express charges by purchasing or trading stamps with one another, of those companies that issued stamps, or labels, such as Pomeroy. The cover shown in Figure 157

Figure 157. A double-rate and, presumably, double-weight letter carried by Pomeroy's Letter Express from Utica to Troy, New York, in July of 1844. U.S. government postage for under 80 miles at this time was 10¢ per single weight. The "Cd" marking (tracing, inset) in red is often found canceling the stamps; its significance is not known.

illustrates such a situation. The stamps are canceled with a manuscript "B" (as established by Richard C. Frajola), the "B" being the marking of Burbank & Co.'s Express at Utica, New York, where the cover originated. Burbank operated from Utica to Kingston, Canada, via Watertown and Sackett's Harbor, New York.

Since Pomeroy operated at Utica, the letter, mailed with Burbank, evidently was given to Pomeroy to be carried to Troy. Whether Burbank supplied the stamps or that they were applied by the sender isn't known, but Burbank canceled them with his "B." The red "Cd" on the cover was applied by Pomeroy.

Pomeroy's stamps sold in 1844 for "20 for $1" (as displayed in tiny print at the bottom of each stamp), so postage on this letter was 10¢ plus whatever fee Burbank charged for handling the letter.

The "20 for $1" price of the stamps, equivalent to 5¢ each, as Pomeroy charged in 1844, was exactly the same as the new Post Office Department postal rate established the following year for single letters carried up to 300 miles. At the time the letter was sent, U.S postage between Utica and Troy would have been 12 1/2¢ for a single letter, so the expressmen's postage considerably undercut the U.S. postage.

It should be recognized that the U.S. postal monopoly, in effect since 1792, at that time covered letter mail only (including newspapers and circulars) as carried over the official post routes of the United States. Nothing excluded the carriage of valuables, packages and such over the same routes by expressmen. In the 1840s, the expressmen commenced to compete actively in the letter mail field as well. They claimed, usually quite correctly in view of the high postal rates then prevailing, that they could carry letters faster and cheaper over the same routes as the Post Office Department. Part of their advantage was that they were not burdened with newspapers, large amounts of free mail, and circulars analogous to the "junk mail" of today. Nor were they burdened with large overhead, in the form of a corporate structure or capital equipment. They kept red tape at a minimum, which is one reason we know so little of the details of their operations.

The establishment of the U.S. Express Mail service was accompanied by legal action, in the name of the postmaster general, against Pomeroy, for violating the postal monopoly by carrying letter mails. Although Pomeroy won the case, in essence all the private expressmen lost. Congress was forced to acknowledge that the expressmen could take over the letter-mail business in the United States (would the congressmen have lost their free mail privileges?) unless stronger laws were passed. Then (as now) the letter-mail business was the "cream," as illustrated by the fact the expressmen preferred it and were willing to challenge the post office to secure it.

Congress took action by reducing the letter-mail rates to 5¢ for under 300 miles and 10¢ for carriage further than that, effective July 1, 1845. In addition, they clarified the law and enacted stiffer penalties for violation of the letter-mail monopoly. Last, which was really the crusher, they declared that all the railroads were post roads of the United States. As such, the railroads could no longer legally carry expressmen with letter mail in their possession.

These changes caused the express companies to abandon the intercity letter-mail business. While the legal penalties were a factor, the reduced postal rates for government-carried letters probably made profit margins unattractive, or at least not worth the risk.

In summary, it was competition — or at least the threat of

competition — that forced the postal service to maintain efficient service at reasonable cost.

Express companies carried valuables before 1900

By the 1850s, the eastern express companies could no longer legally carry letter mails at competitive rates between cities and towns. This was our nation's first illustration of an obvious economic fact: Mail can be carried at far lower rates, and quite profitably, if it is only carried over high-volume routes. An equally obvious corollary is that the more remote post offices, with low volumes of mail (i.e., the sparsely settled parts of the country) would have no mail service at all, or would require subsidy in some manner, if they were to enjoy mail service at the same rates. Thus, the express companies of the 1840s and later "skimmed the cream" (as the saying goes), carrying mail over the most profitable routes and letting the rest go hang.

The Post Office Department, with responsibility to provide mail service wherever Congress decreed and at rates established by law, required a monopoly on letter mail, much higher rates, or some other form of public subsidy. But the legal actions of the 1840s-1860s didn't much impinge on the express companies' bread-and-butter business. Their main activity was carrying valuable letters and packages (including currency, gold and silver) as quickly as possible and with great security, but at far higher rates than the post office charged.

The private letter mails that the express companies carried in the 1840s and 1850s at rates comparable to or lower than the postal rates of the time were distinct from their regular business of securely conveying valuables.

Figure 158 shows the front of a typical valuable letter, demonstrating express company practices from the 1850s on. The reverse is shown in Figure 159. Both front and back are printed as standard forms of the Adams Express Company, Western Division (not to be confused with the earlier California Adams Express). Per the inscriptions, the letter contained $5, which probably wasn't "counted and sealed by" the agent, which would have been the case for larger

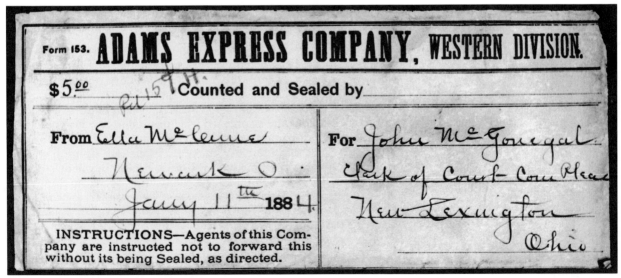

Figure 158. A valuable letter envelope, containing $5 in money, sent via Adams Express Company's Western Division from Newark to New Lexington, Ohio, in 1884. This was the 19th-century version of today's registered letter.

111

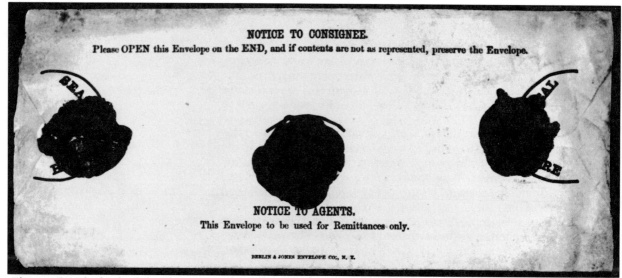

NOTICE TO CONSIGNEE.

Please OPEN this Envelope on the END, and if contents are not as represented, preserve the Envelope.

NOTICE TO AGENTS.

This Envelope to be used for Remittances only.

BERLIN & JONES ENVELOPE CO., N. Y.

Figure 159. The back of the Figure 158 cover, showing black wax seals reading "Adams Express Co., Newark, Ohio/ 34." The printed legend advises the consignee to open the envelope at the end and "if contents are not as represented, preserve the Envelope." It also notes that this type of envelope was to be used for remittances only.

amounts. The letter was sent from Newark, Ohio, to New Lexington, two towns that were directly connected by rail, 35 miles apart. The cover is dated January 11, 1884, with express charges of 15¢ marked as paid.

Why wasn't this letter sent through the post office by registered mail? At that time, in 1884, postage was 2¢ per 1/2 ounce (reduced to 2¢ per ounce the following year). The registry fee was 10¢. This meant a total of 12¢ for 1/2 ounce or 14¢ if the letter weighed between 1/2 and 1 ounce. Either was less than the express fee of 15¢ for a letter that carried only $5. Incidentally, this is the smallest amount I can recall seeing enclosed in an express envelope.

The major reason people used express companies for sending cash or valuables was that until 1898, the post office was not permitted to pay indemnity for lost or rifled registered letters. Even then, indemnification was limited to $10. I presume the private express companies did indemnify senders for lost letters or missing contents. They routinely required the value to be proven when letters were sent, as evident from the printed inscriptions on the envelopes they furnished.

The back of the Figure 158 cover, shown in Figure 159, bears three black wax seals, impressed over printed areas designated for them. The seals are impressed with a number, possibly a clerk's code, as well as the company office name and location. In addition, the letter's printed instructions request that the letter be opened "on the END, and if contents are not as represented, preserve the Envelope." This type of printed envelope was in use at least as early as the 1850s. Continuous use into the 1890s indicates that the system worked and suggests that the express companies didn't often have to pay indemnity for lost or rifled envelopes.

Figure 160 shows another phase of the express company operation — carrying valuable documents between courts and attorneys connected with court cases. Probably the higher costs (believed 25¢ in this case) became part of court costs, although the government

postage on this cover, as a registered letter of 3 or 4 ounces sent in the 1870s, would have been about the same. Either way, this letter probably would have traveled from Toledo to Columbus, Ohio, on the same train. Most likely the express company was chosen over the post office for reasons of security and indemnification.

The label of the United States Express Company on the Figure 160 cover, printed in black on green paper, is shown in Figure 161. It advises that the United States Express Company operated via the New York and Erie Railroad at Buffalo and Dunkirk, New York, Cincinnati and Cleveland, Ohio, St. Louis and Chicago, demonstrating that the express companies followed the railroads and that their network really constituted a separate postal system of its own.

The *American Stampless Cover Catalog*, Volume II, contains a 51-page section on "independent mail service" markings, which lists some express company labels and more of their handstamps. Short biographies are included, and the printed envelopes are mentioned, but not cataloged. Similar material appeared in a Richard C. Frajola auction catalog, in a sale held January 28, 1984. Here an "Eastern Express Mail" section of more than 150 lots illustrated many express company covers from east of the Mississippi River.

Harry M. Konwiser created a catalog of "Independent Mail Routes of the United States" for Volume I, Part 2 of *The Stamp Specialist*, with a supplement in the "Yellow Book" of the same series, published by H.L. Lindquist, New York, in 1940 and 1942. Konwiser also provided the only listing I know of express company labels — in the "Mahogany Book" of the same series, published in 1947. Konwiser's listing, Express Company Labels, speculated that such labels should be listed in the Scott *Specialized Catalogue of United States Stamps*, on the basis that the labels represented "evidence of an imposed tax." Probably the fact that most express labels show no denominations has prevented this from happening.

Personally, I find the express company labels very revealing. For example, until I saw the "Harnden Express, Gallipolis, Ohio," label shown in Figure 161, I had no idea that this eastern pioneer express company, which operated on the East Coast and in Europe, ranged so far west. Harnden probably operated an office at Gallipolis in connection with the steamboat traffic on the Ohio River. Steamboats were being replaced by the railroads in the latter part of the 19th century, but as long as they maintained regular sechedules, they continued to carry mail on some routes. The express companies also used them in the same manner that those companies followed the railroads.

Figure 161. Express company labels, used in Ohio circa 1850-1890. The label at the top is from the Figure 160 cover. The label at the bottom (off cover) shows that the famous Harnden Express Company, normally thought to have operated mainly in New England, also did business in the Ohio Valley.

This chapter is based on the following *Linn's* columns: city carrier covers, June 13, 1983; Express Mail, September 5, 1983, and December 31, 1984; express companies carried valuables before 1900, August 8, 1988.

Chapter 10

Earliest Known Uses

U.S. 10¢ 1847 stamp

An Associated Press news item carried in many papers across the country on September 23, 1989, discussed the authentication of the cover shown in Figure 162. Bearing a horizontal pair of U.S. 10¢ 1847 stamps (Scott 2), the cover was mailed from New York to Indianapolis on July 2, 1847. This is the earliest known use of general-issue U.S. postage stamps. The cover is said to have been found in a law book from the estate of an Indianapolis lawyer. Delmere B. Blackburn and Dr. Harry D. Mark jointly owned the cover. Blackburn died in 1987, and Mark died in August 1989.

The news article brought back memories. I recollect a phone call from J. David Baker, also of Indianapolis, who owned one of the really great U.S. postal history collections. Baker told me that Mark had approached him to learn what the cover was worth. Baker examined the cover and made photographs and color slides.

The result was two articles in the *Chronicle of the U.S. Classic Postal Issues* (usually called the *Chronicle*) for May 1972. The authors were Creighton C. Hart, who edited the 1847 section of the publication, and Susan M. McDonald, who had just become editor-in-chief of the *Chronicle*. Hart discussed the earliest known uses of the first U.S. general-issue postage stamps. McDonald explored the question of what day the stamps could have first been on sale at New York City. This research recognizes that with U.S. classic stamps an "EKU" (earliest known use) and an actual first day of usage are not necessarily the same thing. Hart pointed out that up to the time of this discovery, the EKU of the 5¢ 1847 stamp was a cover postmarked July 7, 1847, and the EKU of the 10¢ was July 9, 1847. Both covers were from New York City.

An official record book in the National Archives shows that the first delivery of 1847 stamps by the printer, Rawdon, Wright, Hatch & Edson of New York, was on July 1, 1847. On this same day, stamps were supplied to the New York post office. Stamps were supplied to the post office at Boston on July 2; Philadelphia on July 12; Washington on July 15; and Baltimore on July 25, 1847. Hart also recorded the earliest uses from those cities.

McDonald, in her article, examined the various stories, previously published in the philatelic press, relating to the actual dates of availability of the 1847 stamps. She noted that most of the stories

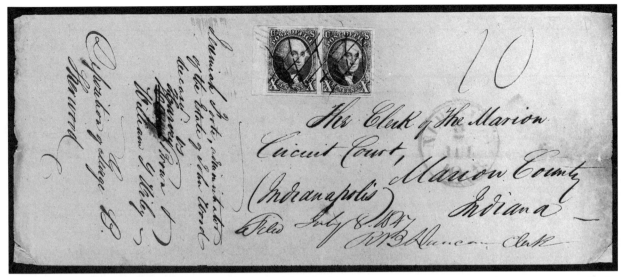

Figure 162. A pair of 10¢ 1847 stamps tied by faint red grid cancels to a cover postmarked July 2, 1847, at New York, addressed to Indianapolis. The two 10¢ stamps prepaid part of a three-times-10¢ rate. Another 10¢ was marked as due and collected upon delivery at Indianapolis. This is the earliest known use of a general-issue U.S. postage stamp.

displayed little research. Those that did, such as articles by Carroll Chase, simply proved previous tales inaccurate without recognizing the manner in which our classic stamps, printed by private contractors, were actually delivered to postmasters. For the 1847 stamps, the same process used with contractors of later years was employed. The Post Office Department sent an agent to the stamp printer. This stamp agent's duty was to inspect and accept stamps and fill postmaster orders relayed from Washington.

Since the stamps were printed in New York City, it followed that New York was the logical place for the 1847 stamps to have been first used. And it is quite clear that they were first available over the post office counter on July 1, 1847.

The Figure 162 cover contained a deposition taken June 30, 1847. Hart and McDonald believe that stamps purchased July 1 were applied to the letter, which was then dropped into the slot at the post office very late on July 1 or early on July 2. Although the cover has a pair of 10¢ stamps to prepay a double-weight letter sent more than 500 miles under the rate structure prevalent in 1847, the letter evidently was weighed by the New York post office and found to be overweight. A due charge of "10" was marked on the cover to be collected at the destination.

As I recollect, Blackburn and Mark were asking around $100,000 at the time the cover was found. The Associated Press article in 1989 reported that the cover "could be worth as much as $1 million." Christie's sold the cover for $132,000 at auction in October 1990.

At the beginning of this chapter, I was careful to say that this cover is the earliest known use of a general-issue U.S. postage stamp. This is because the U.S. Post Office Department, in 1842, purchased the private New York carrier service of Alexander M. Greig, called the "City Despatch Post." Greig was already using stamps, an example of which is shown in Figure 163. Inscribed "CITY DESPATCH POST," these stamps were printed in grayish black ink on grayish to white paper. All were 3¢ denominations, although a second version of the

Figure 163. Greig's City Despatch Post stamp, from a New York carrier service that was purchased by the post office in 1842.

Figure 164. A pair of U.S. City Despatch Post stamps, issued by the New York post office after it acquired the Greig operation. Many consider these the first official U.S. postage stamps.

post operated in 1846 and used 2¢ stamps.

After the U.S. Post Office Department purchased the Greig operation, it issued stamps of its own. They had a similar design but were inscribed "UNITED STATES CITY DESPATCH POST." These stamps were printed in black on grayish paper, and later on various other colors of paper. The original City Despatch Post stamps are listed in Scott's *Specialized Catalogue of United States Stamps* under locals (40L1-8). A brief summary of their history precedes the listing. The United States City Despatch Post stamps are listed under carrier stamps as 6LB1-11, also with introductory matter preceding the listings. A pair is shown in Figure 164. The stamps used by the United States City Despatch Post bear the cancellation of the New York Post Office, usually "U.S." in an octagon. Occasionally, the stamps bear a circle with the date and the words "U.S. CITY DESPATCH POST" or a New York townmark.

The most comprehensive information on these 1842 government issues is in *100 Years Ago*, a monograph by Elliott Perry and Arthur G. Hall, published by the American Philatelic Society in 1942. It is often found included with bundles of handbooks in auctions.

There isn't any doubt that the United States City Despatch Post stamps of 1842 were the first officially authorized U.S. postage stamps. This is shown by surviving correspondence between the New York postmaster and Postmaster General Charles A. Wickliffe. However, the 1842 stamps, which weren't in use very long, were strictly local issues. Whether they were printed under the authority of the postmaster general or just the New York postmaster is uncertain. They weren't in any way valid outside New York City. The distinguishing mark of a general-issue postage stamp is that it is valid throughout the system in which it is used.

The 5¢ and 10¢ 1847 stamps were the first U.S. postage stamps to have this feature. The Figure 162 cover thus represents the earliest known use of a U.S. general-issue postage stamp. It seems doubtful that an earlier date of use — it would have to be July 1, 1847 — will ever be found.

U.S. 1861 stamps

My *Linn's* column for March 14, 1983, displayed the cover shown in Figure 165 and noted that it was considered the earliest known use of the U.S. 3¢ 1861 stamp. Subsequently, the question of

Figure 165. The earliest-known use of the U.S. 3¢ rose pink stamp of 1861 (Scott 64b) on a cover from Baltimore, Maryland, postmarked on Saturday, August 17, 1861.

the "first day" of use of the 3¢ stamp was mentioned by William Hatton in his Basics and Beyond column in *Linn's* for September 29, 1986. There the first-day date was given as August 19, 1861. A letter from Leonard Holmsten in *Linn's* Readers' Opinions section for November 3, 1983, commented that every time he read about the first day of use of the 3¢ 1861 stamp it seemed to be different. He cited a cover sold in Robert A. Siegel's 433rd sale, with an August 17 postmark that was touted as the earliest known date of use of the 3¢ stamp.

The cover noted by Holmsten is shown here in Figure 165. It was sold in a June 1973 Siegel sale, described as a "deep rose pink" stamp tied on a cover with a clear blue Baltimore postmark dated August 17. The 1861 year date is well established by docketing on the cover. The next lot had four more covers with rose pink 3¢ 1861 stamps used from Baltimore in August, September and October 1861. The description didn't say that those covers were a continuation of the same correspondence as the August 17 cover, but they were. The August 17 cover sold for $1,100, and the following lot with the four rose pinks sold for $50 — I hope, to the same buyer.

Figure 166. A loose 1¢ blue 1861 stamp also used from Baltimore on August 17, 1861.

The only other August 17, 1861, usage known on the 1861 stamps is shown in Figure 166, a loose 1¢ 1861 stamp with a clear Baltimore postmark dated August 17, 1861. The postmarks in Figures 165 and 166 aren't from the same instrument. Tracings of similar postmarks are shown in Figure 167. One marking has a year date and one doesn't — but both markings are typical of the several similar Baltimore postmarks in use at that time. So, we can ask, why the confusion about the earliest uses of the 3¢ 1861 stamps?

In my opinion, there are several explanations: the unusual way the 1861 stamps were introduced, factors common with all 19th-century "earliest known uses," and the fact that the 3¢ stamp exists in four distinct 1861 shades, as listed in the catalogs. The different EKUs of the 3¢ 1861 stamps are for different shades.

Taking first things first, the 1861 stamps were put into use as rapidly as the printer could furnish supplies. The contract of Toppan, Carpenter & Company of Philadelphia, the printer of the previous stamp issue, expired in the spring of 1861. New designs of all denominations were required immediately. The old stamps, with considerable quantities in the hands of postmasters in the newly formed Confederacy, had to be rendered invalid. A new printer was selected in the spring of 1861, but it was August before sheets of the new stamps were available.

The new printer, the National Bank Note Company of New York, had problems achieving a satisfactory color for the 3¢ stamp. The wide range of colors would intrigue stamp collectors of later years.

Figure 167. Tracings of types of Baltimore postmarks that were in use in August of 1861.

To replace the old stamps and render them invalid at the same time the new 1861 stamps were furnished, a notice was sent with initial shipments of the new stamps to each post office. The notice required that an exchange period of six days be announced in local newspapers. During this exchange period, the old stamps could be exchanged for the new ones. After the six-day exchange period, during which either issue was valid at that particular post office, the old issue would no longer be accepted for postage on letters or packets mailed at that office. Today, we call the process the "demonetization" of the 1851-57 issues. Larger cities received supplies of the new stamps first. Small post offices often didn't receive the new issues for a month or so afterward. Forwarded covers exist bearing stamps of both issues properly used. These are highly prized.

Figure 168 shows a cover that originated at Emmittsburgh, Maryland, on August 17, 1861, with a 3¢ stamp of 1857 paying the postage to Philadelphia. At Philadelphia, the cover was received and forwarded to Harrisburg with postage prepaid by a new 3¢ 1861 stamp. The cover was postmarked at Philadelphia on Monday, August 19, 1861, the first day the 1861 stamp was available there, and the first day of Philadelphia's six-day exchange period. Since several other cities also had the 3¢ 1861 stamp available on that day, and since some of those stamps were in the rose shades, this accounts for August 19 being considered the earliest known use of the 3¢ 1861 in the rose shade of the basic listing.

The Scott U.S. specialized catalog for 1992 lists no specific date of issuance for any shade of the 3¢ stamp of 1861, although it does show August 17, 1861 as the date the 1¢ stamp was first used. Probably, the dates of August 17, 1861, should be listed for the rose pink, Scott 64b, and August 19 for the rose shades. It is believed that the pinks and pigeon bloods didn't appear quite that soon. August 17 was a Saturday and August 19 a Monday. While Saturday was a full work day in 1861, even major post offices were open but a short time on Sundays. A few rose pinks used August 18 have been recorded.

The postal history collector interested in early uses from the mid-19th century should take the term "first-day cover" with a grain of salt. The earliest known use he acquires today may be a second day or even later use next year. Thus, the term "earliest known use" acknowledges that earlier uses are possible.

The stamps of 1861, in common with the issues before and after,

Figure 168. Posted while the 1857 stamps were just beginning to be replaced with those of 1861, this cover was mailed from Emmittsburgh, Maryland, with a 3¢ 1857 stamp. At Philadelphia, it was forwarded with a new 3¢ 1861 stamp, on August 19, 1861 — the first day the new stamps were available at that city.

were printed by bank note companies that delivered finished sheets to a Post Office Department representative known as the stamp agent, working on their premises. The earliest possible use can be determined from the records of when the first deliveries of a new stamp issue were made. For the 1861 issue, this occurred on Friday, August 16, 1861. While uses of 1861 stamps are thus possible from near New York City on August 16, the August 17 date would seem to be the earliest use of these stamps that will ever be found, since New York City was not allotted supplies of the new stamps until September. This was because the National Bank Note Company couldn't provide enough stamps before then to satisfy the large demand for new stamps expected to be exchanged in the nation's largest city.

This chapter is based on the following *Linn's* **columns: U.S. 10¢ 1847 stamp, November 6, 1989; U.S. 1861 stamps, March 14, 1983, and January 12, 1987.**

Chapter 11

Armed Forces Mail

Banks' Division

One of the interesting features of the Civil War was the number of top ranking military men who, by modern standards, had backgrounds inappropriate to field command. While many of the generals were West Pointers, or at least had varied military field experience, there was also a large proportion of "political generals" with no previous military experience whatsoever. These officers were politicians who had exerted influence to be appointed to high rank in the Army at the beginning of the war. Most of them probably didn't expect the war to last very long and thought it would be nice to run for office again with a military title in front of their names.

While a few of the political generals became outstanding officers, I suspect that as the war progressed, most of them wished they had remained in politics.

When Major General Nathaniel Prentice Banks of Massachusetts became a general, his only war experience was in political combat. He served several terms in Congress, both before and after the war, and was speaker of the House from 1855 to 1857. The fact that it took two months and 133 ballots before he was elected speaker as a compromise candidate simply shows his political ability to be at the right place at the right time. He was also governor of Massachusetts between 1858 and 1861.

Figure 169 shows Banks as a Union general. His appearance is not what humble origins and his nickname of the "Bobbin Boy" (from an early background in the textile mills) would lead us to expect. As an army officer, his only major success was to be in command of Federal forces investing Port Hudson, Louisiana, when it surrendered as a result of Grant's capture of Vicksburg. This opened the Mississippi River and cut the Confederacy into two parts.

Banks was given the thanks of Congress as a result. However, there was very little comment in Congress a year later when Banks was disastrously defeated in his Red River campaign, attempting to capture Texas.

Banks' main claim to fame today is among postal history collectors, as his name appears as part of what are considered our first APO (Army Post Office) postmarks. These read "G.B.D." — for "General Banks' Division" or, later, "Banks' Division."

Figure 170 shows the various types of these markings, which

Figure 169. Major General Nathaniel Prentice Banks.

TYPE	DATE RANGE	COLOR	SEE NOTE
Manuscript	Sept. 1861	——	(1)
A	Sept. 16-Oct. 18, 1861	Black	
B	Oct. 20-Oct. 31, 1861	Black	(2)
C	Nov. 3-Dec. ?, 1861	Black	(3)
C	March 4-March 14, 1862	Blue	(3)
D	March 20-Aug. 17, 1862	Blue	(4)
E	Sept. 9-Nov. 26, 1862	Blue	(5)
f, g, h	Used with various of above		(6)

Notes:
(1) Three covers with a scribbled "G.B.D." have been recorded.
(2) The "B" is inverted in this version. Apparently, the type fell out of the holder of type A and was carelessly inserted in the new instrument.
(3) The type C marking was in use when, apparently, the troops went into winter quarters in late 1861. When the marking reappeared in the spring, it was struck in blue.
(4) This 32-millimeter marking is the most common of all the Banks' Division markings. Strikes on covers mailed after May 1862 show progressively thicker lines from ink incrustation or wear as time passed.
(5) The type E marking is 32 1/2mm, and letters are taller and thinner. Some are also shaped differently than in the type D marking, such as the "D" of "Division."
(6) Auxilliary-rate markings found with different examples of the basic postmarks.

Figure 170. The postal markings of General Banks' Division. See accompanying box for explanation of these markings.

were applied to covers at Banks' Division headquarters while it was in the Shenandoah Valley of Virginia or in Maryland across the Potomac to the north. The uses range from September 1861 until November 1862. The types, range of dates and colors, which I have compiled, are presented in the accompanying box. Usage wasn't continuous, as the troops evidently went into winter quarters from December 1861 until March 1862. Postmarks of Sandy Hook, Maryland, Harper's Ferry, Virginia, or other offices were used on their mail that winter.

It will be noted that the postmark ink color was changed when use of the Banks' Division was resumed in the spring of 1862, so that black markings are from 1861 and blue ones from 1862.

Figure 171 shows a typical early use (October 18, 1861) of the type A "G.B.D." Banks' Division marking. It has neither stamp nor rate, but is simply marked "PAID." It would seem the Banks' Division postmaster was neither well-equipped nor well-aware of the postal regulations.

This all ties in with how the Banks' Division field post office may have been created. General Banks was appointed to command the Department of the Shenandoah in July 1861. In August, this was merged into the newly created Department of the Potomac, which eventually became the Army of the Potomac. The newly created department was divided into "grand" divisions. Banks' command was naturally known as Banks' Division.

Banks, optimistic that his new command would march down the Shenandoah Valley, turn east and take Richmond, desired it to have

Figure 171. The first type (A) marking of the General Banks' Division post office on an all-over blue McClellan patriotic cover. Note the "G.B.D." is struck nicely across the face of General McClellan. No value of rate is expressed with the "PAID."

good mail communications while this momentous act was in progress. So he pulled a few political strings and had a member of his staff, Major Roscoe E. Houghton, appointed postmaster of his division.

The operations of this office, as indicated by the dates of the use of the markings, reflect the division's military operations. As noted, the field post office markings were not in use while the troops were in winter quarters. It is possible to correlate other events with the absence of covers — such as when Stonewall Jackson captured Banks' wagon train. This occurred twice. Banks' troops, which didn't officially bear the Banks' Division title very long, were sometimes called "Stonewall Jackson's Commissary."

The Battle of Second Manassas may have led indirectly to the end of the Banks' Division markings. In a letter written by Postmaster Houghton in October 1862, to the Post Office Department, he commented: "On the 10th of last October a commission was sent me as Special Agent to sell stamps to General Banks' Division. On the late retreat it was destroyed with property belonging to these headquarters." He went on to request that the commission be replaced, but this apparently wasn't done. At least the use of the Banks' Division marking was discontinued soon afterward. Which is to say, Houghton probably "dug up a dead cat." He called the attention of the Post Office Department to his operation at the wrong time.

Banks had been transferred to New Orleans and was out of the picture. Other army mails were processed at the Washington, D.C., post office or at various towns. Banks' Division had not been an official name of any military organization for almost a year, and now it vanished from the postal scene.

Spanish-American War APO markings

The Spanish-American War, fought in Cuba, Puerto Rico and the Philippine Islands, was predominantly a naval war, except for Army operations in Cuba and a few scattered small battles in the other areas. Even in Cuba, after the Spanish fleet came out of Santiago harbor to be destroyed by the U.S. Navy, the war there was over for all practical purposes.

The war in the Philippines was another matter. Admiral George Dewey's squadron destroyed the Spanish fleet at Manila Bay on May 1, 1898, early in the war. The fact that no troops were to arrive for land operations until June 30 allowed the Philippine guerillas under Emilio

Aguinaldo to firmly establish themselves as a third element in the picture. This led to the extended war called the Philippine Insurrection, mostly fought by the U.S. Army with gunboat support.

Covers from the Spanish-American War and the ensuing Philippine Insurrection actually represent our first artifacts from the type of operations that developed into the Army post office (APO) markings of later years. The post offices established with the troops abroad were operated as branches of the New York and San Francisco post offices. Covers from them were the first of this kind from U.S. military operations in foreign lands.

The first troops to arrive in the Philippines landed at Cavite naval base in Manila harbor on July 1, 1898. Later contingents landed just south of Manila, establishing a base called Camp Dewey. Beginning July 16, mail from the troops was consolidated aboard a transport in Manila harbor.

The first post office was established ashore at Cavite on July 30, 1898, as military station number 1 of the San Francisco post office. Station number 1 was moved to Manila on August 14, 1898, the day after Manila fell to the Americans. The Cavite post office was re-established as military station number 2 on September 7, 1898.

Figure 172 shows a cover from aboard *USS Nero*, a navy collier sent from the United States in August with fuel for Dewey's squadron. It bears a handstamped purple straightline "U.S.MIL STA. NO. 2 S.F. CAL/CAVITE, P.I. Dec 1 98." There is no indication of postage, either prepaid or due. The cover is addressed to Clyde, New York, where it was backstamped on January 1, 1899. It bears a hand-drawn, multi-colored depiction of a turreted warship, which wasn't the *Nero* but probably represents the *USS Olympia*, Admiral Dewey's flagship. That vessel was the only turreted warship among the ships of Dewey's squadron at Manila Bay. The cachet is an attractive handpainted design in red, blue, green and yellow. While it lacks either a stamp or due markings, the Figure 172 cover was probably sent collect as a "sailor's letter."

Manila was captured on August 13, 1898, and the Spanish forces capitulated the next day, not knowing that the United States and Spain had signed a protocol to end the war everywhere on August 12. The final treaty led to the U.S. possession of Puerto Rico, Guam and the Philippines, as well as the occupation of Cuba until it could

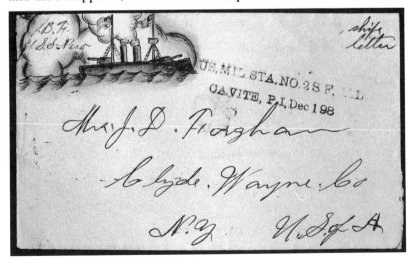

Figure 172. Cover from the *USS Nero*, a navy collier at Cavite naval base in Manila Bay in 1898. The hand-drawn warship (not the *Nero*) is painted in several colors.

Figure 173. A soldier's letter from the Iloilo Harbor military station number 3 on Panay Island in the Philippines, posted to New Jersey in 1899 at the 2¢ domestic rate.

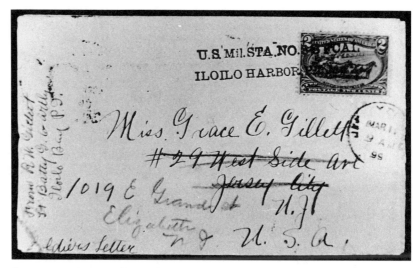

be set up as an independent country.

The Philippine occupation led to numerous military stations, which eventually were converted to offices in the Philippines' own postal system.

Shortly after the war began, Congress passed a law authorizing the establishment of post offices at military posts and camps, including offices involving "expeditions that shall be made" — presumably on foreign soil. In a letter to the secretary of war dated June 25, 1898, the postmaster general established a military mail system to provide smooth handling of mail between the military and the U.S. Post Office Department. This confirmed, for the Philippines, at least, a postmaster general's order of May 24, 1898. This and subsequent acts and orders also extended U.S. domestic mail rates and privileges to all U.S. personnel sending mail through the military post offices.

Figure 173 shows a cover with postage prepaid by a 2¢ Trans-Mississippi stamp, sent from the military station at Iloilo (on Panay Island and at the time the second largest port in the Philippines) in late January 1899. The cover is endorsed as having been sent by a soldier of Battery G of the 6th Artillery at Iloilo Bay and is addressed to Jersey City, New Jersey, whence it was forwarded to Elizabeth on March 1, 1899. Quite a distance for a letter to be carried for 2¢!

Figure 174. Written aboard *USS Monterey* and sent from military station number 2 at Cavite (Philippines) to Vallejo, California, at the 2¢ domestic rate in 1898, this cover bears a large handstamp that satisfies postal regulations.

From the time of the Civil War, U.S. Army and Navy personnel, including Marines, had been permitted to send letters collect at domestic rates without penalty. The postal laws and regulations required that the sender's unit be identified on the cover and that it be signed or "certified" by an officer of the unit to attest its nature as a "soldier's or sailor's letter." About the only change made in the regulations between the Civil War days and the 1880s was that the original act didn't extend the privilege to officers. But by 1887, officers too could send collect letters in such a manner.

Figure 174 on the prevous page shows a cover with a handstamp that satisfies this provision, although the cover is prepaid at the 2¢ domestic rate under the law of 1898. The cover originated aboard *USS Monterey* (Figure 175) and bears a large purple handstamp with the ship's name, a facsimile signature of its captain, and the certification "Sailor's Letter." The handstamp satisfies a requirement of the law of 1898 that the sender's military or naval unit had to be identified to receive the domestic postage rate. Addressed to Vallejo, California (site of the Mare Island navy yard), the cover was mailed at military station number 2 at Cavite on October 4, 1899. Per the backstamp, the cover was about a month in transit.

For those who wish to explore the subject of the markings, the most recent reference I have is Philip Baker's *Postal Markings of United States Military Stations, 1898-1902*, published by the author in 1963. This is now out of print, but I see it often in literature dealers' stocks.

Navy and Marine postmarks

The collecting of U.S. naval ship postmarks has both historical and philatelic aspects. Sometimes they are inseparably intertwined. The postmarks came into being when the first full-fledged U.S. government post offices were established aboard Navy ships. Previously, contents of the ships' letter-collection bags had been processed at ports of call, or handed aboard other ships to reach organized mail systems sooner. Identification of covers sent prior to the use of the naval ship markings is possible from letter headings, endorsements, handstamps or by other means such as docketing.

It was some years before the philatelic world got around to seeing the collecting possibilities of postal markings with U.S. naval ship names. Categorization and cataloging actually didn't get well under way until the 1930s. Since then, there has been a flood of special cacheted covers. There are also many covers with historic rather than philatelic overtones.

This doesn't mean that collectors prior to the 1930s weren't conscious of the unusual aspects of such covers. Figure 176 shows a portion of a cover in which the fine hand of a philatelist probably lurks in the background. Used from aboard *USS Wyoming* at Vera Cruz, Mexico, in 1914, this is a typical U.S. naval post office marking of the period. It is an early use of the most common type of naval postmarks, in which the three-bar killer has slots into which words giving the ship's location or other wording could be inserted. The item is a souvenir of an affair of considerable historical interest, in which a good many of the most important ships of the Navy were involved, supporting the U.S. occupation of Vera Cruz. This took place in the spring of 1914.

Wyoming arrived there in May with a draft of men and stayed until late autumn. *USS Wyoming* was then just two years old and, as

Figure 175. *USS Monterey*, source of the Figure 174 cover, was an updated, twin-turret Civil War-style monitor of the 1890s.

Figure 176. A 2¢ Lincoln memorial stamp of 1909, postmarked aboard the U.S. battleship *Wyoming*, supporting operations at Vera Cruz in 1914. This was some five years after the issuance of the stamp.

Figure 177. A cover from U.S. operations in San Domingo, Dominican Republic, 1916-1924. This censored cover probably dates from 1918.

Figure 178. The postmark of the cover of Figure 177, as nearly as can be determined.

Figure 179. The Navy auxiliary, *USS Prairie*, from which the first troops were landed at San Domingo in 1916.

a 27,000-ton battleship of the period, had steamed to Vera Cruz to deter other powers from interfering in U.S. operations.

The postmark shown in Figure 176, struck in a nice blue on the Lincoln Memorial stamp of 1909, thus was preserved not only as a philatelic item but as a souvenir of a bit of U.S. Navy history.

Figure 177 shows a cover representing a similar situation historically, but without the philatelic overtone. The cover bears the 1¢ and 2¢ U.S. booklet pane stamps of 1914 (Scott 424d and 425e) tied with an only partially legible strike of the postmark shown in Figure 178. The cover is addressed to Pennsylvania and bears a "censored" handstamp and signature of a U.S. Marine captain. The year date of the postmark is either 1916 or 1918; it's too faint to read positively. The presence of the censor markings, required in 1918 because of World War I (and not used in 1916), seem to assure the later date.

The postmark shown in Figure 178 isn't from a Navy ship. It was applied in San Domingo, Dominican Republic, at a post office of the U.S. Marines. The wording between the bars, while unclear, is some version of "Care P.M., N.Y." — to instruct correspondents how to direct letters in reply. U.S. naval forces under Admiral William B. Caperton took control of San Domingo in May 1916. American occupation of the Dominican Republic lasted until 1924, with Marines stationed at various cities in that country. The occupation culminated a series of revolutions and treaties, each ending in another revolution, that began back in the 1880s.

Unlike the Vera Cruz operation of 1914, the U.S. naval operations in San Domingo were relatively small scale. The first landings were on May 5, 1916, being made by U.S. Marines from aboard the *USS Prairie* (Figure 179). The gunboat *USS Castine* was also present, and on May 12, Admiral Caperton showed up in his flagship, the dispatch boat *USS Dolphin*. None of these vessels was a front-line warship. The *Prairie* was the former small passenger liner *El Sol*, which had been converted to a naval auxiliary cruiser for the Spanish American War. *Dolphin*, originally built in the 1880s as an unarmored cruiser, had been one of the "new Navy" of the 1880s and hence was one of our first steel warships. In later years, this vessel had been quite nicely fitted out to convey such notables as the president and

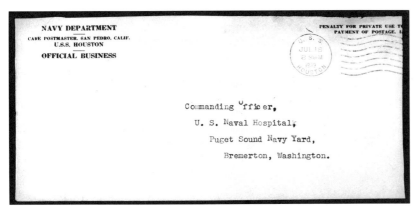

NAVY DEPARTMENT
CARE POSTMASTER, SAN PEDRO, CALIF.
U.S.S. HOUSTON

OFFICIAL BUSINESS

PENALTY FOR PRIVATE USE TO
PAYMENT OF POSTAGE. 1

Commanding Officer,

U. S. Naval Hospital,

Puget Sound Navy Yard,

Bremerton, Washington.

Figure 180. Peacetime penalty envelope from aboard *USS Houston* in 1939, with the machine cancel of the ship's post office.

secretary of the Navy, which probably accounts for Admiral Caperton using such a meek-sounding vessel as a flagship.

Mail from the early operations in the Dominican Republic was handled through the ships' post offices. The 4th Marine Regiment landed in the Dominican Republic in June 1916, and it is presumed their post office was in operation soon after that. Covers with Marine post office markings are known from several towns in the Dominican Republic, with the town names spelled properly in Spanish.

Marine occupation operations were also conducted in Haiti at this time, and similar covers are known from there. In fact, the Marines sent mail from several other activities in Central America and the Caribbean in the first third of the 20th century.

U.S. Navy ship post office markings

The first post offices aboard U.S. Navy ships were established in 1908. But it wasn't until Dr. Francis Locy, a U.S. Navy doctor, established his classification system for the markings that collecting naval covers really caught on.

The 1930s saw a tremendous upsurge in collecting naval ship covers. Few if any covers from the warships of that era (that had post offices) are scarce. Many are in large supply. Most exist on attractive cacheted covers.

Non-souvenir covers such as that pictured in Figure 180 are comparatively scarce. Official business covers such as this are usually legal-size envelopes. Many collectors prefer the smaller, more eye-appealing cacheted examples with Navy ships' postmarks.

The cover in Figure 180 bears the official imprint of *USS Houston* (Figure 181), with a machine cancel applied at the ship's post office in July 1939. *Houston* was one of the prestige Navy ships of the 1930s, from a highly regarded class of heavy cruisers. In January 1939, President Franklin D. Roosevelt was aboard during fleet exercises. When World War II broke out, *Houston* was flagship of the Asiatic Fleet. At the time of Pearl Harbor, she was in the Philippines. *Houston* was sunk by the Japanese, along with most of the rest of a mixed force of Australian, Dutch and U.S. Navy vessels, in the Java Sea in February 1942.

Figure 182 shows tracings of the machine postmark of *Houston*, taken from the cover in Figure 180, and a handstamp applied just one day later, aboard *USS Enterprise*, the famous Word War II aircraft carrier. Such markings contained the names of the ships — up until some months before the U.S. entered the war, when the markings were replaced with markings reading simply "U.S. Navy." Known to

Figure 181. *USS Houston*, whose post office applied the marking on the Figure 180 cover.

Figure 182. Peacetime Navy ship post office markings with the ships' names included.

collectors by a "z" added to the Locy type, these markings can be interesting. Some of the handstampers evidently were made aboard the ships, in response to the order to eliminate the vessels' names from the postmarks.

Postal markings from U.S. Navy ship post offices are listed in the *Catalog of United States Naval Postmarks*, published in loose-leaf sections and normally maintained in print by the Universal Ship Cancellation Society. The catalog uses the Locy postmark classification system, which is based upon the arrangements of ship names, wording and killer bars of the standard types issued to post offices aboard U.S. Navy ships. The catalog lists and gives prices for all known markings (alphabetically by ship names) from the U.S. Navy ships since 1908. It also tells the type of ship and when it was in commission for the Navy. The data also includes dates when shipboard post offices were established and discontinued, which in many cases involves more than one set of dates.

Figure 183 shows two standard types of handstamps used by the U.S. Navy in World War II, issued not only to ships but to post offices at shore stations. Since most covers from servicemen in World War II also bore, as required by regulations, the senders' return addresses — including base or units — most U.S. Navy cancels can be identified as to origin.

In this light, the elimination of origin information from the markings seems a futile gesture. For those postmarks that are standard types, small differences aren't important, but the Locy system helps identify obvious differences. For example, Figure 183 shows the normal type 3 Navy postmark, with three bars widely spaced so that wording could be inserted in slots between the bars. Prior to World War II, this was the norm for most cancels with ship names, although many (if not all) of the larger vessels also had rapid-canceling machines, as exemplified by the *USS Houston* cover in Figure 180.

In mid-1943, or possibly sooner, the standard reverted to the Locy type 2, a four-bar type similar to a style that had been used many years before. The type shown in Figure 183, with stars at the sides, is from aboard the *USS New Jersey* in July 1943. This battleship had just been placed in service; it still survives today.

The three-bar marking in Figure 183 is from aboard the *USS Helena*, a light cruiser sunk in action at Kulu Gulf in the Solomon Islands in July 1943. This marking is called type 3z in the Locy system. The four-bar marking in Figure 183 from the *USS New Jersey* is a type 2z* — the asterisk indicating it has stars. Later World War II versions were mostly type 3z without stars.

Figure 184 shows a machine cancel used by the old battleship *USS Colorado* in 1943. The tracing in Figure 185 may or may not be an improvised die used in a rapid-canceling machine aboard *USS President Jackson*, a Navy transport that operated mostly in the South

Figure 183. The normal type 3 "U.S. NAVY" handstamp of World War II from aboard *USS Helena* (left) and a "U.S. NAVY" marking from *USS New Jersey* (right).

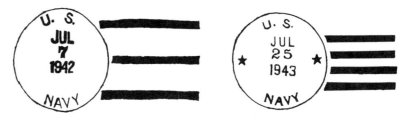

Pacific, after being acquired from the American President Lines.

Under the Locy system, the tracing in Figure 184 is a Locy type 7drz. The "7" refers to the machine cancel and the "d" to its straight bars. The "r" indicates the letters are widely spaced and the "z" that it reads "U.S./Navy" rather than giving a ship's name. In the Locy system, the marking in Figure 185 is cataloged as Fz, the F meaning it wasn't a government-issued type with the "U.S. Navy" wording.

Figures 186, 187 and 188 show handstamps that are designated as provisionals, in that they are apparently adaptations of the standard styles made when the order came to go to the "U.S. Navy" types. It should be recognized, in dealing with these markings, that Navy ships usually had a well-equipped machine shop, with some very talented machinists available. Converting a postmarking handstamper, or even a set of rapid-canceling machine dies, was well within their capabilities. Thus, the markings in Figures 186 and 187 and the left marking in Figure 188 all were adapted from the standard Locy type 3 handstampers by cutting out the ships' names and providing the letters for "U.S. Navy," or the equivalent. None is a standard type.

The marking in Figure 186 (struck in blue) came from aboard a Navy oiler, *USS Cimarron*, then in the Atlantic. Figure 187 shows a marking from a transport, *USS President Adams*, then training U.S. Marines assault troops in New Zealand.

Figure 188 shows provisional markings of a slightly different nature. The May 25 marking in Figure 188 was applied aboard *USS Chenango*, an escort aircraft carrier converted from a fleet oiler, then off the Marshall Islands in the Pacific. This is probably an adaptation of a standard Locy type 3 marking, with the date applied by a separate handstamp — evident from the fact the date crosses the border of the dial, impossible with the standard date inserts.

Figure 188 also shows an unusual marking from a ship with an incredible record of survival. The marking dated September 1, 1942, came from a submarine tender, *USS Holland*. On the surface, it appears to be the standard Locy type 6 handstamp, which is the old-style metal handstamp with duplexed bar killers. However, the handstamp has stars at the side, which isn't listed for the *Holland*.

Holland was at Cavite in the Philippines when the war broke out. She escaped, taking a hazardous trip, servicing her satellite submarines en route, to Australia via New Guinea. At the time the cover was sent, she was in Australia, and was to receive a Presidential Unit Citation for outstanding service during the first months of the war. I strongly suspect the postmarking device was taken from another ship. It is on a very large penalty envelope, with "USS Holland" typed into a printed legend, addressed to the Philadelphia Navy Yard (as are most of the rest of the covers and markings discussed in this chapter).

The *Catalogue of United States Naval Postmarks* has been compiled over a great many years. Its listing of older markings is very comprehensive. While it does list for the *Holland*, as a type 6epz, a

Figure 184. A machine cancel used by the battleship *USS Colorado*.

Figure 185. This may or may not be an improvised die used in a rapid-canceling machine aboard *USS President Jackson*.

Figure 186. A marking from the Navy oiler *USS Cimarron*.

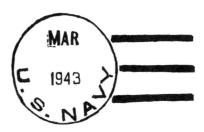

Figure 187. A marking from the transport *USS President Adams*.

Figure 188. Provisional "U.S. NAVY" handstamped postmarks from the escort carrier *USS Chenango* (left) and the submarine tender *Holland* at right.

marking such as that shown here in Figure 188 without the stars, the addition of such seems improbable under the circumstances.

APO locations and postmarks

APO originally and throughout World War II stood for Army Post Office. Since the U.S. Air Force was split off from the Army after World War II, the acronym APO now can stand for either Army or Air Force Post Office. This fact was culled from the explanatory notes section of the fifth edition of *Geographic Locations of U.S. A.P.O.'s, 1941-1984*, published by the War Cover Club. This fifth edition, edited by James Shaffer, follows the pattern of previous editions — with several significant additions, such as reprinting the type chart of Brenner and Baggett originally published by the War Cover Club in 1951 — and as far as I know, not heard of since. I had suggested twice in my *Linn's* column that such a chart was needed and was then advised by George Cosentini of not one but two such efforts. Thus, I was glad to see this reprint, even though it covers only World War II types, since the early efforts are long since out of print.

The main thrust of *Geographic Location* is its first section, "Overseas APOs, 1941 to 1964." This compilation is by numerical sequence of APO numbers. It is very easy to use.

Before exploring this work further, some discussion of the cover shown in Figure 189 will demonstrate its usefulness. Figure 189 is a legal-size envelope addressed to New York bearing a censor marking and an APO number 813 handstamp, dated February 13, 1942. The marking ties a British regular 2 1/2-penny stamp of 1941. This cover was reported by Manoog C. Tatosian as a result of one of my *Linn's* columns about APO markings. I had seen several other examples of British stamps used on covers with U.S. APO markings, but had assumed they were the result of confusion or philatelic foolery. Tatosian's report cast a different light on such usage.

He remarked that as a member of the 63rd Signal Battalion of the U.S. Army, he had been with the first contingent of U.S. troops to

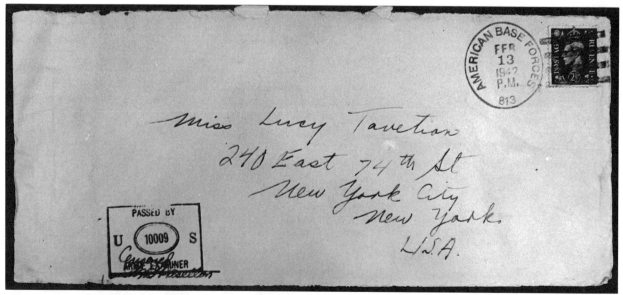

Figure 189. Mailed by a soldier with the first contingent of U.S. troops to be stationed in Europe, this cover bears the APO 813 marking applied at Belfast, Ireland, on February 13, 1942. Note that the cover bears a British stamp.

be stationed in the British Isles (at Belfast, Ireland). Since they had no U.S. stamps, they used British stamps on their mail.

Tatosian also showed a second cover from his correspondence home, also with an APO 813 marking tying a British 2 1/2-penny stamp, dated April 13, 1942. According to *Geographic Locations*, APO 813 was established on January 29, 1942, at Victoria Barracks, Belfast, Northern Ireland, and continued in operation there for an unknown period of time.

Figures 190 and 191 show tracings of two American Base Forces type APO markings, although only the marking in Figure 191 has the designation A.P.O. The tracing in Figure 190 was taken from a cacheted cover dated February 10, 1942, bearing a U.S. 3¢ Virgin Islands stamp of 1937. This was a first day use of the postmark. According to *Geographic Locations*, this post office was established January 29, 1942. I suspect the dates listed are those when such offices were authorized.

The marking traced in Figure 190 is the same as on the February 13 cover shown in Figure 189. This marking also is found on covers from other units of the first contingent, showing British stamps used as late as April 15, 1942.

U.S. servicemen's letters could have been sent free as early as April 1, 1942, but the earliest use I've seen on a free letter with the APO 813 marking, is dated April 17, 1942. There should have been no need for the British stamps after that date.

The tracing in Figure 191 was taken from a cover sent from the 53rd Medical Battalion at APO 813 on May 5, 1942. Not only is the marking new, with the legend APO, but the cover was sent airmail with 6¢ in U.S. stamps. The markings shown in Figures 190 and 191 are listed in the type chart of *Geographic Locations* as types AB 2 and AB 3, which is quite logical. The type chart is based on the Locy Naval Ship system used to categorize U.S. Navy ship postmarks in great detail. It seems to be a useful approach, but there remains the problem of determining just which types were used for each of the approximately 1,000 APOs of World War II — not to mention later establishments.

The early APO markings used at the bases established before the United States entered the war were appropriately worded "American Base Forces," as are the examples in Figures 190 and 191. After the U.S. entry into the war, the wording soon became U.S. Army Postal Service, followed by A.P.O. with a number.

A goodly number of such devices appeared in the spring of 1942. An example is the tracing in Figure 192, from APO 5. However, as noted in the explanatory section of *Geographic Locations*, as of July 1, 1942, a War Department directive required that the numbers not be included in the postmarks.

The removal of the numbers left many of the APO postmarks with a rather lopsided appearance — witness the marking in Figure 193, probably made by the same device as shown in Figure 192. The cover with the postmark shown in Figure 192 is from a soldier of the 11th Infantry (Regiment), stationed at Baldurshagi, Iceland, when the cover was mailed on July 8, 1942.

The tracing in Figure 193 comes from a cover from a member of the 10th Infantry (Regiment) at APO 5. The number is gone from the postmark, which was applied August 8, 1942. According to *Geographic Locations*, APO 5 was assigned to the 5th Infantry Division, and the post office was in Iceland until August 1943. Both the 10th

Figure 190. An American Base Forces marking from APO 813 at Belfast.

Figure 191. Another American Base Forces marking from APO 813.

Figure 192. An APO 5 postmark before the number was removed.

Figure 193. An APO 5 postmark after the number was removed.

Figure 194. An APO number could only be placed in a date slot of markers produced when the handstamps were made with no APO numbers. The APO where this marking was applied can only be suggested from the APO number of the return address.

Figure 195. After the APO numbers were restored to the postmarks, they could only be added in the date slot, as shown here.

This chapter was based on the following *Linn's* columns: Banks' Division, April 14, 1983; Spanish-American War APO markings, March 16, 1987; Navy and Marine postmarks, May 16, 1983; U.S. Navy ship post office markings, February 16, 1987; APO locations and postmarks, November 18, 1985. Thanks to Jim Myerson for doing some research for this chapter on the Marine and Navy uses from the Dominican Republic.

and 11th Infantry Regiments were parts of the 5th Division.

A second War Department directive restored the APO numbers to the postmarks in March 1943.

Devices furnished during the period while the numbers were taboo had the letters APO centered — as shown in the tracing in Figure 194. The APO where this marking was applied can only be suggested from the APO number of the return address.

To complicate matters, for reasons given in the explanatory section of *Geographic Locations*, covers from units in the field were often postmarked at a different APO than that in the return address.

After the APO numbers were restored to the postmarks, they could only be added in the date slot, as shown in the tracing in Figure 195. This particular marking is traced from a cover with a marking applied at APO 612 at Akureyri, Iceland.

The fifth edition of *Geographic Locations* has several other useful features in addition to its main listing and type chart. These include a geographical index with numbers used in various countries and areas, a tabulation of base post offices and other such installations, WWII APOs located in the United States, and a tabulation of the APO numbers assigned to various military units. The compilation has 215 8 1/2- by 11-inch pages, punched for a three ring binder (not furnished).

I probably should stress that although *Geographic Locations* covers U.S. postal history, past issues of the *War Cover Club Bulletin*, the journal of the War Cover Club, have included articles on mails from just about every war that I ever heard of — and some that sent me to the encyclopedia.

And the fact remains that as much as we deplore war, much of our most interesting postal history has stemmed from wartime mails.

Chapter 12

Western Markings

Fort Laramie

Fort Laramie, Wyoming (not to be confused with the present town of Laramie, far south and west of Fort Laramie) stands near the junction of the Laramie and North Platte Rivers. The site was a meeting place for the mountain men and traders of the west from not long after the Lewis and Clark expedition of the early 1800s. Thomas Jefferson, in sending the Lewis and Clark expedition to the Pacific coast, assumed that all the country north of the Spanish possessions in North America on the west coast was acquired in the Louisiana Purchase. This didn't observe British claims, which remained unsettled for years.

Until 1846, the area, known as the Oregon Country, was under joint control of the United States and Great Britain, by an agreement made soon after the War of 1812. Numerous pioneer settlements were made in the Oregon Country during the late 1830s. The wagon trains followed on the heels of the mountain men and traders. The extension of the U.S.-Canadian border along the 49th parallel from the Continental Divide to the Pacific coast, by the U.S.-British "Compromise Treaty" of 1846, settled the situation.

The first U.S. post office in the Oregon Country was opened at

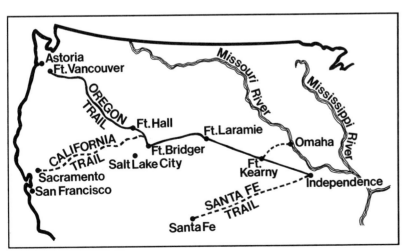

Figure 196. The Oregon Trail, 1830s-1850s.

Figure 197. With an enclosed letter dated at Fort Laramie on May 28, 1852, this is one of but two covers bearing stamps with the early Fort Laramie, O.R., marking. The letter described the journey west, mentioning Council Bluffs, Chimney Rock and Fort Kearny and expecting to reach South Pass on the way to the Oregon Country by covered wagon in 10 days.

Astoria in March 1847. By the mid-1840s, a constant stream of wagon trains was pouring into the Oregon Country.

The site at the junction of the Laramie and North Platte rivers, where a fort had been built by a fur-trading company in 1834, became a key point on the wagon route, soon to be called the Oregon Trail. This is shown by the sketch-map, Figure 196.

In 1849, the U.S. Army sent an expedition of mounted riflemen to establish military posts along the Oregon Trail. In connection with this operation, The U.S. government acquired Fort Laramie from the American Fur Company as a post along the route.

The fort's postal history commenced with the establishment of a post office there on March 14, 1850. Figure 197 shows a dark buff cover bearing the 3¢ brownish-carmine stamp of 1852 and the first Fort Laramie postmark, with a manuscript date of June 15. The cover is addressed to Mount Vernon, Ohio. Since the distance between Fort Laramie and Ohio was less than 3,000 miles, the 3¢ postage reflects the prepaid rate at that time. (For the same service, unpaid, the rate was 5¢.) The cover contains a letter datelined at Fort Laramie on May 28, 1852. The passage of nearly three weeks between the dates of the letter heading and the postmark can be explained: The postmaster at Fort Laramie was following regulations. Letters were to be "rated up" when received, but were not to be postmarked and dated until sent out with a mail.

The letter describes the journey west. The writer remarks he had arrived at Fort Laramie "an hour since." He had left Fort Kearney (see map in Figure 196) 13 days before and expected to go on to South Pass (through the Rockies) in about 10 days on his way to the Oregon Country.

Figure 198 shows Fort Laramie as it appeared to an artist in 1849. Originally built as a log stockade (called Fort Williams) at a different site nearby, the new fort stood on a low bluff and was built on a much larger scale.

Figure 199 shows tracings of the first Fort Laramie postal markings, which were oddities in more than one respect. In Figure 199, "A" is a somewhat stylized tracing of the basic marking, and "B" is a relief type "5" ratemark used on stampless, unpaid covers, reported between 1852 and 1854. Tracing "C" is the way the postmarks were used on at least one cover, the separate "5" being neatly struck in the

Figure 198. Fort Laramie as it appeared to an artist in 1849.

center of the basic postmark of the office. The date was supplied by a large separate handstamp shown as tracing "D." All were in black.

Fewer than 10 Fort Laramie covers have been recorded with these markings. Only two are prepaid with stamps, both sent on June 15, 1852. One, shown in Figure 197, has a manuscript date. The other has the postmark tying the stamp and the large June 15 handstamp date used. The markings read "Ft. Laramie/O.R." The meaning of "O.R." has been variously interpreted to mean either "Oregon" or "Oregon Route." Both versions stem from a differing postal and territorial status requiring some explanation.

As the 19th-century United States grew and territory was acquired, the new areas were at first usually considered to be "unorganized territory" — belonging to the Federal government but with no administrative organization other than the U.S. Army and some representatives of the Office of Indian Affairs. Eventually, Congress would get around to passing acts establishing territorial status, with boundaries outlined. A territorial government would be provided (with a governor appointed by the president) at a designated territorial capital. When enough settlers were in the area, statehood was eventually achieved. The settlers always came before either territorial status or postal services were provided. Postal service usually preceded territorial status.

As the territories were defined from unorganized territory and the states subsequently carved out, boundaries frequently changed. The result was that some areas would be within the boundaries of two or more territories, successively, before finally becoming part of a state. This makes collecting territorial and pre-territorial covers both confusing and interesting.

Fort Laramie is an excellent example of this situation. Lying in what is now eastern Wyoming, it was part of the territory acquired in the Louisiana Purchase of 1803. For years it was in "unorganized territory." Only when Nebraska Territory was organized, in 1854, was Fort Laramie included within the sphere of a territorial administration. In 1863, Fort Laramie was included in Idaho Territory when that area was organized. Then it was shifted to Dakota Territory in another shuffle of boundaries in 1864. It was finally included in Wyoming Territory when that was organized in 1868. It continued there until Wyoming became a state in 1890.

So, when Fort Laramie post office on the Oregon Trail was opened in March 1850, the fort was in unorganized territory administered by the U.S. Army. The Post Office Department had encountered this situation before; it simply attached the Fort Laramie post office to Oregon Territory (organized in 1848) for administrative purposes. Fort Laramie was listed in the Post Office Department papers and lists of the period as being in "Clackemas" County, Oregon Territory. (Today's Clackamas County is located in northwestern Oregon.)

Even though Oregon Territory originally included what is now the states of Washington, Oregon and Idaho, stretching from the Pacific Coast to the Continental Divide, it didn't include eastern Wyoming. So, some postal historians have simply assumed the "O.R." in the first Fort Laramie postmark stood for "Oregon," ignoring the period after "O" and the fact that other Oregon territorial markings read "O.T." for "Oregon Territory."

Most of today's collectors accept the idea the "O.R." stands for "Oregon Route," recognizing the fort was on the Oregon Trail. It can't

Figure 199. The first type of Fort Laramie postmark. The "5" in relief was sometimes struck within the basic office marking with a separate datestamp used. At other times, the postmark was used to cancel the stamp, with no "5" required. These markings are shown in a somewhat cleaned-up form, as normal strikes were usually nearly illegible.

be proven but it sounds better.

As noted, Fort Laramie was included within the boundaries of Nebraska Territory when it was formed in 1854. Postmarks reading "N.T." are known.

Alaska postal history

The compartmentalism of postal history collecting in recent years has disadvantages deplored by many. It also has produced some remarkable in-depth postal history research, conducted by individuals and by organizations. By compartmentalism I mean the collecting of narrow segments of postal history around a given subject. This specialization may be geographic — such as collecting a state, a town or a country. It may be in terms of an issue of stamps, such as the U.S. 1869 issue, or a single stamp, such as the 10¢ 1869.

The advantage lies in the depth of knowledge needed for even the most restricted collection. The scholar will necessarily learn all that can be found about the stamp, and also about the uses. Those collecting covers from a town or county will tie the covers in with history. Such covers will acquire a meaning and a depth not guessed by others. Which is to say, the knowledge gained by exploring a limited subject will have not only depth but breadth.

To properly understand the uses of the 10¢ 1869 stamp, as an example, the collector must understand not only the stamps but foreign mails, territorial uses, ship and domestic waterway uses and many other areas.

What caused a cover with a 10¢ 1869 stamp to be handled in a certain way also applied to the rest of the stamps of that issue and, to a large extent, to the preceding 1861 stamps and the subsequent Bank Note issues. The upshot is that the knowledge acquired will be extensive even though the collection may seem narrow to others.

I don't collect Alaska, owning, as parts of other collections, a few World War II APOs plus perhaps half a dozen other covers. Yet, I find Alaska postal history very interesting.

Figure 200 shows the earliest recorded cover mailed from Alaska after the formal ceremony (on October 18, 1867) transferring the area from Russia to the United States. The cover bears a 3¢ 1861 stamp in a rather pale shade, pen canceled. The cover has a matching manuscript postmark reading "Sitka, R.A., Nov 2d 1867." This is less

Figure 200. With a manuscript postmark, "Sitka, R.A. (Russian America)/Nov 2d 1867," this 3¢ 1861 cover is the earliest recorded cover from Alaska Territory.

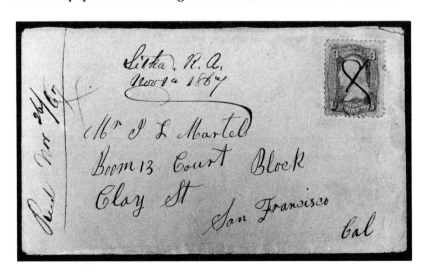

than a month after the formal transfer. The "R.A." stands for "Russian America." Most of the handful of other Alaska postmarks from this period call the area by its official name, "Alaska Territory" or "A.T."

Much has been written about these early Alaska covers and their manuscript postmarks. The record shows that one John H. Kinkead was appointed postmaster of Sitka, as authorized on July 23, 1867. But some authorities say Kinkead was appointed on May 26, 1867. Considering that the first U.S. representatives, an Army garrison for Sitka, didn't arrive until October 9 and didn't go ashore until the official ceremony transferring the area to the United States, one wonders just how the establishment of the Sitka post office was handled. Obviously, Sitka is a long way from Washington, D.C. Appointing a postmaster three months before the area was occupied could have been subject to change once Sitka was a possession of the United States.

The $7 million purchase of Alaska, at the time called "Seward's folly" and similar names, was accomplished by Secretary of State William H. Seward (Figure 201) in a treaty with Russia signed in March 1867. In his *Military Postmarks of Territorial Alaska*, Richard W. Helbock makes clear that the first government of Alaska consisted of a few hundred soldiers at Sitka. This military administration was about all the government Washington provided those first years.

It is believed that most of the early covers were sent by the military, although this is not certain for most of them because of lack of origin designation or content. The fact that a few of the early covers have the territory designated "R.A." in their postmarks (most have the official "A.T.") has caused much discussion.

Figure 201. William H. Seward, who purchased Alaska from Russia for $7 million. He was derided for his efforts.

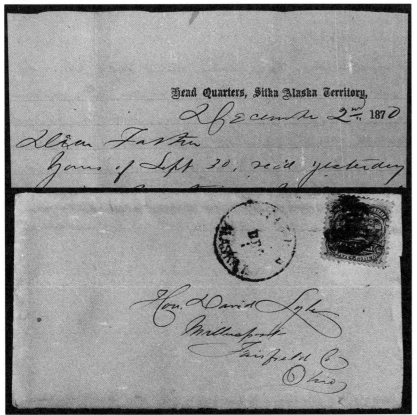

Figure 202. The first Sitka, A.T., postmark, used on a 3¢ 1869 cover sent to Ohio in December 1870. Shown above the cover is the heading of the letter enclosed in the cover.

A nice showing of early Sitka covers with manuscript markings is presented in Joseph Cavagnol's *Postmarked Alaska*, published by the Gossip Printery in 1957. This is the first definitive work on Alaska postal history of which I'm aware.

Inspection of the covers pictured by Cavagnol indicates that at least two persons (perhaps more) applied the manuscript postmarks on these covers over about two years. The distinction between "Russian America" and "Alaska Territory" probably reflects the whim of those writing the postmarks. Whether the first Sitka postmaster appointee, John Kinkead, wrote some of these isn't known. Nor, for that matter, do we know whether he served at all. It is quite probably, however, that the early postmasters were all military people — or at least associated with them, such as a civilian sutler. A sutler's store was the 19th-century counterpart of today's post exchange.

It seems logical that the military would have moved the mails in Alaska in the late 1860s. Certainly most of the mail was military. Such was the situation at most U.S. western military posts of the 19th century, and collectors of western covers are aware that not all the fine details of the postal regulations were observed in the handling of the mails from such posts. Why should Sitka have been different?

Figure 202 shows a cover with a 3¢ 1869 stamp bearing the first Sitka handstamped postmark, which was first used in late 1868, according to Cavagnol. This cover was sent in December 1870. The heading of the enclosed letter, shown in the inset in Figure 202, is dated at Army headquarters, Sitka, on December 2, 1870. This is one of seven or eight Sitka covers bearing 3¢ 1869 stamps, several of which are from this same correspondence. This follows the pattern that most early mails from Alaska were sent by the military.

Not all Alaska covers are as exotic as those shown here; collectors should recognize that every field has its expensive classics.

This chapter is based on the following *Linn's* columns: Fort Laramie, November 28, 1983; Alaska postal history, April 1, 1985.

Chapter 13

Postal Stationery

Act of 1845

Although envelopes were used in France as early as the 16th century, their use in the U.S. mails wasn't practical until 1845. A few stationery stores in New York, Boston and other eastern cities manufactured envelopes in 1840 or earlier, but since people had a good reason not to use them to send letters through the mail at that time, the early envelope operations weren't very successful.

Prior to July 1, 1845, postage on letters was rated on the basis of the number of separate sheets the letter contained, rather than by weight. Use of an envelope automatically caused a letter to be charged double postage.

The act effective July 1, 1845, based rates of postage upon weight, and at the same time greatly reduced postal rates. Suddenly, writing and sending letters became a popular pastime, rather than just a business practice. From mid-1845, the use of envelopes

Figure 203. Locally made envelopes, showing corner cachets, used from Columbus, Ohio, in the early 1850s.

Figure 204. Contents and flap details of the envelopes in Figures 203 and 205. A is part of the flier contained in the upper cover in Figure 203, top. B is the back flap of the upper cover in Figure 203; the flap of the lower cover is identical. C is a duplicate imprint of the upper corner cachet in Figure 203, from the Scott & Bascom's flier shown here. D shows the back flap and wafer seal of the cover in Figure 205.

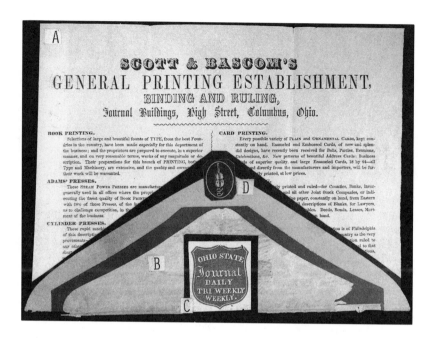

became inevitable, but some years passed before manufacturers could produce envelopes at low cost and in quantities as a standard commercial product. When envelopes began to be used after 1845, they were at first produced by local printers and stationers, in small quantities for local sale.

Figure 203 shows two covers printed and produced by Scott & Bascom's General Printing Establishment of Columbus, Ohio. Figure 204-A shows part of the content of the upper cover of Figure 203. These items shed light on how early envelopes were made — in Columbus, at least. They also show how envelopes can sometimes be used by the postal historian to solve the very problem they caused — permitting the year-dating of covers that have no content.

For some years, I have been making a study of Columbus, Ohio, postal history, including use of envelopes. I discuss it here not because what happened in Columbus was unusual, but because it wasn't. Columbus' story is probably typical of the evolution of envelope use in many U.S. cities.

Envelope use in Columbus began around 1850, insofar as locally produced products were concerned. Most envelopes made locally (there were few or no commercial products offered nationally at this time) were produced in printing establishments or stationery stores. Paper in sheets was stacked perhaps 25 deep, or as high as could be cleanly cut with a sharp pointed knife. With a wood or metal template of the desired shape on top of the pile, the envelopes were created by cutting around the template. A second operation was to apply glue to the end and bottom flaps, and fold. No glue was applied to the top or closing flap. For this purpose, stationery stores sold sealing wax, candles and lucifer matches and sometimes signet rings with which an initial or monogram could be pressed into the wax. Eventually they also handled gummed wafers. Envelopes would be manufactured piecemeal when clerks had no customers to attend to and no other more pressing assignments.

I have heard such envelopes called "homemade," to distinguish them from machine-made products. But envelopes made by stationery stores and printing establishments were really a product of hand manufacturing. They were usually symmetrical and neatly folded.

The two covers shown in Figure 203 apparently were both made by the same Columbus print shop, Scott & Bascom. Part of the content of the upper cover in Figure 203 is shown as A through C in Figure 204, including the top of a large advertising flier that describes their presses and facilities. The flier also advertises the local newspaper, *The Ohio State Journal*, of which William Bascom was editor. His corner card appears, with negative letters reversed out of jet black, on the top cover in Figure 203. A second imprint of the corner card (C inset in Figure 204) appears on the back of the flier. The flier could be folded, addressed and sent as a circular with the cachet showing. An enclosed letter and the faint red Columbus postmark on the cover, with matching red "5," indicates it was sent March 17, 1851.

The lower cover in Figure 203, bearing the corner card of W.A. Gill & Company, is also printed in reversed-out letters on a jet black background, with type matching the cachet on the upper cover. The lower cover has a duplicate of the front corner card imprinted on the back flap, so that the recipient would know the source no matter which side was up. This cover was sent in either 1852 or 1853.

Figure 204 also shows two envelope flaps. The one marked B is from the upper cover in Figure 203. The other, marked D, is from the cover shown in Figure 205. The corner card shown as inset C in Figure 204 came from the otherwise blank back of the flier in Figure 204. It was probably printed from the same cut as the imprint on the upper envelope in Figure 203. Considering that all four of the corner-card imprints on these two covers and contents are identical or similar in makeup and type, and considering that the curvature and shapes of the back flaps are identical, I conclude that both envelopes in Figure 203 were created by the same source.

Figure 205 shows another envelope used from Columbus, bearing a 5¢ 1847 stamp. This envelope was closed by a printed wafer seal showing a violin, shown as D in Figure 204. The Figure 205 cover is the earliest envelope used from Columbus that I've been able to date. Judging from the fact that the stamp is pen canceled, the cover was probably sent on February 15, 1850. Other Columbus covers that I've recorded bearing 1847 stamps show stamps canceled with a red grid in February and April of 1851, although this dating is by no

Figure 205. The pen cancellation on the 5¢ 1847 stamp on this cover, with a red February 15 postmark, indicates the cover was probably sent in 1850. This makes it a very early use of an envelope from Columbus, Ohio. The shape of the flap, printed sealing wafer and high-quality white paper suggest that the envelope was not made locally.

means definitive.

As may be seen by the shape of its back flap, D in Figure 204, the Figure 205 cover differs considerably from the Scott & Bascom products. The paper is a high-quality white, as contrasted with the brown manila types of the local producer. In the absence of similar examples in my Columbus collection, I suspect that the Figure 205 envelope was imported or used by a transient. The wafer on the back of the Figure 205 cover is also unique as a local product.

In any case, considering some 20 envelopes used from Columbus in the 1850-52 era, it appears that envelopes didn't start to be used there much before 1850, and that the first examples were made locally. It wasn't until the first embossed U.S. stamped envelopes were issued, in 1853, that the mass-manufactured envelope became predominant. And the local manufacture of envelopes lasted until some time after the Civil War.

First U.S. embossed stamped envelopes

The first U.S. stamped envelopes were issued in 1853. According to the Scott U.S. specialized catalog, the issue date was July 1, 1853. Some authorities think the envelopes may have been placed in service a few months earlier.

The first printings of these envelopes, produced by George F. Nesbitt of New York (under a contract given him without competitive bidding) bore his impressed seal on the back flap, printed in the same red color as the printed portions of the embossed 3¢ envelope stamps.

Figure 206 shows a photo of such an envelope with its flaps opened. The photo was taken on a light table to show the watermark and laid paper pattern.

Nesbitt was probably the leading manufacturer of stationery in the United States. At a time when envelopes were just beginning to be produced commercially, it seems doubtful that any other manufacturer was considered for this job.

The Post Office Department had been running in the red owing

Figure 206. The first U.S. embossed stamped envelope, with the Nesbitt seal on the flap and the laid lines of the paper horizontal. These stamped envelopes were almost immediately superseded by those with a different watermark.

Figure 207. The second style of Nesbitt stamped envelope, also with the seal on the flap but with laid lines on a diagonal to the envelope design and also to the watermarked "P.O.D./U.S."

to the postal rate reductions of 1851. Prepaid letters sent under 3,000 miles had been reduced to 3¢ per half ounce and those sent further than that to 6¢. Postal officials wished to reduce the large volume of letters carried outside the mails by express companies, steamboats and the like.

In his annual report dated December 4, 1852, Postmaster General Nathan K. Hall commented on this situation, remarking that the Post Office Department was preparing "letter envelopes, with one or more postage stamps impressed thereon." He said that as "letters enclosed in them may be legally sent by private express or other private conveyance, there will remain . . . no excuse for further violation of the laws in that respect."

Thus, government envelopes bearing only steamboat purser's markings or express company imprints, carried completely outside the U.S. mails, were first authorized in 1853. Most of the early uses I have seen are more routine.

Scott's listing of the first envelopes is headed by an interesting parenthetical note: "(Early printings of Nos. U1, U3 on Horizontally Laid Paper)." Scott U1 and U3 are the 3¢ embossed stamped envelopes of 1853, with an embossed bust of Washington on white paper, the difference being in the die types. The cover shown in Figure 206 is one of those with the laid lines running horizontally. Figure 207 shows another early Nesbitt envelope, also with the seal on the flap, with the watermark arrangement that was adopted after the first printing.

Obviously, the government required that the watermark initials "P.O.D./U.S." be placed horizontally, near the center of the envelope.

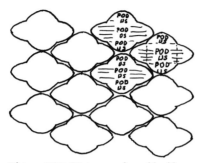

Figure 208. Watermark and knife arrangement for the horizontal-laid-line variety with "P.O.D./U.S." emblems directly above one another.

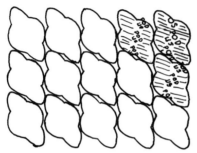

Figure 209. Diagram of the second-type Nesbitt envelope, showing how rearranging the watermark emblem permitted rearranging the knives to produce three more envelopes from the same size sheet of paper.

The key to why the paper change was made almost immediately after the very first printing wasn't recognized until Oscar Salzer worked it out in the 1960s. Previously, collectors thought that the knife arrangement was simply changed, using the same paper.

As may be seen from the sketches of the layouts in Figures 208 and 209, both the knife arrangement and the locations of the wire emblems producing the watermarks had to be changed at the paper mill. The reason — a tribute to Nesbitt's business acumen — was that the change yielded 15 rather than 12 envelopes from the same sheet of paper. This lessened Nesbitt's cost and increased his production at a time when capacity was still severely taxed. At the time, Nesbitt was probably the only manufacturer in the country with the capacity to meet government needs.

When he recognized why the change was made, Salzer got in touch with envelope authority Prescott Holden Thorpe, and also with Tracy W. Simpson, who was then editor of the *Chronicle* of the U.S. Classics Society. A survey by Thorpe produced about a half dozen more examples of the horizontal laid-paper envelopes. Three were postmarked in April (without year dates, as was the normal style of postmark then). This implied use in 1853, suggesting that the catalog date of July 1 is inaccurate. My sketches in Figures 208 and 209 were adapted from larger drawings that appeared in Thorpe's *Envelope World* of August 13, 1963, and in the first pamphlet-sized *Chronicle*, July 1963.

T.J. Alexander, editor of the 1851-61 section of the *Chronicle*, returned to the subject in November 1986. At that time, about a dozen of the envelopes with horizontal laid lines (as in Figure 206) were known.

These varieties are very easy to detect. The laid lines are horizontal and the watermark emblems ("P.O.D./U.S.") repeat directly above one another. On the second type, shown in Figure 207, the laid lines and the emblems are on a diagonal to the envelope rectangle.

To the postal historian, the question is not just when the first envelopes were placed in service, but whether any were used outside the U.S. mails, by express companies or clerks aboard steamboats.

Postcards originated in Europe

In response to various *Linn's* columns, I have received several letters dealing with postcards as postal history. Let's define the subject to avoid misunderstandings. Our U.S. government cards, which commenced in 1873, are designated by official publications and U.S. postal historians as "postal cards." "Postcards" are privately printed cards that require adhesive postage stamps for mailing. Most postcards have a printed picture, greetings or advertising matter on one side and space for the address, with or without a message, on the other side.

Frank Staff's *The Picture Postcard & Its Origins*, the most common reference available to postal history collectors, uses the British definition of postcard, which differs from American usage. The British define the government issues we term postal cards as postcards. The private emissions we call postcards they term "picture postcards," at least in Staff's work, which I suppose is representative or even authoritative.

The picture postcard first appeared in continental Europe, mostly because by the 1860s, some postal administrations found

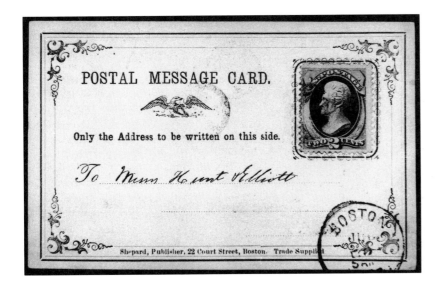

Figure 210. A private mailing or "postal message card" of the 1870s. Such cards, when written messages were present, were charged letter-rate postage prior to 1898.

justification in permitting such cards to pass through the mails at a lower rate than letter mails. The Swiss and Germans, in particular, were publishing picture postcards in color by the 1880s.

England didn't permit privately printed cards to pass through their mails at the same rate as government postal cards until 1894, and the U.S. Post Office stalled for another four years. Both governments made a very good return on postal cards and held off the competition as long as legislative bodies would let them. However, in the United States, as shown in Figure 210, private mailing cards were on the scene as early as the 1870s — even though letter postage was required to transmit them through the mails, unless they were printed matter.

The card shown in Figure 210 bears the wording "Postal Message Card." It was mailed at Boston with a 2¢ Continental stamp in June of 1874 or a later year. The postmark on the card was in use between 1870 and 1877, according to Blake and Davis' *Boston Postal Markings to 1890*. The message side has neither date nor origin. The address on the card has been partially erased, but the "Mass." is readable. Enough survives of the town name to indicate "Boston." Thus, 2¢ postage would be correct for a local letter sent in a city with carrier delivery service.

The first such message cards were produced by Lipman's of Philadelphia in the early 1870s, although they were based upon Charlton's copyright of 1861. Lipman cards are very rare. Charles Fricke of Philadelphia owned at least four examples that were sold in the Richard Frajola sale of September 7, 1985.

The Lipman cards are normal postal-card size, printed with red or green moiré overall and a decorative border. They bear the words "Lipman's Postal Card/Patent Applied For" and, in two lines of very small print, notice of the Charlton copyright of 1861.

The Lipman cards, as indicated by their descriptions in the Frajola catalog, were such that postmasters at offices where they were used may not have been very sure how they were to be rated. Of the three used examples, one was mailed locally in Philadelphia and another, with no town datestamp, is directed to Mount Morris, New York. The earliest, stated to have been sent October 25, 1870, from

Figure 211. Printed on the back of the large (155- by 95-millimeter) Grant government postal card (Scott UX10), this is one of a series of designs celebrating the 1893 Columbian Exposition. The ship portrayed, "BATTLE SHIP 'ILLINOIS,' " was ephemeral in that no ship of that name and exact appearance existed at that time.

Richmond, Indiana, is addressed to New York City. Each bears a 1¢ Bank Note stamp of the early 1870s, and has a printed advertising message. The two later cards were thus accepted as circulars or as miscellaneous third-class matter, under the act of June 8, 1872. This act established a rate of 1¢ for each two ounces for such.

From 1863 until 1872, circulars were rated as third-class matter at 2¢ per three pieces (to the same address) with no other rate seemingly applicable. Thus, the rate on the 1870 card seemingly should have been 2¢.

The issuance of government postal cards in 1873 probably firmed up the situation so that private postcards with written messages were charged full letter postage until Congress took the matter in hand in 1898.

The card shown in Figure 211 may be something of the forerunner of the picture postcard in America, since it is part of a series of "official" cards printed on government postal cards (the large Grant issue of 1891, Scott UX10) that were very popular items celebrating the Chicago World's Fair of 1893. But it still wasn't until May 19, 1898, that Congress declared that privately printed mailing cards could be transmitted through the mails at the same rate as government postal

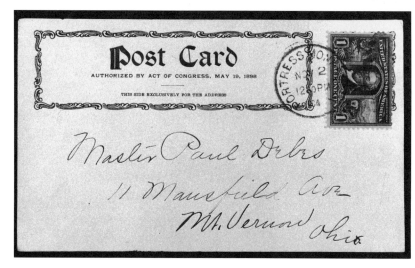

Figure 212. A postcard with the "authorization" legend noting that such could be sent at the same rates as government postal cards by the act of May 19, 1898.

cards, then 1¢ each. And then began the great postcard craze!

Figure 212 shows a card with a printed legend reflecting not only the act of 1898 but the regulations accompanying it. Just as with government postal cards, only the address could be written on the side with the postage stamp. Most postcards printed prior to 1900 and intended for U.S. usage bore similar legends.

The Figure 212 card is a rather late use for reference to the act of Congress. The card bears a Louisiana Purchase 1¢ stamp of 1904 and is postmarked at Fortress Monroe, Virginia, in November 1904. The reverse of the card shows naval personnel drilling aboard the *USS Lancaster* and bears the printed corner address of the Hotel Chamberlin at Fort Monroe.

All postcards sent in the United States until about 1907 bear an imprint, in common with government postal cards, that only the address could be written on the stamp side. Cards sent in 1907 began to show the divided arrangement that prevails today: message written at left and address at right, both on the same side. The legislation authorizing the use of the divided address side went in effect on March 1, 1907, but cards manufactured abroad with divided backs occasionally were sold in the United States before this date.

This chapter is based on the following *Linn's* columns: Act of 1845, September 5, 1988; first U.S. embossed stamped envelopes, April 10, 1989; postcards originated in Europe, August 11 and December 29, 1986. I wish to thank Henry Beecher, Ted Bozarth, Doug Kelsey, Warren Bower, Fred Kozurt, L.E. Lobo, T.E. Range and many others for information regarding the use of postcards in the U.S. mails.

Chapter 14

Illustrated Covers

Mulready envelopes

Over the last few years, the exhibiting status of illustrated covers has frequently been discussed in *Linn's*. There isn't any question about the popularity of illustrated covers. All of us enjoy a pretty cover, whether it be a valentine, a patriotic or an elaborate and beautifully printed cachet on a first-day or special-event cover that just arrived in the mail. Many of us also have closet collections of illustrated advertising covers pertinent to aspects of our personal lives. These might relate to our upbringing, places we've lived, or our profession or avocation.

The rules for exhibiting internationally are laid down by the Swiss-based International Federation of Philately, known by its French initials as FIP. Under FIP rules, "a postal history exhibit may contain, where strictly necessary, maps, prints, decrees and similar associated materials," but these must relate to the subject of the exhibit. I don't know whether this provision would allow use of pictures of ships or photos of a sender of a letter, such as Navy surgeon Dr. Cooke, whose marvelous covers from his service aboard U.S. Navy ships were discussed in my *Linn's* column of January 22, 1990. I can say that I've had several requests for the pictures of Dr. Cooke, and the ships on which he served, from readers sending copies of their

Figure 213. A British 1-penny Mulready envelope, front and back, sent in 1840. The illustrated design shows Britannia sending winged messengers to remote parts of the empire.

148

covers, responding to the offer I made in that column.

I understand that the FIP rules strongly downgrade patriotic, valentine or other illustrated covers. Philatelically inspired cachets are the biggest "no-no" of all, yet stamp collectors continue to collect and enjoy these items. A viewpoint was expressed in *Linn's* Readers' Opinions page that the only objection to condemning illustrated covers comes from Americans, and that this may be because illustrated covers started here. This comment referred to George Ward Linn's pioneering promotion of the cacheted first-day cover for the Harding memorial stamp of 1923. But the cover shown front and back in Figure 213 reminds us that Linn's effort wasn't the world's first illustrated cover.

Figure 213 shows a British Mulready envelope, which was issued concurrently with the famed British Penny Black in May 1840. The design was drawn by William Mulready, whose name appears in fine print at the lower left of the design. According to the Scott catalog caption, the design shows an allegorical figure of Britannia "sending letters to the world." The back of the cover, with the word "POSTAGE" (not saying how much) indicates postage was paid. One penny Mulreadies were printed in black and 2d Mulreadies in blue, matching the colors of the Penny Black and 2d blue stamps. Both values were issued in both envelope (as shown) and lettersheet form, with the denomination in small type at the bottom in front.

On the Figure 213 item, the back bears postmarks (Coleraine, November 6, 1840) and the front has a red Maltese cross cancel at top center, which was the cancel normally used then on the Penny Blacks.

The Mulready was as unpopular as the stamps were popular. In the British spirit of Hogarth and his fellow satiric artists of the previous century, a broad range of caricatures soon appeared. Some of these are illustrated in Robson Lowe's *Encyclopedia of British Empire Postage Stamps*, Volume I. More recently, the subject is fully discussed in Ritchie Bodily and Charless Hahn's *British Pictorial En-*

Figure 214. An 1880s British propaganda envelope, showing William E. Gladstone raising his axe to behead a lady who, by the addition of the stamp, is Queen Victoria. It was one of a series of commercial envelopes, expressing political or other viewpoints, that were available in 19th-century England.

Figure 215. William Ewart Gladstone, in whose face caricaturists found a great subject.

velopes of the 19th Century, published in 1984 by the Collectors Club of Chicago. Many caricature envelopes were sent through the mails, bearing Penny Blacks and subsequent stamps to prepay the postage. Thus, we have illustrated covers from private enterprise as well as the official version. The private parodies were a major force in driving the Mulready designs out of existence. From this colorful start, the British mails of the 19th and early 20th centuries contained a constant stream of illustrated envelopes.

Albeit more savage than normal, Figure 214 shows a typical commercial caricature cover used for political propaganda. It shows a man with an axe, poised ready to swing. As the envelope was sold, a neat blank rectangle suggested the position for the current 1-penny stamp. As Figure 214 shows, the stamp was the 1d of 1881, bearing the head of Queen Victoria. It is probably needless to point out that all the British stamps available showed the head of the queen. Per its postmark, the cover was sent on April 25, 1883. The intense chap wielding the axe is, in caricature, William Ewart Gladstone, famous British Liberal political leader of the 19th century (Figure 215).

This cover, which was lent to me by the late Charles I. Ball, is one of a series of similar caricature envelopes depicting Gladstone, often accompanied by his axe. Ball discussed these in detail in an article in the *15th American Philatelic Congress Book* of 1949.

In my opinion, such billboards of viewpoint, whether political, patriotic, romantic or commercial, passed through the mails and are as much a part of postal history as the designs on stamps and postal stationery.

Postal history collateral

An editorial by Richard W. Helbock, in the September 1987 issue of *La Posta*, quotes a suggestion by railway-marking expert Charles L. Towle that a new term may be needed to describe collateral material exhibited as postal history. The term "collateral" applies to photos of ships, boats and people, enclosed letters and data historically connected with the cover but not necessarily pertinent to the rates and routes of postal history. Helbock discusses this relative to the rules for exhibiting at international shows. These rules are established by the FIP. Helbock notes that FIP rules are very narrow and severely limit showing collateral material.

As a writer, I use a definition of postal history that doesn't necessarily agree with exhibition rules. I find it difficult to define postal history as anything other than the history of the mails. To me, postal history is part of a larger section of our social history — the history of communications. In the same vein, I consider studies of the adhesive stamp as a subcategory of postal history.

The term philately originally was conceived to describe the collecting of adhesive postage stamps, and I consider philately as still being the study of such stamps.

I don't see why people have trouble defining postal history, although Helbock remarks the term has a long history of controversy. Apparently, what is causing the problem isn't the material that applies to the history of the post, or the covers themselves, but the collateral material that often accompanies the covers. And the problem lies in what can be exhibited, not what people wish to collect.

As a writer, I try to include enough background material to set the stage for understanding how a cover was handled. At times, I must admit, I find the information about the people involved with a cover —

Figure 216. This envelope, with a printed corner advertisement of the Missouri River packet *Minnehaha*, was evidently carried off the boat and mailed on Christmas Day, 1857, at Cairo, Illinois — about 150 miles below the steamboat's regular route.

or ships, boats, planes and such that carried it — or historical events, such as battles, wars, explorations or journeys that pertained to the cover, or maps, just too interesting to omit. It also needs to be observed that some printed material on covers — such as patriotic designs, advertising illustrations, and steamboat corner cards or handstamps — really doesn't have a lot to do with the posts, per se.

Figure 216 shows a cover with a printed steamboat advertising imprint of the Missouri River passenger packet *Minnehaha*. The cover entered the mails on Christmas Day, 1857, at Cairo, Illinois, addressed to "Cincinnati Ohio/Walnut Hills Post Office." A similar but not identical *Minnehaha* cover is shown in Dr. James W. Milgram's *Vessel-named Markings on United States Inland and Ocean Waterways, 1810-1890*. That cover, from the illustration, was mailed in 1857 at Kansas (now Kansas City), Missouri, on the Missouri River.

The Missouri River flows into the Mississippi at St. Louis. Cairo lies about 150 miles below, where the Ohio River joins the Mississippi. Respecting the Figure 216 cover, most postal historians would want to explore why this cover, presumably from aboard a Missouri River packet, was mailed at Cairo. Luckily, information about the boat is available in Captain Fred Way's *Way's Packet Directory, 1843-1983*. This large volume lists information, both historical and technical, on all the packet boats of the Mississippi River system that Captain Way knew of, from the advent of photography in America until modern times. A riverboat pilot for many years, Captain Way collected pictures of steamboats of the Mississippi River system. The book is his compilation.

According to this work, the *Minnehaha* was built in 1857. It was running on the Missouri River between St. Louis and St. Joseph, above Kansas City, at the time the Figure 216 cover was sent. Thus, it is apparent that the cover was sent by a passenger who carried the envelope off the boat to mail it at Cairo, possibly as a down-river boat that the passenger had boarded at St. Louis was stopping there. Although the Way directory doesn't show a photo of the *Minnehaha*, it was probably similar to the *Mayflower*, shown in Figure 217 from a Currier & Ives print of 1855. Both boats were of about the same tonnage, design and description, according to Way's directory.

Figure 218 shows a different type of steamboat cover. This bears the clerk's (clerks were pursers on eastern waters) handstamp of the

Figure 217. A Mississippi River steamer similar to the packet steamboat *Minnehaha*.

151

Figure 218. This cover was handed to the clerk of the steamboat *Red Cloud* of the Evansville and Tennessee River Packet Company, plying the Tennessee and Ohio rivers in 1877. The clerk canceled the stamp with the boat's handstamp and delivered it to a post office along the route, to be sent on to St. Louis.

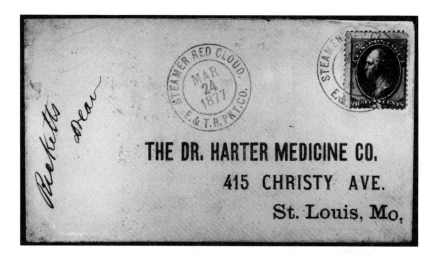

THE DR. HARTER MEDICINE CO.
415 CHRISTY AVE.
St. Louis, Mo.

steamer *Red Cloud*, named after the Indian chieftain who is pictured on the 1987 U.S. 10¢ definitive stamp. The Figure 218 cover bears a 3¢ Bank Note stamp. The clerk's handstamp, dated March 24, 1877, was used to cancel the stamp and then struck separately on the cover.

Milgram, in the work cited previously, pictures this cover (from the photo files of Henry A. Meyer) with a note that this 400-ton steamboat, a side-wheeler built in 1873 for the Evansville and Tennessee River Packet Company, was sold to I.G. Baker & Company for the Missouri River trade in 1877. This is confirmed in Way's directory (which also gives the clerks' names in 1876, plus a great deal of other data) as an 1877 sale, but the cover proves that the sale didn't take place, or at least the boat wasn't transferred, until later than March. In any case, the boat was transferred in time to make three round trips between St. Louis and Fort Benton, Montana, in 1877, including conveying a detachment of Canadian Mounted Police.

I give this detail to show how easy it is to stray far afield from postal history when one is confronted with details that make a subject interesting. It is also noteworthy that in our parochial postal history world, there is much unrecorded data useful to other collecting disciplines — just as their data is useful to us.

It should be understood that the clerk of the *Red Cloud*, who applied the Figure 218 handstamp, wasn't a post office employee. Hence, the handstamp is not a postal route-agent marking. As far as I can learn, the boat didn't have a mail-carrying contract. However, letters were frequently handed to clerks aboard boats, either by passengers or at landings along the route. In the Figure 218 example, the clerk compensated for the mild violation of the postal laws (which required such letters, carried outside the mails, to be in government-stamped envelopes) by simply canceling the stamp with his clerk's handstamp.

Since the *Red Cloud's* route was up the Tennessee River, through Kentucky and Tennessee down into Alabama (the depth of water permitting), we have no way of knowing either where the cover was handed to the clerk, or in what post office it was subsequently deposited to be sent by mail to St. Louis. The receiving post office didn't bother to handstamp the cover, since the ship's clerk had canceled the stamp. From a postal history standpoint, all this non-postal data tells us a good deal about these two covers. A printed corner envelope bearing a steamboat's name really could have been sent from anywhere, but a cover with a clerk's handstamp had to have originated aboard the boat itself. Furthermore, on such covers, the added data lends what Gilbert and Sullivan's Pooh-Bah termed the "corroborative detail that lends artistic verisimilitude to an otherwise bald and unconvincing narrative." Which is to say, the detail keeps many such covers from being suspected as fakes.

Relative to the subject of postal history, such details also underscore how closely our subject is interlocked with other areas of history. As collectors, we can't exactly turn our interest on or off, saying "this I want and can exhibit because it fits the rules," or "this doesn't fit; therefore, I'm not interested."

Going back to the possible need for a new term to be coined so that this kind of material can be exhibited, to me it seems that we don't need a new term, but a better understanding, by all concerned (rules committees, judges and collectors), of what's involved. The rules-makers need to recognize the strong interest among collectors, not only in what is currently termed postal history, but in the collateral material that supports it. These collectors provide much of the financial and exhibitor support that sustains the rules-makers.

It also needs to be recognized that postal history doesn't revolve around the adhesive postage stamp. This fact is still not recognized by many who control the rules. To a postal historian, adhesive stamps are basically one of the means by which postage could be prepaid. Although interesting, and a very important determinant of value, stamps are not the main element the postal historian seeks on covers.

More than ever, stamp exhibiting has become a competition between apples and oranges. To do a fair job in this competition, judges need better definitions of postal history, established by postal historians to whom the stamp isn't the dominating interest. On their part, postal history collectors must recognize that collecting the adhesive stamp got us the hobby we enjoy today. Postal history collectors also need to recognize that postal history exhibits are about the history of the post. The collateral material that we use promotes better understanding of our covers.

Campaign covers

Not many recurrent events in U.S. history show a greater contrast between 19th- and 20th-century practices than a presidential campaign.

Campaign covers that picture candidates were immensely popular in the middle of the last century. The presidential campaigns of 1856-68 marked the high point of use of campaign covers. Of these, covers featuring Abraham Lincoln, from 1860 and 1864, are both the most numerous and the most popular.

In the early 1860s, the country was in the crisis of civil war. The use of campaign covers in 1860 was a precursor of the enormous number of patriotic designs that were to appear during the war. And these, in turn, fostered the attractive designs used in the 1864 presidential campaign.

Seeking a second term on a platform of carrying the war to a successful conclusion, Lincoln, along with Andrew Johnson of Tennessee, was the Union Party candidate. The Union Party was really the Republican Party of 1860 plus some Democrats (like Johnson) who refused to support the Confederate cause.

Figure 219 shows a Lincoln-Johnson campaign cover of 1864,

Figure 219. A 3¢ 1861 stamp on a Lincoln-Johnson campaign cover from the election of 1864.

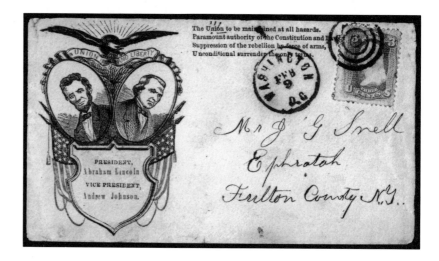

postmarked at Washington in February 1865 — after Lincoln and Johnson had been elected. One of the odd aspects of campaign covers of the 19th century is that many promoting the successful party continued to be used long after the election. Those of the losing party were another matter, as we shall see.

Referring to the standard work on Lincoln and other 19th-century campaign covers, Dr. James W. Milgram's *Abraham Lincoln Illustrated Envelopes and Letter Paper, 1860-65*, which depicts almost 20 designs from the 1864 campaign, I note that the earliest use of an 1864 campaign cover was August 6. Most of the campaign covers show use in October, which was when the campaign peaked. For further data on the Lincoln campaign covers, and in fact, U.S. campaign covers in general, I refer readers to Milgram's book.

The Democrats nominated General George Brinton McClellan for president, with Congressman George Hunt Pendleton of Ohio as his running mate. Formerly commander of the Union armies, McClellan had been fired by Lincoln after the Battle of Antietam in November 1862. Lincoln was said to have commented that McClellan "was an admirable engineer, (who) seems to have a special talent for a stationary engine." Lincoln felt McClellan was a good organizer but lacked heart for battle, so that "he had the slows."

The Democrats' platform called for ending the war immediately, presumably by giving up. Although rejected during the campaign by McClellan, this was the attitude held throughout the war by Pendleton and the "Peace Democrat" element that he represented. Pendleton, a member of Congress from Cincinnati from 1857 to 1865, not only ran for vice president in 1864, but at the same time ran for his old seat in the U.S. House of Representatives. He lost both.

With their candidates exhibiting widely divergent views, the Democrats aroused little enthusiasm other than among those tired of war or already opposed to Lincoln. Some of the surviving McClellan-Pendleton campaign covers show this, as witness the cover in Figure 220. This cover — which has a counterpart in the same format showing Lincoln and Johnson — shows McClellan and Pendleton together in the center with a box on each side. The box at the right is for the stamp. The box at left bears a legend reading, "Where 'Little Mack' leads, the heart of the people will follow." However, whoever sent it from Auburn, New York, in October 1864, when the campaign

Figure 220. Another 3¢ 1861 stamp, here on a McClellan-Pendleton campaign cover from 1864. The sender altered its commentary to show both opposition and disrespect.

was at its hottest, marked up the cover so that the slogan reads, "Where 'Little Mack' leads, the people up Salt River," — "Salt River" being the 19th-century counterpart of the well-known 20th-century creek up which people sometimes find themselves without a paddle.

Figure 221 shows two more McClellan campaign covers of identical design. I suspect that both were sent after the election was decided, although only the one at the right has a legible postmark. This was mailed in December 1864 from Whitestone (Queens County), New York. Whether he was defiantly expressing political sentiments or just needed an envelope, the sender of the cover at the left in Figure 221 (the cover is addressed to Middleville, New York) placed the 3¢ 1861 stamp directly over McClellan's face. I suspect he was simply using up envelopes.

Outside the newspapers, most of which were openly biased, using editorials, cartoons and detailed reports on the speeches and activities of their favorite candidates, the campaign cover and broadsides were about the only way that political sentiment could be

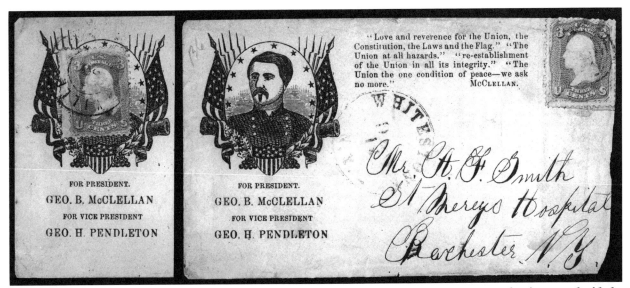

Figure 221. Two examples of the same McClellan-Pendleton design, posted after the 1864 election was decided, showing that our economy-minded ancestors didn't waste envelopes, even if the envelopes showed support for a loser.

Figure 222. An immaculate brown gloved arm extends through a tattered hole in the front of this cover, to present a card with Adlers Gloves' address and return legend. Printed in brown, black and green.

publicly flaunted. Of course there was no radio or television, but there were also no national news syndicates. Newspapers sent exchange copies to one another so that editors could crib articles. Some news was reported by telegraph, but not frequently or consistently.

Thus, the campaign covers of the 19th century survive as colorful souvenirs of an entirely different approach to getting elected.

Turn-of-the-century advertising covers

Figure 222 shows an illustrated advertising cover from Adlers Gloves of New York, sent around the turn of the century. It is printed in brown, green and black. The brown is used to create a moiré background that appears tan. The design is very eye-catching. An arm with a brown gloved hand apparently protrudes through a ragged hole in the envelope front. The hand holds a card with Adlers' address.

The back of the cover, with a black design over the tan moiré background, notes that Alders' gloves are sold by reliable dealers at $1.50 — probably then a high price even for quality gloves.

The cover, addressed to Sheboygan, Wisconsin, bears a New York Station D handstamp with killer attached, dated March 21. The year date, between hub and killer, isn't clear, but is probably 1896. The stamp is probably the watermarked 2¢ type III carmine issue of 1895.

The clever design, with the arm reaching through the seemingly rough torn hole in the front of the envelope, has a very realistic appearance. The shredded paper edges around the hole are carefully drawn. If it were not for the scale of hand compared to envelope, the design could be mistaken for the real thing.

The design is an example of a style of super-realistic artwork, popular in the gilded age, called "trompe l'oeil" — pronounced "tromp loy" and literally meaning "deceiving the eye." Several 19th-century artists were well known for their lifelike paintings with trompe-l'oeil features. Among them were Antonio Gianlisi of Italy, Wallerant Vaillant of the Netherlands, Marcos Correa of Spain and William Harnett of the United States.

Figure 223. William Harnett's *Old Models*, while not a trompe-l'oeil design, was carefully detailed — as illustrated on this U.S. commemorative stamp issued in 1969.

Harnett's *Old Models*, not a trompe-l'oeil design but vividly realistic, was pictured on a 6¢ U.S. commemorative stamp in 1969. The stamp is shown in Figure 223.

Born in Ireland in 1848, Harnett was brought to Philadelphia at

156

Figure 224. The attempted trompe-l'oeil or illusionary effect of this illustrated design is a pencil thrust through the paper of the cover front, with the view of Joseph Dixon manufacturing works seen through the hole.

an early age. He studied art and engraving there and in New York. He visited Germany for four years, beginning in 1878, and probably learned the art of extreme realism and the trompe-l'oeil approach while in Europe.

The traditional example of the perfect trompe-l'oeil effort is when a viewer attempts to brush off a fly painted upon the nose of the subject in a portrait.

Probably the major user of the trompe-l'oeil approach in advertising covers was the Joseph Dixon Crucible Company of New Jersey. Figure 224 shows an attractive cover of this type with the Dixon imprint. The cover was sent from San Francisco January 3, 1900, and is addressed to Stockton, California. The design depicts the center of the envelope as torn away, to frame the Dixon works in New Jersey pictured in pale green beyond in the distance. The envelope shows a brown Dixon pencil with yellow imprint and black lead pushed through the torn, shadowed edges of the hole. A black crucible is pictured at lower left. The effect is somewhat unrealistic because of the uniform pale green color of the distant view of the plant.

Figure 225 shows a more believable Dixon trompe-l'oeil design, simpler and life-size. Here, the pencil is brown with black lead and black imprint. The tattered edges of the hole are supported in concept by shadows, creating an illusion of folds in the paper.

Figure 225. This simple Joseph Dixon Crucible Company envelope is effective as an illusionary trompe-l'oeil design. The life-size scale of the pencil and the printed shadows on the envelope make the paper seem crumpled around the pencil.

157

The cover, with a 1¢ blue stamp of 1895, evidently contained a circular. It has no origin postmark, although it does have a Dixon corner card with a Jersey City location. Several other similar Dixon designs exist, but not all have the trompe-l'oeil effect of the pencil thrust through the front of the envelope.

A run through the *American Illustrated Cover Catalog* failed to reveal any users of trompe-l'oeil artwork other than Adlers Gloves and Joseph Dixon Crucible Company. While popular as art or as art novelty, the trompe-l'oeil concept was probably very difficult to use effectively in a format as small as an envelope front. Objects portrayed, attempting to create an illusion that they were resting on the cover or thrust through it, had to be realistically sized in comparison with the envelope.

Not too many advertised products were of a size and nature to work well on a trompe-l'oeil envelope. However, when it does work, such as in some of the Dixon designs, it is a definite eye-catcher — which is what advertising designs are all about.

This chapter is based on the following *Linn's* **columns: Mulready envelopes, March 5, 1990; postal history collateral, November 23, 1987; campaign covers, October 17, 1988; advertising covers, October 21, 1985.**

Chapter 15

The Free Mails

Free franking started in England

The free-mail concept has always aroused a great deal of interest. It has many aspects. There are free franks, penalty envelopes and those with a legend noting that postage was paid by such-and-such a government agency.

The free frank has always attracted the most attention. The term refers to the signature of a public official on a cover serving in lieu of postage. The cover is thus "free" to the sender. The personalities of the individuals whose franking signatures appear on such covers are as attractive to postal historians as they are to autograph or manuscript collectors. This factor, coupled with the inherent interest of postal history artifacts, has made frank collecting very attractive.

In recent years, franks have normally taken the form of printed facsimile signatures or, rarely, signatures reproduced by hand-stamps or mechanical devices. Today's congressional franks are nearly all printed facsimile signatures. There is really no reason that congressional mail could not be sent under a penalty clause or postage accounted for by means other than the sender's name. But the signature-franked cover, even bearing a facsimile, has a strong political aspect.

Legislative franks with written signatures are a traditional part of the congressional scene. Signatures of all the important members of Congress prior to 1873 are available theoretically. These include some great names: Henry Clay, Daniel Webster, John C. Calhoun, James Madison and, in later years, William H. Seward and Jefferson Davis. While all of these men franked from other than congressional posts, their franks are more readily available from congressional years than otherwise.

The franking privilege started in America by being brought from England as part of the British mail system. In England, it had a long tradition, originally stemming from 1652, in the Parliamentary period of the Cromwellian era. After the Restoration, with King Charles II on the throne, the postal system was under the control of and operated for the financial benefit of the Crown. From 1661 until 1764, authority for franking was granted under Royal Warrant from the Crown to the House of Commons and the other branches of the government.

In 1764, control of the British Post Office revenue passed from Crown to State. Only after 1764 can specific laws and regulations be

Figure 225. Free-franked cover of British House of Commons Member Charles James Fox, from his country home at Chertsey to Edinburgh, Scotland, in 1803.

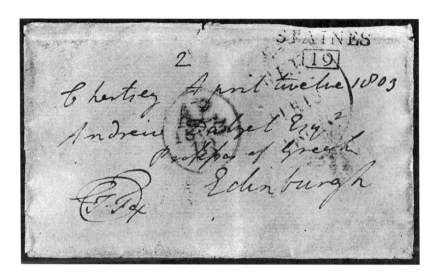

Figure 226. A tracing of a FREE handstamp similar to the nearly illegible red marking on the free-franked cover in Figure 225.

Figure 227. Charles James Fox.

found in the acts of Parliament relative to the details of free franking letters. Franking continued in England until January 10, 1840. It was abolished in connection with the cheap postage acts of Parliament that ushered in the first stamps, the Penny Black and Twopence Blue.

Figure 225 shows a franked cover of Charles James Fox, a well-known member of the House of Commons. The cover bears Fox's monogramlike franking signature at the lower left and also, in his own hand, a legend, "Chertsey, April twelve 1803." The address, directing the letter to a professor of Greek at Edinburgh, is also in Fox's hand. The manuscript "2" above the legend will be discussed momentarily.

The name, "Chertsey," isn't a postmark, but was in compliance with a British postal regulation aimed at reducing abuse of the franking privilege. This regulation stated that franked covers had to be endorsed with the place and time of sending. If the franker was not within 20 miles of the endorsed location on that or the previous day, the frank was not considered valid, and full postage was charged.

Chertsey was the site of Fox's country home, St. Anne's Hill. The letter was placed in the official government General Post at Staines, after being taken from Chertsey to Staines by a "farmed" or private post. This probably accounts for the manuscript "2" above the legend written by Fox, but it may also be Fox's count on the number of free letters he sent that day. Another part of the law governing franking was that frankers were permitted no more than 10 letters sent (and 15 received) free each day.

Operations of the British General Post Office in this era were limited to carriage of mails over six main post roads, radiating like spokes of a wheel from London. These were supplemented by various cross post roads and some by-post roads, branching from the main roads to large towns. Except for mails carried on the cross post roads, letters on adjacent main roads passed through London.

The net effect was twofold. First, most letters were charged for the distance carried to London plus the distance from London to destination. From about 1785 until after 1829, the townmarks of the post towns had the distance from London included in the handstamp. This was to simplify computation and collection of postage at the towns to which letters were addressed. Second, there were large areas of England, remote from London, to which the service of the General

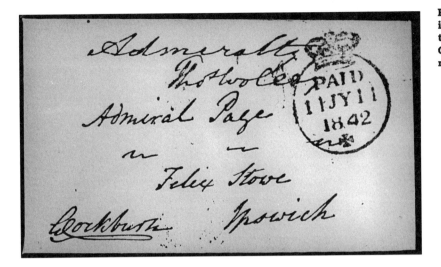

Post Office was not extended.

Returning to Fox's franked cover, the boxed "19" with the Staines postmark on the cover front means that Staines was 19 miles from London. Oddly, Cary's survey of 1802, and other tables of distances, show the post route distance as 16 miles. The thimble datestamp of AP/1803/16 was also applied (in red) at Staines. Staines was located on the great Western Post Road. When the letter reached London, it was checked by the inspector of free letters and the "free" handstamp, similar to that shown in Figure 226, was applied. This verified the cover's status as a free letter.

Charles James Fox was a younger son (younger sons didn't inherit titles) of Lord Holland, and was elected to Parliament before he was 20 years old. He was once described as "generous to a fault, utterly dissolute, profoundly witty, obsessed with gambling, soaked with alcohol and indestructibly radical." By way of verification of this description, his father, in 1774, paid Fox's accumulated gambling debts of some £140,000.

Fox was one of the greatest speakers in the history of Parliament. During the American Revolution, he supported the cause of the revolting colonies against England. His picture is shown in Figure 227.

Figure 228 shows a cover, signed but not a frank, sent by an Englishman whose actions were as unfriendly to American interest as Charles James Fox was supportive. This is Admiral Lord George Cockburn, K.B., who burned Washington during the War of 1812. His picture, with the burning city in the background, is shown in Figure 229. As was then customary, the background of the painting shows the subject's greatest accomplishment.

The cover shown in Figure 228 carries Cockburn's signature as Senior Naval Lord of the British Admiralty. Sent in 1842, after franking was abolished, the signature apparently certifies the official nature of the letter to justify the "PAID" crown official stamp on the cover. The term "stamp," as used here, might be defined as that which accounts for the postage, just as does the term "frank" or an adhesive postage stamp.

Based upon the present-day criticism for apparent abuse of their franking privileges by Congressional frankers by overusing it in election years, perhaps the British laws of 1800 might offer a good

Figure 229. Admiral Lord George Cockburn, posed before his crowning achievement, the burning of the city of Washington.

solution to the problem. Representatives could have the choice of using the same types of penalty (or "postage paid by") envelopes the rest of the government used, or they could use franks signed by their own hands. Thus, neither printed facsimiles nor mechanical devices such as Autopens would be acceptable, and writer's cramp would limit the number of franks produced. Or, would it still be necessary, as the British Post Office found, to also limit by law the numbers sent daily?

Free-frank designation misused

In my columns in *Linn's*, I have noted examples of misuse of the terms "frank" and "franking privilege" in both auction catalogs and articles written by friends. When I commented to that effect, one friend replied, after finally understanding what was meant, that I should explain the concept. Correctly used, the terms apply to covers bearing the signature of a public official, where the signature serves in lieu of a postage stamp.

The terms "frank" and "franking" aren't just the product of some collector's imagination. They stem from our postal laws and regulations, as they came down to us from the English codes in Colonial days. The U.S. federal postal laws from their earliest versions, responding to progressive and continuous abuse of the free-mail privilege, became stricter with each revision. Controls were placed on the government positions that had the franking privilege, as to whether each could frank personal mail or only that pertaining to the duties of their office. Weight limits also were imposed.

Auction houses and some writers have a tendency at times to assume that any cover bearing the signature of a public official or military man is a free-franked cover. But there are other reasons signatures appear on covers. A signature is by no means an automatic indication of free franking.

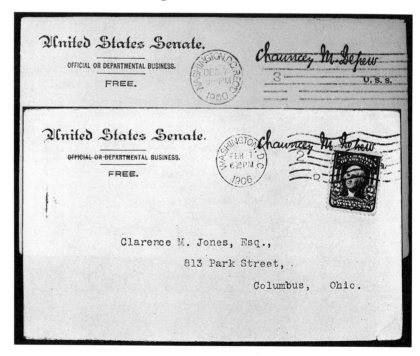

Figure 230. Two covers, sent six years apart, with identical imprints, including the facsimile signature of U.S. Senator Chauncy M. Depew. Only the lower cover bears a stamp.

162

Figure 230 shows a pair of covers to illustrate what "frank" or "free frank" means. Both bear the signature of U.S. Senator Chauncy M. Depew of New York (Figure 231). Both also bear identical imprints "United States Senate/Official or Departmental Business/FREE," together with the printed facsimile of Depew's signature and "U.S.S." However, the cover on the bottom has the legend "Official or Departmental Business" scratched out and a 2¢ stamp of 1903 placed just below the facsimile signature. Thus, the upper cover is franked by the facsimile signature, together with the statement including "FREE." The lower cover is franked by the stamp, since the letter evidently wasn't sent on official government business. Each accounted for the postage required to carry the letter, or to "frank" it through the mails.

In the 1896 Postal Laws & Regulations, Section 217 cited the act of January 12, 1895, "extending the franking privileges as follows: The Vice President, Member and Members-Elect of and Delegates and Delegates-Elect to Congress shall have the privilege of sending free through the mails and under their frank, any mail matter to any Government official or to any person, correspondence, not exceeding one ounce in weight, upon departmental or official business." Paragraph 4 of the same section noted, "The name of the franking Senator, Representative or territorial Delegate, written or impressed, must appear on the envelope of the letter, in connection with the initials of his office and be preceded by the word 'Free.'" These two provisions explain the legends on the covers shown in Figure 230.

It should be noted that by this act, a handwritten signature wasn't necessary. An "impressed" or facsimile signature was all that was required. The act of 1895 actually renewed the franking privilege of the Congress after a 22-year hiatus on franking letter mails.

Effective July 1, 1873, the franking privileges of the president, vice-president and all members of the executive departments were also abolished. Official stamps and, later, penalty envelopes were substituted. Since the beginning of the federal government, the Congress, president and vice president could have franked personal mail or whatever they wished. There were weight limitations, and the franking had to be by written signature of the franker. The members of the executive departments, with the occasional exception of the members of the cabinet, could frank only on official business. The Postal Laws & Regulations usually spelled out just what positions had the franking privilege and on what basis. For example, in an act approved July 5, 1838, "to increase the present military establishment of the United States," Section 21 read, "And be it further enacted, That all letters and packages on public business, to and from the Commanding General, the Colonel of Ordnance, the Surgeon General, and the head of the Topographical Corps, shall be free of postage."

In the major revision of the postal laws made by the act effective in 1825, which was to control the franking privilege for the next 20 years, the only U.S. Army officers listed as having the privilege were the adjutant general, commissary general, inspectors general, quarter master general, paymaster general and the adjutant generals of the militia of each state. Their franking privileges included the right to send and receive mail free. Each was subject to certain other limitations that varied from time to time.

As the Army was increased, reduced or reorganized, the acts of Congress making the changes usually included necessary amend-

Figure 231. Chauncy M. Depew

Figure 232. The signature of "a.(cting)" Colonel Zachary Taylor on this cover mailed at Prairie du Chien, in Michigan Territory, in 1829, was intended to certify the official nature of the letter so that it could be transmitted through the mails free. The franking privilege rested in the addressee.

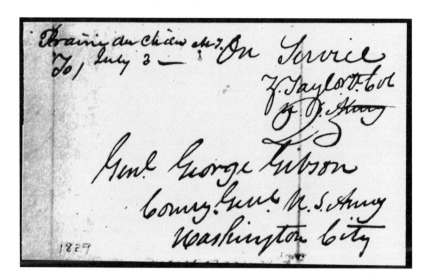

ments or authorizations to the franking privilege. The important aspect was that mail on official business could be sent or received free.

From the death of General George Washington in 1799 until the act of 1838, no commanding general of the Army had the franking privilege — mostly because although the Army had a senior major general, he wasn't in command of the entire Army. Also, no field officer of the U.S. Army had the franking privilege. This fact isn't known to all today, and it causes the confusion and misdescribing noted earlier. Let's look at two prominent examples.

Figure 232 shows a cover bearing the signature of "Z. Taylor, a.(cting) Col./U.S. Army" with the legend "On Service," which was the military term for official business. In 1829, Taylor was lieutenant colonel of the 1st Regiment of Infantry. He was promoted to colonel on April 4, 1832. The cover bears the manuscript postmark of Prairie du Chien, M.T. (Michigan Territory) and is addressed to "Genl George Gibson, Comy Genl, U.S. Army, Washington City." The postmaster at Prairie du Chien (now Wisconsin) rated the cover at 25¢ for carriage over 400 miles. The cover actually originated at Fort Snelling, in what is now Minnesota, on June 14, 1829. A description with the cover remarked that the cover should have gone free because it was on official business, which is correct. However, the description continued to remark that "Taylor's frank constitutes the earliest marking from that office." This strays a bit in accuracy relative to the franking privilege. Zachary Taylor (Figure 233), as a U.S. Army officer, didn't possess the franking privilege. The only time in his life that he could legally frank his mail was as president of the United States.

The Figure 232 letter was addressed to the commissary general of the U.S. Army. This position did have the franking privilege. The most important aspect of that privilege, in the prestamp era, was the right to receive official mail free. Taylor's signature and statement "On Service" was to attest to the official nature of his letter, so that postmasters at originating offices wouldn't charge postage. Many such military letters exist, bearing signatures of ranks from second lieutenant on up.

It should be recognized that the franking privilege, under the law, was granted to the position in the government and not to the individual occupying it.

Figure 233. Zachary Taylor

164

Covers occasionally are offered identified as a free frank of Robert E. Lee, when he was a young lieutenant serving on the staff of the chief engineer of the U.S. Army in Washington in the 1830s, or as commander of the Confederate Army of Northern Virginia. While the signatures may be perfectly genuine, they cannot be free franks, since Lee never held a post authorized to frank mail. From the days when he was on the staff of the chief engineer of the Army, about 1834 to 1837, Lee's signature may be found on official covers with a scribble that can be interpreted as "Lt Assistant in charge." I have seen four or five of these covers. All bear a second signature of an official of the War Department, such as Elbert R. Herring, Superintendent of Indian Affairs, or J.L. Edwards, Commissioner of Pensions, both of whom had the privilege of franking letters at that time. Even had Lee been the senior officer of the engineering service of the Army in the office that particular day, he still could not have used the franking privilege. He was transferred to St. Louis in 1837, and the chief engineer, then Colonel Charles Gratiot, didn't receive the franking privilege until a few years later. Thus, Lee's signature on covers sent while he was in the chief engineer's office in Washington are simply to attest to or identify those letters as being on official business, so that another official, with the franking privilege, could be advised to supply his franking signature.

Lee's signed letters as a Confederate general are another matter. Most of them were carried by military courier to Richmond. Those that were placed in the mails bear, or at least should bear, a Confederate postage stamp. Only a few officials of the Confederate Post Office possessed the franking privilege. One of the major reasons Confederate Postmaster General John Reagan operated his mail service in the black was because the service wasn't required to carry huge amounts of free-franked letters. While Lee's signature on his letters sent from the Army of Northern Virginia certainly earned the attention of the couriers who carried them, they weren't franks, since they didn't account for the postage, none being involved.

The problem of recognizing what is and isn't a frank exists mainly because franks of famous men are collected as autographed covers, not as postal history. The fact that the covers aren't really "free franks" does not affect their value in the marketplace. But, to the postal historian, calling them "free franks" creates the same reaction produced in the collector of 3¢ 1861 stamps when he is offered a common rose shade as a pigeon blood pink. That's similar to the reaction of one of Lee's Atlanta colonels listening to "Marching Through Georgia!"

Official stamps replaced franking privilege

Ulysses S. Grant was president of the United States (1869-77) when Official departmental stamps replaced the franking privilege of the executive branch of the government.

In the early years, only the chief executive possessed the franking privilege in the presidential office. Nonetheless, covers franked by incumbent presidents are very rare. Most of the early presidents had one or more secretaries, but none of those before Buchanan's term possessed the franking privilege. However, before 1855, mail could be (and usually was) sent collect. This meant that the president franked mail only when he desired to send letters free. Nearly all such mail was personal, political or family-oriented.

After 1856, most official mail from the presidential office was

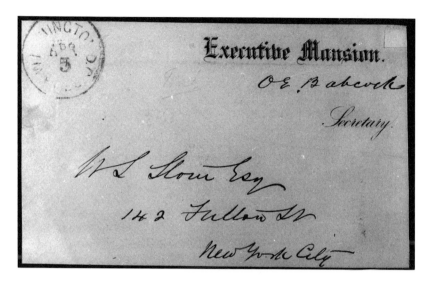

Figure 234. Franked by Grant's presidential secretary Orville E. Babcock, to New York City, year unknown. Babcock was a general on Grant's staff during the Civil War.

franked by the private secretaries. Lincoln had three secretaries. Franks of two, Nicolay and Hay, are known. Andrew Johnson had a much larger personal staff. Franks of at least a half dozen of his secretaries are known.

Ulysses S. Grant brought into the presidential office a large staff, mainly aides from his military years. Franks of most of these are known. Written franks were used for the presidential mail from March 1869 until the privilege was abolished on July 1, 1873. Only a very few franks of U.S. Grant are known. The few that do exist are mostly on official printed envelopes (such as that shown in Figure 234) with the word "Secretary" marked out. These undoubtedly carried personal mail. It should be understood that the presidential franking privilege, which applied also to presidential secretaries, was a personal privilege. It wasn't limited to official mail.

The cover shown in Figure 234 bears the franking signature of General Orville E. Babcock. Babcock and General Horace Porter, also a presidential secretary, were probably the two aides upon whom Grant relied most heavily, both during his last Civil War years and as president. Babcock, shown in Figure 235, was a Vermonter. He graduated from West Point, ranking third in the class of 1856. As with most West Point graduates with high academic standing at the time, he entered the Corps of Engineers. Due to the limited number of posts available, he was not made a second lieutenant until 1861. During the war, Babcock achieved a high reputation, becoming a lieutenant-colonel on Grant's staff in early 1864. The association with Grant lasted until 1876.

Figure 236 shows a cover directed to Louisville, Kentucky, and franked with a 3¢ Executive departmental stamp. It has an enclosed letter with a printed "Executive Mansion" heading dated March 31, 1874. (It wasn't officially called the White House until some 30 years later.) The letter thanks the addressee for sending a picture of Grant's father and is signed by Levi P. Luckey, "Secretary."

In the 1871 *U.S. Register*, the presidential staff is listed with Babcock, Porter and General Frederick T. Dent (Grant's brother-in-law) as secretaries, Robert M. Douglas (son of Stephen A. Douglas, of Lincoln-Douglas debate fame) as private secretary, and Levi P. Luckey as assistant private secretary. Culver C. Sniffen and William H. Crook

Figure 235. General Orville E. Babcock was a Vermonter and a West Point graduate.

Figure 236. A 3¢ carmine Executive Department Official stamp, used to frank mail from President Ulysses S. Grant's office in 1874. The content thanks the addressee for sending a picture of Grant's father.

are listed as executive clerks.

I have seen franks of all these except Luckey and Crook. Luckey's frank has been reported.

Unquestionably, the use of the Official stamps reduced the work load a good deal, considering that all the signatures to frank letters had to be hand-signed after 1869, due to an enactment of Congress attempting to prevent frauds.

All of Grant's staff went on to other things by the end of his administration, except Crook. He had entered the Executive Mansion in 1864 as a police bodyguard, but soon was made a clerk. He continued through five administrations and produced a biography of those years around the turn of the century.

Babcock and Luckey came to a sticky end together. In 1876, a St. Louis grand jury indicted Babcock in connection with the Whiskey Ring scandals. Although he was acquitted, probably correctly so, both he and Luckey, who was also involved, left the presidential office soon after.

Shortly before the end of Grant's administration, Grant appointed Babcock to be superintendent of the Light House Board, and Luckey was given a subordinate position in the same office. These were not sinecures. In 1884, Babcock and Luckey were on an inspection trip at Key West, Florida, when the boat they were in went down in a storm. Both drowned. Babcock's body was washed up on the beach a few days later.

The Executive Department Official stamps are rarer, both on and off cover, than those of any other department because fewer were printed. Between 1873 and 1877, only slightly under 55,000, valued at under $2,000, were used. Next lowest were the Justice and State departments, each with fewer than a half million — about 10 times as many stamps.

Other than the covers with the Official stamps sent during the Grant administration, the only other covers bearing Executive Department Official stamps are from the first two years of the administration of Rutherford B. Hayes. Letters sent from the Executive Mansion during the later years of the Hayes administration bore the regular Bank Note stamps or had a form of penalty imprint.

Penalty envelopes

From the beginnings of our government, an important separa-

Figure 237. The first type of Official penalty-clause envelope, used by the Post Office Department as early as 1878. This example was used to mail stamps to Dakota Territory in 1886.

tion of the franking privilege existed. The legislative branch, until 1873, could send all mail free, whether official or personal. However, laws passed by the legislative branch limited the franking privilege of the executive branch — with a few exceptions — to mail sent on official business. The exceptions were the presidential and, at times, the vice president's offices; and also, only at times, cabinet members. For most of the years until 1873, the postmasters throughout the country were also permitted to send all their mail, up to a half ounce in weight, under their free frank. This was part of their compensation.

In 1873, the franking privilege was abolished. The executive branch was given Official postage stamps and stationery for their official mail. The legislative branch declared they would pay their own postage, using regular postage stamps for the purpose.

Within a few years, the legislators commenced restoring their franking privilege, but only for printed matter sent on official business. The departmental Official stamps were succeeded, beginning in 1877, by what we call penalty-clause mail. In 1877, the Post Office

Figure 238. A typical penalty envelope of the early 1880s, as provided by the Navy's Bureau of Ordnance to its field offices.

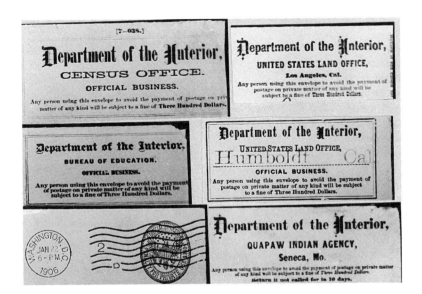

Figure 239. A sampling of penalty-clause imprints used by offices of the Department of the Interior. Each provided its own design with appropriate wording.

Department and the Executive Mansion were authorized to use a penalty-clause statement in lieu of postage stamps, subject to some restrictions not imposed later.

In 1879, the scope of the penalty-clause concept was extended to cover most of the executive and judicial branches of the government. The penalty clause, still familiar to the present generation, is a declaration on Official envelopes (or labels) that a penalty of $300 would be imposed on anyone using the envelope for private mail.

Basically, free franking had been abolished because of abuses. Additionally, for those executive departments that sent very large volumes of mail, use of handwritten franking signatures was expensive and time-consuming — and still didn't necessarily solve the problem of misuse of the privilege.

The Official postage stamps probably lessened the problem to some degree, although the distribution and accounting of the stamps, as well as their application, was also somewhat costly.

The penalty-clause concept cut to the heart of the problem for the executive departments, by letting each office provide its own version of the penalty clause, so long as it contained the key wording. This was effective and inexpensive.

Figure 237 shows an envelope that represents a transition between the Official stamps and postal stationery and the use of penalty clauses. This is a cover with a printed design including the requisite penalty clause, but used as an Official envelope. Envelopes of this type are listed in the Scott U.S. specialized catalog as Official postal stationery, Scott UO14-17. None of these shows any denominations or money value, nor any way to account for equivalent postal charges, which is a characteristic of all penalty-clause mail.

The envelope shown in Figure 237 was used to mail correspondence to the postmaster of Fargo, Dakota Territory, in 1886. Thus, the Post Office Department, with its official penalty-clause postal stationery, attained a degree of standardization of the usage.

Other departments of the government didn't deem this idea useful. Every office, in Washington or in the field, of every department, seemed to design and print its own customized penalty imprint or had

Figure 240. A sampling of imprinted and handstamped penalty-clause legends from the War and Navy departments.

Figure 241. The *USS Michigan*, whose imprint appears at upper right in Figure 240.

This chapter is based on the following *Linn's* columns: free franking started in England, March 21, 1983; free-frank designation misuse, April 21, 1986; Official stamps replaced franking privilege, October 24, 1983; penalty envelopes, May 25, 1987.

handstamps made, according to individual needs and ideas. Figure 238 shows a typical early example of a pretty penalty-clause imprint, on a drop letter sent by the Navy Department's Bureau of Ordnance, Boston office, in 1881. The cover bears a Bureau of Ordnance coat of arms design, with crossed cannon and an anchor. The penalty-clause legend runs vertically up the edge of the cover. The naval ordnance bureau probably furnished such envelopes to field offices.

Figure 239 shows a group of penalty-clause imprints of the Department of the Interior. The three at the left were used at Washington, those at the right from the field. All are printed. Some are printed at upper left of the envelopes and others at upper right. The black lines indicate the edges of the envelopes.

The Census Office and Bureau of Education imprints are on covers posted in 1881. The seal-like affair at lower left, with a 1906 Washington postmark, was sent from the office of the Secretary of the Interior. The right-hand group are on envelopes sent in the 1880s and 1890s. Two have Official Interior Department stamps used to account for registry fees, which weren't covered by the penalty-clause imprint.

Figure 240 shows Navy and War departments penalty-clause uses. The first two imprints from the top are printed; the other two are handstamps. The three Navy items are from aboard U.S. Navy ships, the *Constellation* imprint being from her service as a Naval Academy school ship. The *USS Michigan* handstamp is in pale purple on a cover postmarked at Buffalo, New York, in the 1880s.

The *Michigan* (Figure 241), an iron sidewheeler built in 1844, was the U.S. Navy's first iron-hulled warship. For the better part of a century, it was the only warship on the Great Lakes.

Penalty imprints of one style or another are still with us today, although they appear to have been largely superseded by the "postage paid by" and other imprints.

Author's Afterword and Acknowledgments

In his introduction, *Linn's* Editor-Publisher Michael Laurence outlines some of the problems we encountered in creating this book, and some of the concepts applied in attempting to solve the problems.

Handbooks usually treat a narrow subject in considerable depth, but this Sampler is just the opposite. It touches a wide range of representative postal history subjects in a superficial way. As some of the chapters should make clear, the book uses a dictionary (rather than a stamp show) definition of postal history. In my dictionary, postal history is very simply the history of the mails.

The chapters don't attempt to provide full coverage of any subject. Much more could have been said about most of the subjects covered. More undoubtedly will be said, in the future, about nearly all of them.

Although many references are given in the text, a bibliography isn't included, largely because of the ephemeral nature of philatelic publishing. Printings are usually small, and sources and prices change rapidly. Rather than publish names, addresses and prices in a work that may or may not remain in print for some years, it seemed better to refer readers to dealers in philatelic literature. Such dealers advertise their services and publish periodic pricelists. Frequently they can also provide works not listed in the pricelists. They are a good source of out-of-print publications.

From the beginning, response to my *Linn's* columns has been heavy, sometimes producing dozens of letters a week. Some of the respondents have provided important corrections, and others have added useful data that led to more columns. Still others have asked questions of considerable general interest, so that these questions too have sparked more columns further exploring a subject.

The following listing includes the names of most of those who wrote in response to the columns on which this work is based. The listing also includes names of frequent contributors to the column, and the names of those to whom I've gone at times to borrow covers to photograph, or for a greater depth of knowledge than I had available. While the many reference works mentioned in the text have been the major sources, the individuals named below have all made valuable contributions.

The real problem in compiling such a list concerns names inadvertently omitted. I am not a good record keeper in this regard, nor is my memory in this respect entirely dependable. Thus, I know I owe apologies to many whose names should have appeared here but aren't included.

Albrecht, Carl
Allen, Thomas F.
Alexander, Thomas J.
Bahry, Major Ted, USMC
Baldridge, Bob
*Ball, Charles I.
Barber, Dan
Bednarczyk, Stanley P. Jr.
Beecher, Henry
Birks, Michael
Botham, Michael
Bower, Warren
Bozarth, Ted
Cammarata, Carl J.
Christofferson, Paul
Clark, Douglas C.
Clarke, Tom
Cole, Edwin
Cole, James M.
Collins, Leroy
Cusick, Allison
DeHaas, Ron
Dickson, Frederick S.
Dreschel, Edwin
Dyke, Rod
Fassbender, Michael
Fenn, Bert
Fiset, Louis
Frajola, Richard C. Jr.
Gallagher, Scott
Gallup, Harold
Gault, Paul
Hahn, Calvet M.
*Hahn, Joseph
*Hanmer, Russell F.
Hart, Creighton C.
Hartmann, Leonard H.
Harvey, Edward T.
Hatton, William H.
Hines, Edward
Hines, Dr. Terrence
Hirschinger, Tom
Hoak, Frank M. III
Huggins, Roland
Jennings, Clyde
Jersey, Stanley C.
Johnson, Cary E.
Johnson, John L. Jr.
Johnstone, Dr. Donald B.
Jones, Julian
Kaplan, Earl

Kay, John
Kelsey, Douglas A.
Kaufmann, Patricia
Kimball, Warren F. Jr.
Kozurt, Fred
Laurence, Michael
Levi, Frank S.
Lightfoot, Fred
Lobo, T.E.
Longabach, Gordon A.
Manchester, Diana
Manchester, Jason
Mayo, L.D.
McDonald, Susan M.
McGee, John
Michael, William
Milgram, Dr. James W.
Morrissey, Michael J.
Murch, Captain Robert W., USNR
Myerson, James P.
Newton, Frank Q.
Payne, Robert J.
*Persson, N. Leonard
Phillips, David G.
Piller, Stanley
Pittard, Henry
Pulver, Dale
Range, T.E.
Risvold, Floyd E.
Schreiber, Michael
Schroeder, Paul T.
Schumacher, Paul
Silver, Philip
Spaulding, Dr. Robert M.
Stambaugh, Richard
Staubus, Dr. Alfred E.
Stehle, Randy
Stets, Robert J.
Stone, Robert G.
Sutherland, Greg
Taylor, Thomas O.
Tillinghast, James
Todsen, Dr. Thomas K.
*Towle, Charles L.
Truax, Robert
Van Dam, Theodore
Wegner, Thomas R.
Welch, Bill
Williamson, Dr. James
Winter, Captain Richard F.
*Now deceased

Linn's Postal History Columns

The following is a listing of Richard B. Graham's Postal History columns, which have appeared weekly in *Linn's Stamp News* since 1982. This listing was compiled by Douglas A. Kelsey.

Number	Date	Headline or subject	Notes
	1982		
1	11/15	Mute cover yields year date after analysis	Navy Agency, Baltimore, Md.
2	11/22	Covers from the Sherman brothers illustrate the franking privilege	Free franks
3	11/29	Constant plate varieties discovered on 4¢ Stagecoach coil stamps	Transportation coils
4	12/6	Fort "ABE" Lincoln marking puzzling	Western forts
5	12/13	Revenue stamps used on parcels are scarce relics of world war	World War I
6	12/20	Route agents markings were applied on steamboats as well as on trains	
7	12/27	Declaration of war with Spain produced markings showing interruption of mail	Auxiliary markings; war covers
	1983		
8	1/3	Republic of Texas covers hard to spot	Texas Republic free frank
9	1/10	Civil War could have begun at Fort Pickens	Florida
10	1/17	Covers from Vancouver Island testify to Wells, Fargo's operations in Canada	Western expresses
11	1/24	Civil War patriotic envelopes survive in more than 8,000 different types	
12	1/31	Illustrated covers segment unto itself	Railroad and fire engines
13	2/7	Readers respond to "free frank" privilege	Free franks
14	2/14	Military information in captured letters recognized as problem during Civil War	Confederate soldier's letters
15	2/21	Docketing indicates letter traveled to Fort "Abe" Lincoln from conservationist George Bird Grinnell	Western forts
16	2/28	Used White Plains from aboard U.S.S. Seattle	Defining postal history, Navy mail
17	3/7	Covers show how Alexandria shifted from District of Columbia back to Virginia	Preadhesive postal history
18	3/14	First-day cover collecting evolved from seeking earliest known uses	
19	3/21	Tradition of U.S. legislative free franking has its roots in Britain's Cromwell era	U.S. and British free-frank privilege
20	3/28	Understanding origin markings aids classic U.S. cover analysis	Virginia postal history
21	4/4	Bank's Division, during Civil War, source of first APO postal markings	
22	4/11	Research plus luck combine to decipher early naval cover from Hawaii to New York	Maritime mail
23	4/18	Pioneering work on "steamship letters" will enhance a postal history library	Book review
24	4/25	Studying covers in chronological order effective technique in detecting fakes	Self-expertizing covers, Hartford, Connecticut
25	5/2	Stampless U.S.-British treaty covers are both understandable and inexpensive	Transatlantic mail
26	5/9	Dinosaur bones and the Little Big Horn: Reader response adds details to record	Western mails
27	5/16	United States Navy, Marine postmarks show activities of those forces abroad	
28	5/23	Postmasters' whimsical carvings created sought-after fancy cancels	19th-century fancy cancels
29	5/30	Markings from railway post offices weren't always applied on trains	Waterway RPOs
30	6/6	Revenue use on parcel post clarified; local mail agent function explained	Reader response column
31	6/13	Covers show how postal monopoly replaced private carrier service	Private posts
32	6/20	Army, post office disagreed for 120 years on Fort or Fortress Monroe in Virginia	
33	6/27	Some early covers between U.S. coasts used route designation as illustration	Western covers
34	7/4	Reader response contributes to record	1850s Virginia and railroad markings
35	7/11	Tips on how to recognize scarce covers from Admiral Dewey's squadron at Manila	Spanish-American War
36	7/18	Complex forms, frequent paperwork show 19th-century postmaster's job no sinecure	PO administration
37	7/25	Sole surviving signer of the Declaration Charles Carroll had unique franking status	Free-frank privileges

Number	Date	Headline	Notes
38	8/1	Civil War "roses" cherished by collectors	Novel "rose" enclosure
39	8/8	Railway agents moonlighting as postmasters used ticket daters to make postal markings	Railway station agent markings
40	8/15	Hawaii: Early covers, stamps and history had close ties with U.S.	
41	8/22	U.S. marine shore station markings pose questions, need cataloging	Military mail
42	8/29	Two covers in U.S.-British mails show many similarities and one big difference	Transatlantic mail
43	9/5	Post Office express mail service in 1840s was in response to private competition	Private posts
44	9/12	Kelleys Island cachet-postmark typifies unusual events on Lake Erie islands	19th-century Ohio
45	9/19	From riches to rags: the story of the founding of the legendary Pony Express	Central Overland and Pikes Peak
46	9/26	Business and politics deeply involved in development of the Pony Express	Wells, Fargo
47	10/3	V-Mail solved wartime logistical problems	World War II
48	10/10	Pennsylvania legislative precancels used at Harrisburg in the late 1860s	
49	10/17	Covers from the Northwest Territory are scarce and not easily recognized	Territorial Great Lakes area
50	10/24	Official stamps replace franking privilege during presidency of Ulysses S. Grant	
51	10/31	"U.S. SHIP" and "SHIP-3" rate markings peculiar to mails of Civil War era	
52	11/7	Readers respond about marine mails, transatlantic rates and purpose of the column	
53	11/14	The famous "B. Free Franklin" signature: Why did Franklin use it on his free mail?	
54	11/21	Post office attempt at weather reporting produced scarce backstamp markings	Auxiliary markings
55	11/28	Fort Laramie, outpost on Oregon trail, illustrates shifting territorial boundaries	Western mail
56	12/5	Name-of-boat covers are a popular postal history collecting specialty	Inland waterway
57	12/12	Newspapers, periodicals and postal history	Second-class mail
58	12/19	Skinner-Eno book on U.S. fancy cancels a giant step in the right direction; reader response; modern Official covers	19th-century fancy cancels
59	12/26	An earlier version of today's fast mail: U.S. eastern express mails of 1836-39	
	1984		
60	1/2	Stamp affixing and vending machines have their roots in the 19th century	Meter mail and private coils; Mailomats
61	1/9	Streetcar post office markings easier to collect than streetcars	Streetcar RPOs
62	1/16	Small town printer J.A. Howells added poetry to Civil War envelopes	
63	1/23	Early transpacific mail markings: China and Japan steam service	
64	1/30	Reader responses: further discussion of V-Mail and Harrisburg precancels; legislative signatures on covers	
65	2/6	Spanish-American war covers illustrate beginning of U.S. administration of Guam	U.S. possessions
66	2/13	A very unusual Civil War valentine	Soldier's farewell
67	2/20	Covers depict battle between post office and private intercity express companies	Private expresses
68	2/27	Ship letter charges explained: first a fee and then a rate	Maritime mails
69	3/5	American Expeditionary Forces, 1917-23	World War I
70	3/12	Mails from the U.S. to France in the 1850s	Transatlantic mail
71	3/19	Covers span P.T. Barnum's colorful career	Illustrated covers
72	3/26	Postmarks of rural free delivery system	
73	4/2	Readers respond to B. Free Franklin, V-Mails, weather report backstamps	
74	4/9	Fancy postmarks existed long before stamps	Preadhesive covers
75	4/16	Earliest U.S. registered mail covers show fee paid in cash, not by stamps	Registered mail and rates
76	4/23	Turn of the century special events covers	Fairs, carnivals, etc.
77	4/30	Mystery still surrounds manufacturer of first United States machine canceler	Machine cancels
78	5/7	Readers respond on wagon trains, newspaper stamps, mailing machines (Mailomats)	
79	5/14	Sanitary Commission during Civil War combined USO and Red Cross services	
80	5/21	Duplexed postmarking devices used on stampless covers as early as 1830s	Attached rates, Norton patent
81	5/28	Marine postmarks from Dominican Republic	Military mail
82	6/4	Collection and distribution wagons: horse-drawn postal sorting vehicles	
83	6/11	U.S.-French treaty mails from 1857-1869	Transatlantic mails
84	6/18	Personal mail by diplomatic pouch, 1928-60	
85	6/25	Covers salvaged from wrecked mail ships	Interrupted mail
86	7/2	Early U.S. railroad route agent postmarks	
87	7/9	Readers respond on weather report cards, streetcars, mysterious valentine hat; registry fees	Romeo and Juliet valentine
88	7/16	Classic precancels as postal history	Book review
89	7/23	Early patent canceling devices were intended to cut stamp fibers	Patent cancels
90	7/30	Now almost forgotten, 1940 destroyer swap produced controversy as well as covers	Navy postmarks, WWII
91	8/6	Covers from bases involved in 1940 destroyer swap	WWII APOs
92	8/13	Free mail to U.S. soldiers in Mexican War	
93	8/20	Readers respond about presidential mail, poems on Howell's patriotic envelopes	Regular U.S.stamps on President Hayes' personal mail
94	8/27	Airmail service to foreign countries	U.S. contract routes

Number	Date	Headline	Notes
95	9/3	Maryland prestamp cover collecting upgraded by new D. Homer Kendall work	Book review
96	9/10	Personal mail from 19th-century diplomats	Franking privilege
97	9/17	Mailomats and other meter imprints	Meter stamped mail
98	9/24	More on U.S. registered mail in the 1870s mail	Fee change of 1875
99	10/1	Readers respond on sanitary commissions; diplomatic pouch	Non-UPU Katanga mail
100	10/8	Mid-19th century presidential campaigns employed envelopes to promote candidates	Illustrated covers
101	10/15	Covers from Civil War blockade ships provide fascinating historical insights	
102	10/22	Ocean letters, transmitted by radio, recall the era of transatlantic liners	
103	10/29	B.F. Stevens: antiquarian, bookseller and U.S. Despatch Agent in London	Forwarders
104	11/5	Large and important, "Letters of Gold" is a fresh approach to postal history	Book review, California postal history
105	11/12	Military absentee voting produced interesting covers in two major wars	Civil War; WWII
106	11/19	Free franked covers show capital's move from Philadelphia to Washington in 1800	Franking privilege
107	11/26	Collection and distribution wagons to be subject of forthcoming MPOS monograph	Also machine cancels; monograph reviewed
108	12/3	Forwarders added speed and reliability to 19th-century international mail	Rowe's book reviewed
109	12/10	Unusual datestamps of mid 19th century most frequently found from small towns	Fancy cancels
110	12/17	Airmail crash covers difficult to find	Interrupted mail
111	12/24	Topical cover collecting can reflect collector's hobby or business interests	Illustrated covers; steam engines
112	12/31	New light on Pomeroy's Express markings; earliest known railroad route agent cover	Private express
	1985		
113	1/7	They don't come in fine condition, but train wreck covers are highly collectible	Interrupted mail
114	1/14	As postal officials, the Zevely brothers created some highly collectible covers	Stampless covers, free franks
115	1/21	North Atlantic convoy route of 1940-41	WWII
116	1/28	Early circular rates can create confusion	
117	2/4	Few covers show book and newspaper rates	
118	2/11	Philadelphia centennial exposition produced world's first commemorative postal issues	Postmarks, expositions
119	2/18	Nisei internment camps of World War II	WWII
120	2/25	19th-century postal celebrations generated modern style souvenirs	U.S. and British
121	3/4	WWII Caribbean U.S. base postmarks	Military mail
122	3/11	Presidential franks not always autographs	Franking privilege
123	3/18	Telegraph covers from the 19th century	
124	3/25	WWII Philippine commonwealth covers	
125	4/1	Collecting states such as Alaska offers fascinating insights into postal history	Alaska
126	4/8	Collecting pneumatic mail tube covers	Chicago postal history
127	4/15	Nisei story prompts reader response	WWII
128	4/22	Steamship markings on early U.S. covers	
129	4/29	Detroit and Algonac steamboat markings show RFD service via lake steamer	
130	5/6	U.S. foreign airmail covers from 1930s similar to classic international covers	International airmail rates and covers
131	5/13	Macabre Civil War patriotic lettersheet illuminates grim side of war sentiments	
132	5/20	"Fictitious" and "fraudulent" auxiliary markings	P.L. and R
133	5/27	19th-century illustrated advertising covers portray details not well understood today	Illustrated covers
134	6/3	U.S. naval covers from the Yangtze Patrol	U.S. Navy in China
135	6/10	1850s cover from California has both postal history and philatelic appeal	Registered mail, western mails
136	6/17	Quaker dated postmarks: Who made them?	Stampless covers
137	6/24	19th-century postal special events covers	U.S.; Canada
138	7/1	New book details Suez Canal Co. stamps and covers	Book review
139	7/8	Foreign airmail contract routes of 1940s	
140	7/15	Mail between U.S. and Canada, 1851-1868	
141	7/22	19th-century college postmarks and covers	
142	7/29	More information on pneumatic tube mails	Chicago; Philadelphia
143	8/5	Covers from Civil War prison camps	Censored covers
144	8/12	Maps help interpret territorial covers; Arizona; New Mexico	Western mails
145	8/19	Nisei relocation centers of World War II	
146	8/26	Collecting hometown postal history	Columbus, Ohio
147	9/2	Colton's 1856 U.S. post office directory	Reference book
148	9/9	U.S. machine postmarks from the 1890s	
149	9/16	New York foreign mail cancels from 1870s make handsome postal history collectibles	Fancy cancels
150	9/23	20th-century ancillary postal markings	
151	9/30	19th-century auxiliary post markings	
152	10/7	Flag cancels an inexpensive collection	Machine cancels

Number	Date	Headline	Notes
153	10/14	First reliable international mail service grew from U.S.-U.K. postal treaty of 1848	Transatlantic mails
154	10/21	Turn-of-the-century advertising covers feature deceptive trompe l'oeil designs	Illustrated covers
155	10/28	New edition of stampless cover catalog, Volume 1	Book review
156	11/4	19th-century circular and book rates	Circular rate table
157	11/11	Unusual markings show post office concern with security of registered mail system	
158	11/18	APO locations and postmarks of WWII	Book review
159	11/25	Forwarding rules evolved in 19th century	
160	12/2	World War II APOs in occupied Europe	AMG covers
161	12/9	High rates on early stampless covers	War of 1812 rate, etc.
162	12/16	Sick chicken and trompe l'oeil covers	Illustrated covers
163	12/23	Postal history columnist reveals his sources	References
164	12/30	J. David Baker collection contained unusual and exotic classic U.S. covers	Exotic covers of 1869 issue
	1986		
165	1/6	Beginning of U.S. special delivery mail	
166	1/13	Fancy cancels on U.S. stamps, 1870-1900	
167	1/20	Early airmail routes to Latin America	
168	1/27	More on trompe l'oeil illustrated covers; circular rates; auxiliary and ancillary markings	
169	2/3	Postmaster Colburn of Leominster, Mass., carefully created interesting covers	"3" cancels and "Due 3" adhesive labels
170	2/10	Introduction to collecting machine cancels	Barry machine cancels
171	2/17	U.S. naval mission to Brazil, 1923-40	Naval shore stations and diplomatic pouch mail
172	2/24	Cross border covers between U.S.-Canada	
173	3/3	Early and recent U.S. territorial covers; reader response	Western mails; old and recent
174	3/10	New book on Minnesota territorial covers	Book review
175	3/17	Covers from faraway places: the Galapagos	
176	3/24	Appropriation by Congress in 1882 created many similar fancy cancels	Duplexes
177	3/31	Collection and distribution wagons	Book review
178	4/7	Polar philately: Byrd Antarctic ventures	
179	4/14	Detroit's unusual waterborne post offices	Waterway RFD and RPO
180	4/21	"Free frank" designation often misused	
181	4/28	Zeppelin flights created interesting covers	German-South American service
182	5/5	Leavitt machine markings, rare on covers, are most frequently found on postal cards	Machine cancels
183	5/12	Highlights of Chicago's postal history	Also see Ameripex columns
184	5/19	New book on railroad markings available; U.S. Route and Station Agent Markings (Towle)	Book review
185	5/26	Postcard shows Doane duplex markings	
186	6/2	More on auxiliary and ancillary markings	
187	6/9	Early slogans advertising stamp shows	Machine cancels
188	6/16	Dead letter office prior to Civil War	
189	6/23	U.S. despatch agency markings, 1866-1916	Forwarders
190	6/30	Galapagos revisited via reader response	
191	7/7	Markings from St. Louis World's Fair	Machine slogan cancels
192	7/14	Readers contribute on diplomatic mails	Naval mission to Brazil
193	7/21	Purser handstamps and route agent postmarks	Name-of-boat markings
194	7/28	More on 19th-century steamboat covers	
195	8/4	Barr-Fyke rapid canceling machine markings	Machine cancels
196	8/11	Postcards originated in Europe in 1860s	
197	8/18	Stateside army posts of World War I	Military mail
198	8/25	"Way" markings on mail ashore and afloat	
199	9/1	Weekly airmail across the South Atlantic	Catapult mails
200	9/8	Pictorial ship markings on incoming covers	Auxiliary markings
201	9/15	Holcomb of Mallet Creek: postmark supplier	Should be "Holcomb"
202	9/22	Camp Sherman typical WWI army camp	Military mail
203	9/29	Cover tales: Postmasters and the presidency	
204	10/6	Early U.S. machine cancels with slogans	
205	10/13	Dietz Confederate catalog causes controversy	Book review
206	10/20	A look at the 1913 U.S. parcel post system	
207	10/27	19th-century presidential widows franks	Madison; Lincoln
208	11/3	Terminus marks recall railroad construction	Idaho; Montana
209	11/10	Recap of U.S. naval mission to Brazil	
210	11/17	New books and publication of interest	Confederate bibliography, Streetcar RPOs
211	11/24	Prepaid and due stamps, then and now	
212	12/1	Rural Free Delivery: history and markings	Rural stations

Linn's Postal History Columns

Number	Date	Headline	Notes
213	12/8	Handbook on Alaska territorial postmarks	Book review, Alaska
214	12/15	Columbus, Ohio, "prison bar grid" myth	Fancy cancel
215	12/22	New exposition station markings handbook	Book review
216	12/29	Sparkling cards bring New Year greetings	Postcards and P.L. and R
	1987		
217	1/5	Early army post offices in the Pacific; WWII	Australia; Christmas Island
218	1/12	Earliest known uses of U.S. 1861 stamps	
219	1/19	Ephemeral post office; trompe l'oeil covers	Railroad POs, illustrated covers
220	1/26	When working, Time Machine cancelers created markings accurate to the minute	Machine cancels
221	2/2	Free franks of modern presidential widows	Kennedy; Truman; Eisenhower
222	2/9	Unusual handling of registered mail creates need for unusual postal markings	
223	2/16	U.S. Navy ship post office markings of WWII	
224	2/23	Express mail service in the War of 1812	
225	3/2	"Advertised" markings date to before 1800	Auxiliary markings
226	3/9	Strife creates "mails suspended" covers	19th and 20th century
227	3/16	APO markings from Spanish-American War	Military mail
228	3/23	WWII in the Pacific: Hawaii, 1941-42	
229	3/30	New York supplementary mail markings	Auxiliary markings
230	4/6	Obsolete postal terms survive on covers	Ancillary markings
231	4/13	Presidential widows' franks: 1881-1948	McKinley; Garfield; Cleveland
232	4/20	Due stamps affixed at delivering office	Postage due
233	4/27	Time to buy these reference books is now	Resources
234	5/4	Postal evolution of "fraudulent" markings	Ancillary markings
235	5/11	Reader response: additions and corrections	1812 express, Brazil naval mission
236	5/18	How first-day covers become postal history	"Fractured" FDCs
237	5/25	Penalty envelopes succeeded Official stamps	Official mail
238	6/1	Canada Small Queens offer wide variety	
239	6/8	New society forms from two cancel groups	Machine cancels
240	6/15	New book explores U.S. cover collecting	Book review
241	6/22	Civil War prison mail from Camp Chase, Ohio	
242	6/29	Presidential widow's franks of Helen Taft	Franking privilege
243	7/6	Apologies, explanations and precautions	Auxiliary markings
244	7/13	200th anniversary of Northwest Ordinance	Territorial midwest
245	7/20	Two new specialist catalogs on markings	Book review: HPOs and Doanes
246	7/27	Stock postmarking devices of the 1860s	
247	8/3	Markings on covers damaged in the mails	Ancillary markings
248	8/10	Attracted by free mailing privileges, merchants moonlighted as postmasters	Franking privilege
249	8/17	Covers from remote South Atlantic islands	Ascension, Tristan da Cunha
250	8/24	19th-century postmarks with county names	
251	8/31	French colonies in the South Pacific, 1941 (WWII)	New Caledonia and Tahiti
252	9/7	Town postmarks with the postmaster's name	
253	9/14	Free franks of the constitutional convention	1787
254	9/21	Automation produces more apology markings	Ancillary markings
255	9/28	WWII in the Pacific: the Line Islands (Palmyra Island)	Navy shore station
256	10/5	Courthouse covers bear lots of postage	
257	10/12	Publicity from philatelic covers prompts better mail service for remote islands	Tristan da Cunha, Tonga
258	10/19	Dead Letter Office article: reader response	Minor letters
259	10/26	Covers show Ohio River flood emergencies	Modern postal history
260	11/2	Steamship RPO routes to Alaskan goldfields	Waterway RPOs
261	11/9	Five years of columns prompt reflections; data sought on Baby machine cancels	Machine cancels
262	11/16	In review: long-awaited second volume of "American Stampless Cover Catalog"	Book review
263	11/23	Steamboat covers, postal history collateral	
264	11/30	Covers from Guam under U.S. Naval administration	
265	12/7	Illustrated covers: topical postal history	Brooklyn Bridge
266	12/14	In review: book on Gold Rush mail agents	Book review
267	12/21	Covers marked by several forwarders	Forwarding agents
268	12/28	RPO markings from Lake Winnipesaukee	Waterway RPOs
	1988		
269	1/4	City branch and station marks of the 1860s	
270	1/11	Free franks of three presidential widows	Harrison; Roosevelt; Harding
271	1/18	Difficulties in rating heavy pre-1845 covers	Rates, stampless
272	1/25	World War II in the South Pacific: Tonga; British administration	APOs, FPOs
273	2/1	Return letter envelopes of the 1860s	Dead Letter Office
274	2/8	Personal mail via diplomatic pouch, 1913-1966	
275	2/15	Fourth-class post office markers, 1880-85	
276	2/22	Free franks of three presidential widows	Wilson; Coolidge; Roosevelt
277	2/29	Fancy cancels from the Small Bank Note era	Book review

Number	Date	Headline	Notes
278	3/7	New light on Ohio flood emergency mails	Reader response
279	3/14	New books on Confederate Richmond; postcard markings	Book reviews
280	3/21	U.S.-British treaty mails, 1848-1868	Transatlantic
281	3/28	John Deere "spoker" on 7.1¢ Tractor stamp	Bulk mails; stamp design
282	4/4	Aguinaldo and the Philippine insurrection	
283	4/11	Homemade postmarks on U.S. 3¢ 1861 covers	
284	4/18	WWII in the Pacific: Fiji Islands bases	APOs; British administration
285	4/25	Much-forwarded cover shows 1890s PO policies	
286	5/2	U.S.-U.K. printed-matter rates, 1849-1900	
287	5/9	New monographs on Louisville postal history; waterways POs	Book reviews: Waterway RPOs
288	5/16	Gunboats along the Yangtze: 1903-1939	U.S. Navy in China
289	5/23	Wesson's "time-on-the-bottom" handstamps	Distinctive postmarks
290	5/30	Machine cancels: promising collecting area	Groth-Constantine
291	6/6	Depreciated currency markings of 1863-78: philatelic artifacts of Civil War inflation	Incoming foreign mails
292	6/13	Recent monographs on postal history subjects	Book reviews: WII POD, "fraudulent"
293	6/20	Censor marks on Civil War prisoner mail	
294	6/27	Ancillary markings show unusual handling	Interrupted mail
295	7/4	U.S. sea post office markings, 1893-1917	Maritime mail
296	7/11	Reader responses: 7.1¢ Tractor design	Illustrated covers; first-day covers
297	7/18	"Paquebot" succeeded ship letter markings	
298	7/25	Society publications aid in researching covers	French-Indo China; U.S. Navy-Tripoli
299	8/1	Extension of clipper airmail service in 1937, Hong Kong airmail	
300	8/8	Express companies carried valuables	Private expresses
301	8/15	War in the South Pacific: New Hebrides, French administration	APO; FPO; WWII
302	8/22	Stamps served as money during Civil War	Postage currency
303	8/29	Mixed-franking covers take several forms	Foreign mails
304	9/5	Act of 1845 caused envelope use to spread	
305	9/12	Navy crewman created multi-ship covers	Cinderella naval postmarks
306	9/19	Ohio River flood mails; diplomatic pouch	Readers response
307	9/26	Express companies followed the railroads	Private expresses
308	10/3	New catalog of Doremus machine cancels	Book review
309	10/10	U.S. mail censorship during World War II	
310	10/17	Campaign covers from the election of 1864	Illustrated covers
311	10/24	Census of Black Jack stamps used in Vermont	
312	10/31	U.S. domestic airmail rates, 1918-1926	
313	11/7	Soldiers' absentee balloting in Civil War	
314	11/14	Free mails of the Pan American Union	
315	11/21	Early hotel handstamps and corner cards	Illustrated covers
316	11/28	Books on German and U.S. seapost markings	Resources
317	12/5	1851-55 rates: 3¢ if prepaid, 5¢ if collect	Postmarks with rates
318	12/12	More on covers with "Paquebot" markings	
319	12/19	Some covers bear items not meant to pay postage	Cinderellas
320	12/26	World War II Christmas greeting via V-Mail	On V-Mail enclosures
	1989		
321	1/2	Ornate U.S. propaganda envelopes from the 1850s	Illustrated covers
322	1/9	Two new monographs on machine cancels	Book reviews
323	1/16	The beginnings of free returned letters	
324	1/23	Congressional free franks: 1775 and 1919	Franking privilege
325	1/30	Triple rate eliminated for a short period	Mid-19th century
326	2/6	Kansas-Nebraska series as postal history	
327	2/13	French maritime packet markings of the 1890s	Seaposts
328	2/20	Charge markings on stampless-era covers	
329	2/27	Automatic affixing machines, then and now	Coil stamps on covers
330	3/6	The life and markings of William G. Barry	Machine cancels
331	3/13	Fancy cancellations from the Bank Note era	
332	3/20	WWII in the Pacific: Guadalcanal, 1942-43	Military mail
333	3/27	"Gold Fever" a new approach to postal history	Book review
334	4/3	Facsimile franks of presidential widows	Jacqueline and Ethel Kennedy
335	4/10	First U.S. embossed stamped envelopes	Postal stationery
336	4/17	New catalog of classic precancels to 1907	Book review
337	4/24	Liberty series: fractional-denominated stamps and rates	Bulk-rate mails
338	5/1	19th-century transatlantic sailing packets	Pre-treaty period
339	5/8	Wordy handstamps made by postmasters	Ancillary markings
340	5/15	Illustrated covers: Colorado and tractors	Book review
341	5/22	Non-profit, bulk-rate mail, 1965-1982	Fractional denominated rates
342	5/29	Abuses of congressional free franking	

Number	Date	Headline	Notes
343	6/5	Two new books continue earlier efforts	Book review: Prexies, machine cancels
344	6/12	Nesbitt envelopes used outside the mails	Express, waterway
345	6/19	Markings from U.S. Marines in Haiti	Military mail
346	6/26	Drop letters stayed at one post office	
347	7/3	World War II in the Pacific: Midway Islands	Military mail
348	7/10	The first governmental postal cards	
349	7/17	World War II and the War Cover Club	32nd U.S. Infantry Division
350	7/24	Wheel-of-fortune cancels were widely used	Fancy cancels
351	7/31	Foreign mail with U.S. special delivery	
352	8/7	Franking privileges of congressional, president's widows	Julia Dent Grant
353	8/14	Third class: early bulk and permit mail	
354	8/21	Two transatlantic covers, two useful books	Resources
355	8/28	Construction machinery on illustrated covers	Thematic postal history
356	9/4	United States Marines flew the mails in Haiti	Airmail postal history
357	9/11	Numbering of registered letters, 1865-1900	
358	9/18	Early international airmail to Europe	Airmail postal history
359	9/25	Private labels used to prevent loss of letters	National Return Letter Association
360	10/2	Two new reference books, both interesting	Book reviews: CSA, machine cancels
361	10/9	Congressional franking blackout: 1873-95	Franking privilege
362	10/16	Military mail from Korea: hubba-hubba	Military airmail privilege
363	10/23	Unpaid letters under Universal Postal Union	
364	10/30	New first-class mail permit stamp catalog	Bulk mail
365	11/6	Earliest known use of a U.S. general issue	10¢ 1847 cover
366	11/13	Evolution of the Universal Postal Union	UPU, Washington, 1989
367	11/20	Stampless covers from Washington, 1795-1847	UPU, Washington, 1989
368	11/27	PMG Blair and his postal accomplishments	UPU, Washington, 1989
369	12/4	Government mail from Washington after 1878	Penalty envelopes
370	12/11	New books on U.S. stamps and postal history	Book reviews: UPU mail, Brookman
371	12/18	Revised Herst-Sampson, new Montana book	Book reviews
372	12/25	1897 UPU rules forced lower postcard rate	
	1990		
373	1/1	Fancy cancellations from the Bank Note era	
374	1/8	Opera-glass markings applied at New York	Auxiliary markings
375	1/15	Permit mailing; more on Virgil Brand covers; 2¢ Louisiana Purchase FDC	Bulk mails; FDCs
376	1/22	Surgeon Cooke carefully dated his covers	Incoming foreign mails covers
377	1/29	Providence automated post office a U.S. first	Modern postal history
378	2/5	New catalog of Arizona statehood postmarks	Book review: Arizona postal history
379	2/12	Saint Valentine's Day and valentine cards	
380	2/19	Covers evoke Samoa's turbulent history	
381	2/26	Linn's Almanac a useful postal history reference	Rate tables, etc.
382	3/5	Illustrated covers began with Mulready	
383	3/12	WWII: South Atlantic air route to Cairo	Airmail postal history
384	3/19	Patriotic covers with corps insignia	Civil War
385	3/26	New editions of two useful reference books	Book review: machine cancels, pre-UPU foreign letter rates
386	4/2	How the United States census uses the mails	Free franks
387	4/9	Red Cross international mails during WWII	
388	4/16	New from two state postal history societies	Ohio, New Hampshire
389	4/23	French-line transatlantic seapost covers	
390	4/30	Early census takers were federal marshals	
391	5/7	World War II: Southwest Pacific Theater	Military mail
392	5/14	New work on Groth-Constantine cancels	Machine cancels
393	5/21	The census and the mails in 1870 and 1880	
394	5/28	More on Intelex markings; diplomatic pouch	
395	6/4	Congressional mail and post offices: 1873-95	
396	6/11	More on South Atlantic route APO covers	WWII route to Middle East
397	6/18	Odd-shaped envelopes usually short-lived	
398	6/25	Rabaul: key Japanese base throughout WWII	
399	7/2	Arizona territorial catalog	Book review
400	7/9	Philatelic covers from the 19th century	Columbians, etc.
401	7/16	New catalog on Philadelphia postmarks	Book review
402	7/23	U.S. stamps used abroad: St. Thomas, DWI	
403	7/30	Weather-forecast backstamps had short life	Auxiliary markings
404	8/6	Charles Towle's railroad post office catalogs	
405	8/13	County and postmaster's name postmarks	

Number	Date	Headline	Notes
406	8/20	Reader response: Civil War Corps insignia patriotics	
407	8/27	More on WWII Red Cross message scheme	Censored mail; WWII
408	9/3	WWII: New Guinea missionary covers	British administration
409	9/10	New South Carolina postal history handbook	Book review
410	9/17	Marines in Nicaragua; philatelic covers	Readers response (philatelic covers)
411	9/24	The beginnings of duplex handstamp cancels	Norton patents
412	10/1	U.S. 2¢ rate to England began around 1910	
413	10/8	New books feature regional postal history	California, Illinois
414	10/15	U.S. Outlook and Transo window envelopes	
415	10/22	Barr-Fyke and Universal machine cancels	Monographs reviewed
416	10/29	British stamps used in Malta and Gibraltar	
417	11/5	U.S. Customs inspection of letter packages	Auxiliary markings
418	11/12	Seebecks on cover are fine postal history	
419	11/19	More on covers from U.S. Navy Surgeon Cooke	
420	11/26	False frankings explained in PNC handbook	Book review
421	12/3	History often illuminates postal history	Amos Kendall; U.S. Navy in China, 1932
422	12/10	Wesson Time-on-the-Bottom handstamps	Monograph reviewed
423	12/17	Early U.S. airmail postal rates	
424	12/24	Christmas cards, stamps and rates, 1933-71	
425	12/31	Reader responses; 2¢ steamship rate; customs covers	
	1991		
426	1/7	James Monroe and his franked mail	
427	1/14	U.S. international reply and message cards	UPU mails
428	1/21	Philadelphia postmark catalog	Monograph reviewed
429	1/28	Postal history in daily mails; current rates	Oversize cards and letters
430	2/4	19th-century window envelopes	
431	2/11	Postal history of the A.E.F., WWI	New book reviewed
432	2/18	Illustrated covers with railway themes	
433	2/25	Bishop marks and Dockwra-style markings	
434	3/4	New Machine Cancel Society Handbook	Handbook reviewed
435	3/11	Reader response; Christmas card rates; Hubba-Hubba covers; window envelopes	Korean War
436	3/18	Carriers, locals and independent mails	New society periodical
437	3/25	Bisected U.S. stamps	
438	4/1	Colorado Post Offices; U.S. Postal Relations in the Western Hemisphere	Books reviewed
439	4/8	U.S. mail agency at Vera Cruz in 1914	
440	4/15	Receiving backstamps and markings, 1879-1913	
441	4/22	Intermec meter strips and Autopost stamps	Modern express & priority mails
442	4/29	Gilded-era branch and station post offices	
443	5/6	Certified mail fee services, 1955-91	
444	5/13	High-value stamps on cover, 1890-1900	Columbians
445	5/20	Combat Infantry Division Mail of WWII	New book reviewed
446	5/27	Demonetization of the stamps of 1851-61	
447	6/3	Parcel Post began in 1913 and thrived	Auxiliary services
448	6/10	Handling of recovered plundered mail	Auxiliary markings
449	6/17	New and old references on flag cancels	
450	6/24	Suspension Bridge, N.Y., and J. Roebling	U.S.-Canadian mails
451	7/1	More on postal laws and regulations	
452	7/8	Butaritari Island: Gilbert & Ellice group	WWII and prior
453	7/15	Perfection, Tilton markings	Machine cancels handbook reviewed
454	7/22	Early Steam and Steamboat markings	
455	7/29	WWII in the Pacific: Gilberts retaken	
456	8/5	Pan Americans used to and from abroad	
457	8/12	New book on N.Y. Foreign Mail cancels	Bank note-era fancy cancels
458	8/19	Steamship company mail and postal laws	
459	8/26	WWII markings of ships of the new Navy	
460	9/2	Lowe Leewards volume; Stets 1794 study	Book review
461	9/9	Demonetization; flags; Suspension Bridge	
462	9/16	Early U.S. postage dues and their usage	Book review
463	9/23	Censorship of U.S. civilian mail in WWII	Book review
464	9/30	Navy covers from Japanese post offices	19th century
465	10/7	Money shipment registry tags, 1932-55	High-value stamps on cover
466	10/14	Government-issue auxiliary handstamps	
467	10/21	WWII in the Pacific: Marshalls retaken	
468	10/28	Confederate patriotics and their usage	Book review
469	11/4	Airmail special delivery stamps on cover	
470	11/11	New book on New York provisional stamp	Book review

Linn's Postal History Columns

Number	Date	Headline	Notes
471	11/18	WWII in the Pacific: Guadalcanal 1943-46	
472	11/25	U.S. canceling devices that cut and punch	Patent cancels
473	12/2	World War II in the Pacific: Pearl Harbor	Salvaged mail
474	12/9	Hampden and Pneumatic machine cancels	Handbooks reviewed
475	12/16	Rural Free Delivery station post offices	
476	12/23	Santa on stamps; an 1893 cover to Santa	
477	12/30	19th-century Cleveland, Ohio, markings	Handbook reviewed

Columns from Linn's Ameripex daily special show issues, 1986
(All on Chicago postal history)

Number	Date	Headline	Notes
AX1	5/22	Chicago postal history prior to 1856	
AX2	5/23	Chicago's postal history in the 1850s	
AX3	5/24	Chicago postal history from 1860-61 reflects the city's increasing importance	
AX4	5/25	Foreign covers from Chicago prior to UPU	
AX5	5/26	Chicago domestic mail in the mid-1860s	Chicago branch POs
AX6	5/27	Chicago postal history during Civil War	
AX7	5/28	Development of Chicago as railroad center	
AX8	5/29	Chicago postal history from 1870-1890	
AX9	5/30	Chicago's World Columbian Exposition and other events of the gilded era	

Index